Myrtle Beach
and South Carolina's
Grand Strand

Myrtle Beach and South Carolina's Grand Strand

INCLUDES WILMINGTON AND THE NC LOWCOUNTRY

A Great Destination

Renée Wright

The Countryman Press ✳ Woodstock, Vermont

For Joan, who took me to the Carolina Coast for the very first time,
and for Bill, who taught me to shag (even though he called it the Beach bop).
And, as always, for my Mom, who makes it all possible.

ISBN 978-1-58157-111-0

Interior photographs by the author unless otherwise specified
Book design by Joanna Bodenweber
Composition by Eugenie S. Delaney
Maps by Erin Greb Cartography, © The Countryman Press

Published by The Countryman Press, P.O. Box 748, Woodstock, VT 05091
Distributed by W. W. Norton & Company, Inc., 500 Fifth Avenue, New York, NY 10110

Acknowledgements

MANY PEOPLE CONTRIBUTED TO WRITING THIS BOOK. Irene Karas Long introduced me to Kure Beach and shared stories of fishing on its pier. Linda George took me to my first SOS. Stephanie Agniel told me about the quiet pleasures of Sunset Island. Caitlin Snead taught me to swirl a wand. My sister Karen and Paul Rogoshewski displayed admirable stamina testing mini-golf courses and tasting steamed oysters all along the coast.

A special thanks to Connie Nelson at the Wilmington/Cape Fear Coast Convention & Visitors Bureau and Kimberly Miles at the Myrtle Beach Area Convention & Visitors Bureau. Both provided invaluable help and advice. Thanks also to Sally Hogan at the Georgetown County Tourism Management Commission; Eric Grubb at the Brunswick County Tourism Development Authority; Lauren Frye at Bald Head Island Marketing; Phil Werz, Annette Shepherd, and Nancy Greene at The Brandon Agency; Heather Mill and Seagren Doran at MBooth; Monique Newton and many others at LHWH; and Martin Armes working with MMI Public Relations. All provided information that found its way into these pages.

A big shout-out goes to food writers Liz Biro in Wilmington and Becky Billingsley in Myrtle Beach. Both do amazing jobs keeping up with day-to-day changes in the food industry in their cities.

Without the hard work of lots of folks at Countryman Press and W.W. Norton, including Kim Grant, Kermit Hummel, Lisa Sacks, Doug Yeager, Jennifer Thompson and Abby Collier, this book would never have reached the press.

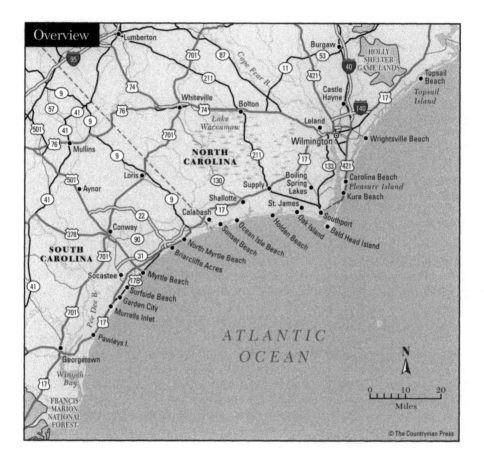

Contents

Introduction

STRETCHING BARELY 100 MILES along US 17, the laid-back Carolina coast between Wilmington, North Carolina, and Georgetown, South Carolina, offers visitors a wide variety of vacation options, something for every age and interest. This is the golf capital of the East, with more than 100 courses welcoming golfers year-round. Colonial seaports and fishing villages where the seafood comes straight off the boat rub shoulders with the cosmopolitan dining and shopping scenes of Wilmington, the film capital of the East Coast, and Myrtle Beach, one of the top beach and family destinations in the country.

Ten of *Golf Digest's* top 100 courses in the world are located in this region, more than any other destination. Amusement parks, roller coasters, and water slides overlook the surf. Over 50 miniature golf courses make this the minigolf capital of the world.

This comprehensive guide helps you find your favorite spot along the Carolina coast, the place that delivers the vacation you're looking for, whether you're in search of a trophy fish, a hole in one, a thrill ride, a quiet week in a surfside cottage, or a meal created by a top chef. Event suggestions guide you from internationally acclaimed film festivals to boil-offs of the local bog stew.

Recommendations lead you down blackwater rivers and through maritime forests on unique eco-adventures. And you'll discover the shag—the local dance that anyone can learn.

LEFT: Surf fishing requires only a rod, reel, bait, and license.

The Way This Book Works

TO MAKE YOUR VISIT to the Carolina Lowcountry easier, we've divided our book into sections that will guide you to places that match your interests. Generally, the destinations are arranged north to south along the coast. There are special sections on Wilmington, North Carolina, and Georgetown and Conway in South Carolina, all brimming with history. The chapter on the Grand Strand forms the heart of our book, exploring the many family friendly and golfer options available in Myrtle Beach and its surrounding towns. Other sections look at each fishing village, island, and beach from Wrightsville Beach in the north to Pawleys Island in the south. Many of these make wonderful day trips, even if you're staying on another part of the Strand.

In several regions, we suggest 48-hour itineraries that make sure you see the best and most iconic sights at each destination. Short Don't Miss lists help you explore in more depth.

In the History & Nature section, you'll find information on the unique ecology of the region and about Carolina bays (reputedly created by meteors), blackwater rivers, and local culture, from Native American tribes to the dance called the shag. We also list some Wilder Places where you can plunge more deeply into the wilderness that lurks just beyond the bright lights of the amusement parks.

Maybe it's those meteors, but the Carolina coast can be hard to navigate. Nearly all the major roads are in one form or another part of US 17, the major north-south road through the region. Others head off into the swamps and end up where you least expect.

Our Transportation section offers you some guidance with suggested routes, including the major airports serving the region and some waterways you can follow to explore by boat.

FINDING YOUR PLACE ON THE CAROLINA COAST

Most visitors to the Carolina coast come looking for one thing—a beach vacation. The long, white-sand beaches that stretch from Wrightsville Beach, North Carolina, to Pawleys Island, South Carolina provide the perfect venue. But there are many other choices to be made.

The Carolina coast boasts many wonderful seafood dishes.

If you're looking for maximum choices when it comes to family activities, popular dining, souvenir shopping, and nightlife, combined with beautiful beaches, your best bet is to head for one of the region's classic beach destinations. Myrtle Beach can't be beat for family activities, chain restaurants, and big shopping opportunities. The Boardwalk at Carolina Beach in North Carolina offers many similar attractions on a smaller, more laid-back scale.

North Myrtle Beach is home to a concentrated nightlife scene that appeals to adults and retirees, plus a real old-fashioned summer pavilion with rides, dancing, and all the burgers you can eat.

If you're looking for a quieter spot, choose one of the North Carolina beaches or head south to Surfside or Litchfield. For a real, old-fashioned summer getaway, look to the islands where vacation cottages still dominate the oceanfront—places such as Kure Beach, Holden, Sunset, or Pawleys—that have hosted family vacations for generations.

If culture and creative food options are high on your list, you can't do better than Wilmington, North Carolina. With many of the same features as its busier sister city, Charleston, Wilmington has the history, top chefs, and ghosts to compete on the national stage, along with a booming film industry that brings prosperity—and stars—to the region.

Or spend time in a quiet village dating back to the Colonial era. Southport, North Carolina, has been compared to Beaufort, South Carolina, before Oprah moved in. Georgetown, just north of Charleston, is South Carolina's third-oldest city and the best place to investigate the history of the rice plantations that made South Carolina the richest of the United States before the Civil War.

Key to Icons

🖉 child-friendly establishment

🏦 extra value establishment

🐾 pet-friendly establishment

♿ wheelchair accessibility

☂ rainy-day activity

⚭ hosts weddings/civil unions

🍸 bar/nightspot

▼ caters to gay clientele

((ı)) WiFi access

♻ Eco-friendly establishment

Throughout the region, you'll find golf courses to suit all abilities. Brunswick County, on the North Carolina–South Carolina border, is an area of concentrated golf options. Or choose one of the world-class stay-and-play plantations set at the Strand's southern end, in Litchfield Beach and Pawleys Island.

Just a few decades ago, most of these coastal communities became ghost towns when the summer crowds departed. But today, many are year-round destinations, with plenty for visitors to do in the off-season. Many people find the beach even better when the crowds depart and the locals come out to play.

History & Nature

BY THE TIME THE SIX SHIPS commanded by Lucas Vázquez de Ayllón sailed along the sandy beaches of the Carolina barrier islands looking for a place to found a Spanish colony in 1526, Native American tribes had been living along this coast for thousands of years. They camped beneath the old live oak trees, many hundreds of years old; fished in the marshes; and feasted on oysters, piling the shells into huge hills that still dot the coast.

Historians believe Ayllón explored the Cape Fear area and Winyah Bay but failed to found a permanent colony. The native tribes would be left in peace for nearly 150 years until the English arrived to stay.

Charles II granted the entire territory that's today both North and South Carolina to eight of his cronies, known to history as the lords proprietors, in 1663. Settlements soon followed. Sir John Yeamans established a short-lived settlement on the Cape Fear River in 1665. Many of the surviving colonists helped found Charles Towne, the Carolinas' first permanent town, in 1670.

The colonists soon found the swampy land of the Lowcountry ideal for rice cultivation, and by 1730, Charleston, Georgetown, and other Carolina ports shipped over 20 million pounds of rice annually. The numbers of enslaved Africans, needed for the highly labor intensive cultivation of rice, multiplied as well, and by 1740, nearly 90 percent of the population of South Carolina was black.

Indigo became an important cash crop after Mrs. Eliza Lucas Pinckney managed to successfully grow a crop in 1742. The blue dye nearly overtook rice as a cash crop, thanks to price supports from the British government, but nearly disappeared after the Revolutionary War.

Rice cultivation was not as successful along the Cape Fear River, where peanuts and naval stores were the major commercial products, and North Carolina gradually emerged as a unique entity with its own interests. In 1729, North and South Carolina became separate colonies, each ruled by its own royal governors.

LEFT: Century-old live oaks create shade and splendor in the Carolina Lowcountry.

15

nd Indigo-dyed Silk Thread

Roasted oysters remain a popular Lowcountry meal from Native American days.

Indigo, used to make a blue dye, rivaled rice as a cash crop in early Colonial days.

NATIVE AMERICANS OF THE CAROLINA COAST

Initially extending a welcome to the English settlers, the tribes living along the Carolina coast soon found themselves at odds with the newcomers because of land disputes, the disappearance of deer, and the Indian slave trade. These differences came to a head during the Tuscarora War (1711–13) and the bloody Yamasee War (1715–17), involving many confederated tribes. After years of defeats, many of the survivors moved away or simply disappeared into the swamps.

Although decimated by war and disease, several groups of Native Americans have managed to remain in the area of their traditional homelands to the present day. The Waccamaw Indian People (843-358-6877; www.waccamawindians.us) live closest to Myrtle Beach. Their arts festival and pauwaw is held every November at their tribal grounds, located just off US 501 in Aynor.

If you like this . . . the Pee Dee Indian Tribe of South Carolina (843-523-6790; www.peedeeindiantribeofsc.com) hosts an annual powwow every April at its tribal grounds in McColl, north of Bennettsville.

Another branch of the Waccamaw Indians, the Waccamaw Siouan Tribe (910-655-8778; www.waccamaw-siouan.com) lives in North Carolina on the edge of the Green Swamp, about 37 miles west of Wilmington. It holds its annual powwow in October.

The largest remaining tribe in the region is the Lumbee (www.lumbeetribe .com), living along the border between North and South Carolina on the shores of the Lumbee River. They have a long history of resistance to oppression, stretching from the guerrilla war waged by legendary folk hero Henry Berry Lowrie against the Confederacy to an armed confrontation with the Ku Klux Klan in 1958. The Lumbee Regional Development Association (910-521-8602; www.lumbee.org) sponsors a fall powwow in October.

Deep swamps made the Swamp Fox impossible to catch.

Fast fact: The **Museum of the Native American Resource Center** (910-521-6282; www.uncp.edu/nativemuseum), located on the campus of the University of North Carolina at Pembroke, has exhibits and films on tribes all over the United States, with an emphasis on the history and culture of the Lumbee and other local tribes. Pembroke is just 10 miles west of I-95 on US 74. Admission to the museum is free.

Did you know? Much of what we know of the life and customs of the Native American tribes in the Carolinas before their cultures dissolved in the face of English settlement comes from the work of naturalist John Lawson, who toured the region in the early 1700s. His book *A New Voyage to Carolina* was published in 1709. Lawson died in 1711, an early casualty of the Tuscarora War.

FRANCIS MARION: THE SWAMP FOX

No name looms larger in Lowcountry legend than that of Francis Marion, hero of the Revolutionary War. Born into a family of French Huguenot plantation owners, Marion grew up near Georgetown and took command of the local patriot forces after all the other American officers were captured when Charleston surrendered to the British. (Marion had been out of town nursing a broken ankle.)

Charged with setting up a spy ring, the young officer and the men he recruited perfected a guerilla style of warfare, attacking British and Loyalist patrols then disappearing into the surrounding swamps, a tactic that earned him the name the Swamp Fox. The U.S. Army Rangers consider him one of their founders.

Marion is credited with an important role in winning the Revolution in the South, and many places in South Carolina are named in his honor, including Francis Marion University (www.fmarion.edu) in Florence; Marion County (www.marionsc.org), just west of Horry County; and its county seat, the city of Marion (www.marionsc.gov), where a statue of the Swamp Fox stands in front of the county courthouse. The Marion County Museum (843-423-8299; www.marionsc.org) contains exhibits on the life of this favorite son.

If you like this . . . Olde Towne Marion (843-423-9918; www.theswampfox.com) sponsors the FoxTrot Festival every May, with Revolutionary reenactors, musket firing demonstrations, and an encampment in Courthouse Square.

The USS *North Carolina* was one of the most decorated ships in World War II.

WORLD WAR II

The Carolina coast played an important part in World War II and was actually under threat of attack by submarines during much of the war. Kure Beach in North Carolina was shelled by a U-boat in 1943.

The shipyard in Wilmington built over 200 Liberty ships for the war effort, and several prisoner of war camps were located nearby. The self-guided World War II Trail for Wilmington and Southeastern North Carolina visits more than 45 historic sites, including the USS *North Carolina*, berthed across from Wilmington's historic downtown, the Historic Hannah Block USO, Fort Fisher, Camp Lejeune, the Missiles & More Museum on Topsail Island, and many other memorials, markers, and museums related to World War II. Ask for a trail map at Wilmington visitor centers or download a copy at www.wilburjones.com, the website of the area's foremost military historian.

In South Carolina, Myrtle Beach emerged as an important site for air force activity. The air base is now Myrtle Beach International Airport, but Warbird Park and other memorials recall the war days.

World War II played another important role in the region's development. Wrightsville Beach, Carolina Beach, Ocean Drive, and Myrtle Beach developed as entertainment spots for servicemen on leave, places where they could meet their sweethearts, walk on the sand, and forget the war for awhile.

BEACH MUSIC AND THE SHAG

As the Jazz Age turned into the Big Band era, and the Charleston gave way to the swing, folks along the Carolina coast were already developing their own unique dance form, the shag. A shag contest was advertised as early as 1932 on Wrightsville Beach, but most historians of the shag agree that the dance didn't approach its modern form

Quick tip: To get an idea of the swamps where Marion and his men took shelter, visit the **Francis Marion National Forest** (843-928-3368; www.fs.fed.us).

Did you know? Francis Marion is closely associated with the area around Lake Marion, just west of the Grand Strand, where his plantation now lies under the waters. To find out more, follow the **Swamp Fox Murals Trail** (www.swampfoxtrail.com) along historic US 301 through the towns of Summerton, Manning, Paxville, and Turbeville, South Carolina, where over two dozen paintings on the buildings in the historic downtowns tell the story of the Southern campaign of the Revolution. US 301 parallels I-95 north of Lake Marion.

The O.D. Pavilion is the last of the open-air shag palaces that once lined the coast.

until the postwar years, when returning GIs, lifeguards, and local teens gathered in the open-air pavilions that then lined the coast to dance to the jukebox and make memories that would last a lifetime.

Many of the records they danced to had been acquired at the black-only beaches that existed back then in the days of segregation: Seabreeze, just north of Carolina Beach, and Atlantic Beach, just south of Ocean Drive, were two such beaches, and they hosted an active nightlife of their own, with dancing till all hours to jukeboxes stocked with the latest rhythm and blues hits. Like most things forbidden, this so-called race music, with its driving backbeat and cool lyrics, became the sound that seeped into the young shaggers' souls, a memory they took home with them from vacation and came back to find again the next summer.

The shag as it developed on the coast owed a lot to the old swing moves of the 1940s, but slowed down and adapted to hot summer nights. Sometimes described as a lazy jitterbug, the shag survived the disco years, reemerging as a major force in Grand Strand tourism with the first Society of Stranders reunion (www.shag dance.com) in 1980. (See our Grand Strand chapter for a rundown of shag clubs and culture in Ocean Drive.)

Since then, the shag movement has grown, with clubs and dancehalls up and down the coast, and has spawned an entire beach music industry (www.bmai.net), with bands writing and recording new songs for shagging. The dance has spread beyond the coast, with shag clubs in cities across the South and beyond. Visit the Shag Tour website (www.shagtour.com) to find a shag club or lessons near you. The Shag Preservation Association (www.shagspa.com) sponsors contests where you can see the best dancers demonstrate their moves.

Many radio stations play beach music as well, and you can listen to them online. 'Fessa Hook, one of the top beach DJs and shag historians, streams Beach Music Top 40 countdowns on his website, www.beachshag.com. Or listen live to 94.9 The Surf (www.949thesurf.com), the official radio station of the Society of Stranders, based in North Myrtle Beach.

Beach Music Classics

While every aficionado of the shag has their own list of favorite tunes, these records have stood the test of time and still appear on playlists at shag clubs today.

Sixty Minute Man—Billy Ward and the Dominoes
Give Me Just A Little More Time—Chairmen of the Board
Be Young, Be Foolish, Be Happy—The Tams
Ms. Grace—The Tymes
I Love Beach Music—The Embers
Stay—Maurice Williams & the Zodiacs

Penny loafers remain the shaggers' favorite footwear.

My Girl—Temptations
Under the Boardwalk—The Drifters
One Mint Julep—The Clovers
With This Ring—The Platters

In 2011 the Beach Music Hall of Fame (www.beachmusichof.com) inducted its first class of classic songs and beach music pioneers, including Fats Domino, Louis Jordan, Ruth Brown, and The Clovers. Hall of Fame ceremonies are scheduled every May at Coastal Carolina University's Wheelwright Auditorium (843-349-2502; www.coastal.edu), where an ongoing exhibit honors the inductees.

THE CAPE FEAR ARCH: CAROLINA BAYS, CARNIVOROUS PLANTS, AND BLACKWATER RIVERS

Beyond the sandy beaches, the earliest explorers of the Carolina Lowcountry found unique geological features known today by the name Carolina bays or pocosins, derived from an Algonquian Indian word meaning "swamp on a hill."

Most bays are oval depressions in the earth, typically with a sandy ridge that's particularly noticeable on the southeastern edge. Many of the Carolina bays don't contain standing water, but the ground is typically wet and boggy. The water and soil inside a pocosin is extremely acidic, containing thick layers of peat. Bay trees, vines, and briars survive best in this nutrient poor soil. Some pocosins contain pine trees; others are rimmed with cypress.

Found scattered all along the southern Atlantic seaboard, these bays are most numerous in eastern North Carolina, where thousands have been identified. Scientists have never definitively proved their origin, but theories

Quick tip: Visit the website of the **Beach Music Hall of Fame** (www.beachmusichof.com) to hear classic recordings and find out much more about beach music and shag history.

Fast fact: The shag is the state dance of both North and South Carolina.

abound, ranging from the building habits of giant prehistoric beavers to sudden floods at the end of the last Ice Age. Many people believe they're the result of an ancient asteroid shower, thus the popular name Meteor Lakes.

Some plants in the bays have developed unusual behaviors to supplement their diets. This ecosystem is the evolutionary cradle of carnivorous plants, including the Venus flytrap, and the less-well-known pitcher plant and sundew.

Rivers in the coastal plain can be described as either red water or blackwater. Red water rivers come down from the Piedmont carrying a load of reddish clay and silt. Blackwater rivers originate and flow entirely in the coastal plain. Their dark waters come from tannins released into the water by decaying foliage. Shades vary from an orangey-tea color to a deep rich color reminiscent of blackstrap molasses.

Fast fact: Local legend holds that the Venus flytrap, which is native to the 60 miles surrounding Wilmington, North Carolina, came to earth with the same meteor shower said to have formed the Carolina bays.

Did you know? Carolina bays take their name from the many varieties of bay trees that find the acidic soil to their liking.

Native Wildlife

The beaches of the Carolina coast are as popular with sea turtles as they are with tourists. Numerous female loggerheads and other endangered sea turtles come on shore each summer to lay their eggs. To protect these nests, volunteers patrol the beaches, tracking and monitoring turtle activity during the May to August nesting season.

Volunteers walk Sunset Beach every morning looking for sea turtle nests.

Many of the volunteer groups that operate on the islands along the Carolina coast also offer educational opportunities to help the public understand how they can help these endangered creatures survive. Contact them to find out how you can help, or to report turtle sightings.

In North Carolina, the following groups work to protect sea turtles: the Wrightsville Beach Sea Turtle Project (910-791-4541; www.turtles.wrightsville-beach.info); the Pleasure Island Sea Turtle Project (1-888-290-1065; www.seaturtleproject.org), covering Kure and Carolina Beaches; the Bald Head Island Conservancy (910-338-0911; www.bhic.org); the Holden Beach Turtle Watch Project

(910-754-0766; www.hbturtlewatch.org); and the Sunset Beach Turtle Watch (910-579-5862; www.sunsetbeachturtles.org).

Over the border, the South Carolina United Turtle Enthusiasts organization (www.debordieuscute.org) monitors the beaches from Georgetown to North Myrtle Beach and hosts educational programs at the Hobcaw Barony. The Burroughs and Chapin Center for Marine and Wetland Studies (www.coastal.edu/cmws) at Coastal Carolina University oversees preservation efforts on Waties Island, an undeveloped barrier island on the border between North and South Carolina.

Injured turtles are brought to the ☃ ☂ Karen Beasley Sea Turtle Rescue & Rehabilitation Center (910-328-3377; www.seaturtlehospital.org) at the southern end of Topsail Island, North Carolina. Located about 40 miles north of Wilmington, this is one of the only sea turtle hospitals in the United States. Tours of the facility are available from June to August, but hours vary so call before you go. Kemp's Ridley, Green, and Loggerhead turtles, all endangered, are typically among the resident patients. The occasional release days, when turtles are returned to the wild, are community-wide celebrations.

Wilder Places
Between 35 and 45 million years ago, forces within the earth led to a massive uplift of limestone and sand along what's now the Carolina coast. Called the Cape Fear Arch, this uplift stretches from Cape Fear in North Carolina to Cape Romain in South Carolina, and inland as far as Fayetteville. Off shore, the uplift creates the gently curved and shallow Long Bay. On shore, it's home to a unique set of ecosystems, including longleaf pine savannas, Carolina bays, blackwater streams, tidal swamps, and ancient fossil dunes.

Many rare and endangered plant and animal species call the area home, including the world's only native Venus flytraps and the oldest trees east of the Rocky Mountains, bald cypresses over 1,700 years old.

Beyond the resorts and cities, a great deal of the Carolina coast is protected in nature preserves, wildlife refuges, and national forests. These provide a wide variety of recreational options, including excellent birdwatching, hiking, paddling, mountain biking, horseback riding, and hunting. The Cape Fear Arch Conservation Collaboration (www.capefeararch.org) details many of these options. Others are listed below.

The Carolina Coast is a noted birding destination.

Environmental Education Centers
The ♿ Waccamaw National Wildlife Refuge Environmental Education Center (843-527-8069; www.fws.gov/waccamaw) is situated on US 701 between Conway and Georgetown. In addition to exhibits on local animals and plant life, the center provides access to a self-guided nature trail and hiking along the Great Pee Dee River.

Red wolves can be seen at the Sewee Environmental Center

At the ♂ ♿ Hobcaw Barony Discovery Center (843-546-4623; www.hobcawbarony.org), just north of Georgetown, exhibits introduce the ongoing environmental research being conducted at the North Inlet–Winyah Bay National Estuarine Research Reserve (www.northinlet.sc.edu).

South of Georgetown along US 17, the ♂ ♿ Sewee Visitor & Environmental Education Center (843-928-3368; www.fs.fed.us) contains interpretive displays on the unique ecosystems of the Francis Marion National Forest and Cape Romain National Wildlife Refuge (843-928-3264; www.fws.gov/caperomain). A mile-long loop trail leads through a butterfly garden to an enclosure that's home to a family of red wolves.

If you like this . . . visit the nearby Sewee Shell Ring Interpretive Trail, where a boardwalk encircles a prehistoric shell ring believed to be 4,000 years old.

The ♂ ♿ Playcard Environmental Educational Center (843-756-1277; www.horrycountyschools.net/departments/learningservices/playcard_center), in Loris, South Carolina, has exhibits on logging, early farming, and Indian culture, as well as the Braille Nature Trail. Contact the center to arrange a visit. Playcard also hosts Swampfest, a public open house, every November.

North Carolina Wilder Places
About 20 miles to the south of Wilmington, off US 17 on NC 87, the Boiling Spring Lakes Preserve (910-395-5000; www.nature.org) contains the remnants of an ancient dune system and several Carolina bays. A 3-mile nature trail begins behind the City of Boiling Spring Lakes Community Center.

Continue south on US 17 to Supply, then head northwest on NC 211, the Green Swamp Byway, for a drive through the heart of the Green Swamp Preserve (910-395-5000; www.nature.org), one of the most ecologically diverse spots on the continent. A nature trail begins at the parking lot

Quick tip: The community of **Boiling Spring Lakes** (910-845-3693; www.cityofbsl.org) is the place to go if you prefer to swim in freshwater lakes. Four city parks offer free beaches for swimming. Visit the city's webpage for directions.

Did you know? The Green Swamp has reputedly been the home to a variety of isolated communities, from Lost Colony survivors to pirates to runaway slaves. One of the best documented is Crusoe Island, said to have been founded by plantation owners escaping the revolution in Haiti. Read *Into the Sound Country*, by Bland and Ann Cary Simpson (University of North Carolina Press, 1997) for more info on the Green Swamp's rich ecology and mysterious inhabitants.

about 5.5 miles from the US 17 junction. The byway continues for about 30 miles to Lake Waccamaw.

Not all Carolina bays contain lakes, but some do, thanks to springs and seeps rising from the underlying water table. Lake Waccamaw in North Carolina is the largest of these lakes and the most unusual. Limestone deposits have neutralized the acidic waters of Waccamaw, making it a suitable habitat for a variety of fish and amphibians found nowhere else. At ⬥ Lake Waccamaw State Park (910-646-4748; www.ncparks.gov), several trails and boardwalks begin near the visitor center, including one that leads to a fishing pier. Boating, picnicking, and wilderness camping are popular activities. The park is located about 35 miles west of Wilmington off US 74.

The longleaf pine is the only habitat of the endangered red-cockaded woodpecker.

Several more Carolina bays are found in Jones Lake State Park (910-588-4550; www.ncparks.gov), along with hiking trails, a primitive campground, a picnic area, and a beach. You can swim in the lake's tea-colored water, launch your kayak, or rent a canoe or paddleboat at the boathouse, open Memorial Day to Labor Day.

If you like this . . . interpretive trails at ☙ Turnbull Creek Educational State Forest (910-588-4161; www.ncesf.org) include a talking tree for kids.

Much closer to Wilmington, about 10 miles from the Cape Fear Memorial Bridge, off US 17 on Rock Creek Road, UNCW's Ev-Henwood Nature Preserve (910-962-3107; www.uncw .edu) offers 15 trails and old logging roads through the forest bordering pristine Town Creek. Two of the trails are self-guided with plant labels and exhibits. Download a guide from the university website.

Quick tip: Across the 7-mile-long lake from the state park, the town of **Lake Waccamaw** (910-646-3700; www.lakewaccamaw.com) offers a variety of modern services, including dining and shopping. The free **Lake Waccamaw Depot Museum** (910-646-1992; www .lakewaccamawdepotmuseum.com) contains exhibits on the area's unique ecology and its history as a railroad center and summer resort. For more information, contact the **Columbus County Tourism Bureau** (1-800-845-8419; www .discovercolumbuscounty.org).

South Carolina Wilder Places

Just across the Intracoastal Waterway from Myrtle Beach, the Lewis Ocean Bay Heritage Preserve (843-546-3226; www.dnr.sc.gov) contains 23 Carolina bays, as well as bald eagles, red-cockaded woodpeckers, and South Carolina's largest population of black bears. Hiking, driving, and horse trails lead through this natural gem, just off US 501.

Little Pee Dee State Park (843-774-8872; www.southcarolinaparks.com), off SC 57 in Dillon, contains 54-acre Lake Norton, a water-filled Carolina bay. Recreational opportunities include a nature trail to a beaver pond; fishing on the river and lake; camping for tents and RVs; a boat ramp; and jon boats, canoes, and kayaks available for rent.

If you like this . . . Cartwheel Bay Heritage Preserve (843-546-3226; www .dnr.sc.gov) in Nichols is one of the few Carolina bay/longleaf pine savanna complexes in South Carolina, with excellent birding, plus Venus flytraps, pitcher plants, and other wildflowers.

Situated close to the Grand Strand, the Cox Ferry Lake Recreation Area (843-527-8069; www.fws.gov/waccamaw), along the Waccamaw River off SC 544 in Conway, has nature trails ideal for birding, hiking, or biking.

Located between the Waccamaw and Great Pee Dee Rivers near Brookgreen Gardens, Sandy Island Preserve (843-937-8807; www.nature.org, www.sctrails.net) is accessible only by boat. Easy hiking trails on the island loop through several rare ecosystems, including a mature longleaf pine forest over 100 years old, home to the endangered red-cockaded woodpecker.

For a look at an untouched wilderness, make arrangements to visit the Tom Yawkey Wildlife Center Heritage Preserve (843-546-6814; www.dnr.sc.gov, www.yawkeyfoundation.org), near Georgetown, accessible by guided tour only, September–May. Call for reservations, preferably 4–6 months in advance.

Nearly 259,000 acres between Georgetown and Charleston are preserved as part of the Francis Marion National Forest (843-928-3368; www.fs.fed.us). Numerous trails cross this vast forest including some of the best off-road biking tracks in the coastal region. The South Tibwin Hiking Trail is noted for its birding, and the 40-mile Wambaw Cycle Trail is open to motorcycles and off-road vehicles. Several paddle trails explore the creeks and canals in this wilderness. Primitive camping is permitted in several areas, and RV sites with full hookups are available at the Buck Hall Recreation Area on the Intracoastal Waterway.

Alligators are a frequent sight on golf courses and along rivers.

If you like this . . . the I'on Swamp Interpretive Trail in the Francis Marion National Forest provides a fascinating glimpse into the heart of the swamp, where Marion and his men themselves might have hidden.

Transportation

ROUTES TO AND THROUGH THE LOWCOUNTRY

MORE THAN MOST PLACES, travel on the Carolina coast is dominated by bridges. One bridge on and off an island—or an outdated swing bridge—limits traffic and preserves the small-town character that many visitors treasure. A modern high-rise bridge that soars above the Intracoastal Waterway (ICW) can speed development as it eases access.

A few years ago, only US 501 and SC 9 brought traffic across the ICW to the Grand Strand. The old route from Conway straight to the heart of Myrtle Beach, US 501 witnessed legendary traffic jams on busy summer weekends.

As tourism grew, South Carolina took action, and now a network of new highways and a bevy of bridges connect the Grand Strand with the mainland. When traffic backed up on the US 17 Bypass, Horry County built a parallel four-lane highway (SC 31/Carolina Bays Parkway) on the west side of the ICW. Bridges at Main Street in Ocean Drive and SC 22/Conway Connector in Restaurant Row ease pressure on US 17 leading north. SC 544 and SC 707 are shortcuts to the South Strand.

The situation is similar over the state line in North Carolina. US 17 is the main highway along this coast as it is in South Carolina, and has been upgraded to four-lane status along much of its route. Several new bridges cross the Cape Fear

> **Fast fact:** US 17 follows the route of the old Kings Highway that stretched over 1,300 miles connecting Charleston with Boston in colonial days and is still the major route along the Carolina Coast. In 1791 George Washington spent the night at several taverns and plantations along the Kings Highway, then just a sandy track, during his tour of the South. Today US 17 is mostly four-lanes between Jacksonville, North Carolina, home of the U.S. Marine Corps base Camp Lejeune, and Charleston, South Carolina, with many bypasses around urban areas.

LEFT: Increasing numbers of Grand Strand visitors arrive by air.

27

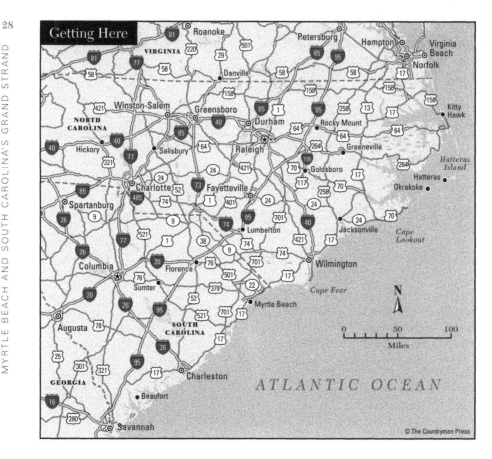

© The Countryman Press

River, steering traffic around Wilmington's historic downtown, adding to its pedestrian-friendly character. That great cross-country corridor, I-40, dead-ends just north of downtown Wilmington, making this end of the coast easily accessible from I-95 and destinations all over the eastern part of the country.

Interstate access to the Grand Strand is a bit more problematic. I-20 ends in Florence, about 70 miles west of Myrtle Beach. Plans are in the works for I-73, which splits from I-77 near Winston-Salem, North Carolina, to extend all the way to the ocean.

LEFT: Dizzy Gillespie is honored in Cheraw, his hometown.

South of the Border welcomes visitors to South Carolina and the North Strand.

By Air

Two major airports bracket this coast, Wilmington International (ILM) and Myrtle Beach International (MYR).

& (p) Myrtle Beach International/MYR (843-448-1589; www.fly myrtlebeach.com) is one of the fastest-growing airports in the country, with nonstop flights to more than a dozen destinations. Airlines serving MYR include Delta, Continental, and US Airways, as well as low-cost carriers Spirit (www.spirit.com), Direct Air (www.visitdirectair.com), and Allegiant (www.allegiantair.com). Toronto-based Porter Airlines (www.flyporter.com) provides seasonal service from Canada, and several international carriers offer flights from Europe. A bar and grill and a branch of the Myrtle Beach Welcome Center (843-626-7444; www .visitmyrtlebeach.com) are in the arrivals area.

& (p) Wilmington International Airport/ILM (910-341-4125; www.flyilm.com) provides a low-stress alternative, with direct flights from more than seven major cities around the country, and is a favorite spot to pass customs for private pilots returning from the Caribbean. The Tailwind Deli & Bar (910-343-9881) is in the main lobby.

Fast fact: ILM is known locally as a prime spot to watch for celebrities flying in to make movies at the local Screen Gems Studios.

Quick tip: Drivers headed for Myrtle Beach from the Charlotte area can speed up their trip by following SC 38, a freshly built four-lane highway that splits off from US 52/US 1 in Cheraw (birthplace of jazz great Dizzy Gillespie). Named the Blenheim Highway, since it passes the birthplace of the iconic ginger ale, SC 38 joins US 501, just before it crosses the Little Pee Dee River.

Did you know? Since 1949, Pedro and his huge sombrero, one of the iconic sights along I-95, have greeted vacationers at **South of the Border** (1-800-845-6011; www.thesouthoftheborder.com). Humorous billboards sporting Pedro's sayings line the highway for hundreds of miles, speeding many a trip with laughter. Stop and enjoy a hot tamale with Pedro and get a bird's-eye view from the top of the Sombrero Tower. If you're headed for the North Strand from points north, this is the place to get off the interstate and head down SC 9 to Cherry Grove.

Several general aviation airports offer facilities for private pilots. In North Carolina, Cape Fear Regional Jetport (910-457-6483; www.capefear jetport.com), between Southport and Oak Island, and Odell Williamson Municipal Airport (910-579-6152; www.oibgov.com), owned by the Town of Ocean Isle Beach, provide access to the north and south ends of Brunswick County.

Brunswick Air (910-363-4334; www.brunswickair.com) conducts family-friendly scenic tours from Cape Fear Regional. For an adrenaline rush, take a leap with Skydive Coastal Carolinas (910-457-1039; www.sky divecoastalcarolinas.com), also based at the jetport.

The Grand Strand Airport, a county-owned facility along the ICW in North Myrtle Beach, has an instrument landing system and control tower, but is considered more challenging for inexperienced pilots due to frequent crosswinds. Ramp 66 (843-272-5337 or 1-800-433-8918; www.ramp66.com) operates a fixed base facility here. Several flight-seeing companies offer scenic tours of Grand Strand, including Long Bay Aviation (843-437-7731; www.flyoib.com) and Classic Air Ventures (843-340-5079; www.coastalbiplanetours.com), with flights in an open-cockpit biplane.

Other general aviation airports in South Carolina include Conway-Horry County Airport (843-397-9111) on US 378, 5 miles west of Conway, and the unattended Loris-Twin Cities Airport on US 701, both in Horry County; and the Georgetown County Airport (843-527-8017; www.georgetowncountyairport.com), halfway between Myrtle Beach and Charleston.

> **Quick tip:** Several golf courses, including the award-winning Witch, are located just minutes from Myrtle Beach International Airport, if you'd like to fit in a final round before your flight.

> **Did you know? Myrtle Beach Transportation** (843-449-4445; www.myrtlebeachtransportation .com) offers shuttle service to Myrtle Beach International Airport from Brunswick County in North Carolina to Charleston, South Carolina, as well as shuttles to hotels, restaurants, and golf courses, 24 hours a day.

A car ferry connects Fort Fisher and Southport, North Carolina.

By Boat or Ferry

Many visitors arrive on the Carolina coast by boat. The Atlantic Intracoastal Waterway (ICW) runs behind the many islands in the region, separating them from the mainland. Numerous marinas line the ICW in both North and South Carolina, offering transient slips, as well as boat and Jet Ski rentals, charter and headboat fishing, water-front dining, and other amenities that appeal even to those who don't own their own boats. See our destination chapters for suggestions on where to find waterfront fun.

One inexpensive and fun way to get out on the water is to take a ferry from Southport in North Carolina. The state-operated ❀ ♿ Fort Fisher–Southport Ferry (910-457-6942; www.ncferry.org) makes seasonal trips linking Pleasure Island with Brunswick County. Or take the passenger ferry to ❀ ♿ Bald Head Island (910-457-5003; www.baldheadisland.com) for a day of ecologically oriented pleasures.

By Automobile and Motorcycle

Both major airports in the region, and many general aviation facilities, offer a wide selection of cars from national rental companies. See their websites for more suggestions.

Myrtle Beach Harley Davidson (843-369-5555; www.myrtlebeachharley.com) rents motorcycles by the day or week. Rallies are held in the fall and spring.

Many scenic byway routes have been identified in the region. Detailed directions for North Carolina Scenic Byways can be found at www.ncdot.org/travel /scenic/. Information on South Carolina trails is found at www.sctrails.net.

By Bicycle or on Foot

Several trails cross the Carolina coast. The East Coast Greenway (www.green way.org) runs through the region, with several off-road portions completed. Bike maps for North Carolina can be ordered free or downloaded from the North Carolina Department of Transportation website (877-DOT-4YOU; www.ncdot.org/transit/bicycle). South Carolina biking and hiking trails are detailed at www.sctrails.net.

Biking is a popular way to get around on the Carolina coast.

North and South Carolina both have trails that cross the state from west to east. North Carolina's Mountains-to-Sea Trail (www.ncmst.org), suitable for hiking or biking, stretches 1,000 miles from the Great Smoky Mountains to the Outer Banks. South Carolina's Palmetto Trail (www.palmettoconservation.org) will eventually be more than 425 miles long and is open for hiking, mountain biking, and horseback riding. Its eastern terminus is at Buck Hall Recreation Area in the Francis Marion Forest (843-336-3248; www.fs.fed.us), south of Georgetown.

By Bus and Train

No direct railroad service is currently available to either Wilmington or Myrtle Beach. However, AMTRAK (1-800-872-7245; www.amtrak.com) provides daily service along the Eastern Seaboard on the Silver Meteor and Palmetto routes, with stops at Fayetteville, North Carolina, and Dillon, Florence, Kingstree, and Charleston in South Carolina.

Southport is a popular stop for boaters traveling the ICW.

Buses operated by Greyhound Lines, Inc. (1-800-231-2222; www.greyhound .com), stop in Wilmington, North Carolina, Georgetown, South Carolina, and downtown Myrtle Beach.

Within Wilmington, Wave Transit (910-343-0106; www.wavetransit.com) runs daily routes throughout the city, including a bus to Monkey Junction. The entire Wave fleet is equipped with bicycle racks. Many local attractions can be reached by bus; however, no service is available to Wrightsville Beach or Pleasure Island.

On the Grand Strand, the Coast RTA (843-488-0865; www.coastrta.com) provides connecting bus service from Myrtle Beach to Conway, Surfside Beach, Murrells Inlet, Pawleys Island, and Georgetown. An hourly shuttle travels along Ocean Boulevard in Myrtle Beach, with stops at many hotels and restaurants. Another route runs from Broadway at the Beach to the Charleston Visitor Center (1-800-774-0006; www.charlestoncvb.com), where you can connect with free Carta trolleys (843-724-7420; www.ridecarta.com) that circle Charleston's historic district.

Fast fact: Wave Transit's free trolley circles downtown Wilmington.

Quick tip: Maps to completed portions of the Waccamaw River Paddle Trail, as well as other water routes, can be found at www.ncsu .edu/paddletrails/ and www.sctrails .net.

With numerous red water and blackwater rivers, thousands of acres of salt marsh, the ICW, and the unique tidal estuary of Winyah Bay, the Carolina coast makes the ideal destination for paddling vacations.

A Blue Trail (www.americanrivers.org) is under development on the Waccamaw, one of the longest blackwater rivers in the world. When complete, it will stretch from the river's origin at Lake Waccamaw in North Carolina to its mouth at Winyah Bay in South Carolina, a distance of 150 miles, with primitive camping along the way.

A boat trip through the Nature Conservancy's Black River Preserve (910-395-5000; www.nature.org) near Wilmington is a peaceful float past ancient Spanish moss-draped bald cypress, some of the oldest trees east of the Rockies, wading birds, and several diverse ecosystems. See the Nature Conservancy's website for suggested put-ins or sign up for a cruise with the Audubon Society (910-686-7527; nc.audubon.org) aboard the SS *Moffitt*.

Other rivers with paddle trails in North Carolina include the Lumber (910-628-4564; www.ncparks.gov), designated a National Wild and Scenic River (www.rivers.gov); Town Creek; Lockwoods Folly; the Shallotte; and the Cape Fear itself. For detailed maps of North Carolina paddle trails, including directions for kayaking to Bald Head Island, visit www.ncsu.edu/paddletrails/.

In South Carolina, established paddle trails follow the Little Pee Dee (843-546-3226; www.dnr.sc.gov) through Horry and Marion Counties, and the Black River (843-546-8436) in Georgetown County. Details and maps at www.sctrails.net.

If you want to venture a bit farther afield, consider the Old Santee Canal Park (www.oldsanteecanalpark.org) in Moncks Corner (canoe rentals available) or the Woods Bay State Natural Area (843-659-4445; www.southcarolinaparks.com) in Olanta, near I-95 exit 141, where you can rent a canoe to follow a 1-mile paddle trail around a Carolina bay.

Kayaks are the best way to explore the region's blackwater swamps.   Karen Wright

Wilmington

HOLLYWOOD EAST

SITUATED ON BLUFFS along the eastern side of the Cape Fear River, Wilmington, North Carolina's first great metropolis, looks, as it always has, to the river. The city's charm radiates through the historic district, some 230 blocks of homes and businesses, most built before and just after the Civil War. Horse-drawn carriages tour the streets, while paddlewheel riverboats ply the river.

Eminently walkable, downtown Wilmington's sidewalks are lined with house museums, trendy restaurants, bed & breakfast inns, hot nightspots, galleries, and boutiques. Streets slope gently down to the water, where the Riverwalk, a mile-long boardwalk along the Cape Fear, provides scenic views of boat traffic and the mighty USS *North Carolina*, berthed on the far shore.

Founded in 1729, the town that would become Wilmington always took its meaning and purpose from the river. By the mid-1700s the city was a major port with ships from around the world docking to take on loads of vital naval stores—tar, pitch, and turpentine—produced upriver in the endless forests of longleaf pines that covered the Sand Hills.

Sailors looked for the Dram Tree, a prominent cypress along the riverbank, where they were allowed a ration of rum to celebrate the successful navigation of the shifting sands of Frying Pan Shoals. Extending 20 miles offshore, the shallows gave meaning to the name of the river's mouth—Cape Fear.

> ### Top 5 Don't Miss: Wilmington
>
> - Enjoy a glass of wine on the Riverwalk.
> - Visit the USS *North Carolina*.
> - Cruise the Cape Fear River on the *Henrietta III*.
> - Tour the historic district in a horse-drawn carriage.
> - Dine on a deck by the Intracoastal Waterway (ICW).

LEFT: A stroll on the Riverwalk gives views of both public art and the USS *North Carolina*.

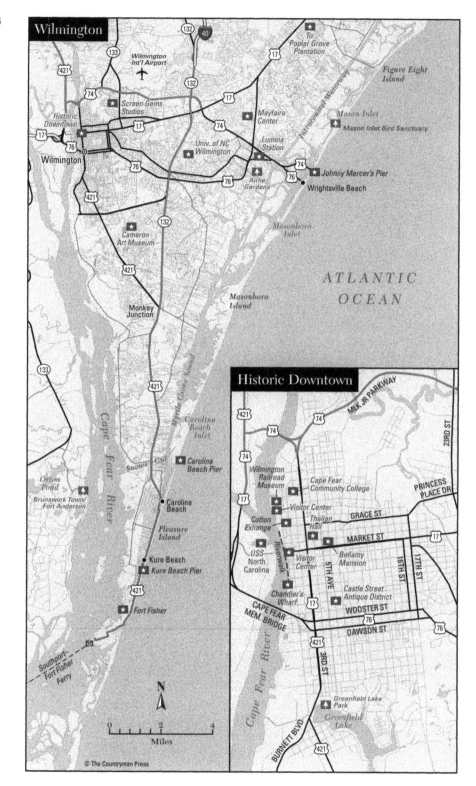

Wilmington

To Poplar Grove Plantation

Figure Eight Island

Wilmington Int'l Airport

Screen Gems Studios

Historic Downtown

Wilmington

Mayfaire Center

Mason Inlet

Mason Inlet Bird Sanctuary

Univ. of NC Wilmington

Lumina Station

Johnny Mercer's Pier

Wrightsville Beach

Airlie Gardens

Cameron Art Museum

Masonboro Inlet

ATLANTIC OCEAN

Masonboro Island

Monkey Junction

Carolina Beach Inlet

Carolina Beach Pier

Snows Cut

Carolina Beach

Cape Fear River

Pleasure Island

Orton Pond

Brunswick Town/ Fort Anderson

Kure Beach

Kure Beach Pier

Fort Fisher

Southport- Fort Fisher Ferry

N

0   2   4
Miles

© The Countryman Press

Historic Downtown

MLK JR PARKWAY

23RD ST

Wilmington Railroad Museum

Cape Fear Community College

PRINCESS PLACE DR

Visitor Center

GRACE ST

Cotton Exchange

Thalian Hall

MARKET ST

USS North Carolina

Visitor Center

Bellamy Mansion

16TH ST

17TH ST

Chandler's Wharf

Castle Street Antique District

WOOSTER ST

CAPE FEAR MEM. BRIDGE

DAWSON ST

Cape Fear River

3RD ST

Greenfield Lake Park

Greenfield Lake

BURNETT BLVD

Fast facts:

• Before being named for Spencer Compton, the Earl of Wilmington, in 1740, Wilmington was called New Liverpool, and many of its downtown streets are named after counterparts there.

• The ﴾ **Fort Fisher Historic Site** (910-458-5538; www.nchistoricsites.org), with restored gun batteries, a visitor center, and guided and self-guided walking tours, sits at the southern end of Pleasure Island on US 421, just before the **Fort Fisher–Southport Ferry** (910-457-6942; www.ncferry.org). Admission is free. The adjacent **Fort Fisher State Recreation Area** (910-458-5798; www.ncparks.gov) has a pleasant beach with lifeguards during summer.

• Flora McDonald, heroine of the Bonnie Prince Charlie saga in Scotland, played a part in the fight at Moore's Creek Bridge, rallying the Highlanders to battle. At the time, she was living in the Cross Creek community, today's Fayetteville, where many expatriate Scots received land grants.

• Wrightsville, Carolina, and Kure Beaches share New Hanover County with the Wilmington metropolitan area. For more information on all the county's attractions, contact the **Wilmington/Cape Fear Coast Convention and Visitors Bureau** (910-341-4030 or 877-406-2356; www.capefearcoast.com), located at 505 Nutt Street, Wilmington, NC 28401.

Local residents were early patriots, defying the Stamp Act from 1765. In February 1776, a band of 1,000 patriot soldiers defeated a loyalist force at the Battle of Moore's Creek Bridge, 20 miles north of Wilmington, ending British rule of North Carolina.

Today the ﴾ Battle of Moore's Creek Bridge National Battlefield (910-283-5591; www.nps.gov/mocr), the nation's smallest battlefield park, preserves the site of the bridge where the loyalist Highlander forces, armed with broadswords, charged the Americans who met them with deadly musket fire. Visitor center exhibits and trails are free and open daily.

At the time of the Civil War, Wilmington was the largest city in North Carolina and played a vital role in the Confederacy. By 1865 every major port in the South had been captured or closed, except for Wilmington, defended by a series of gun batteries along the river, including the largest of them all, Fort Fisher. Guarding the mouth of the Cape Fear River, this immense fortification, called the Gibraltar of the South, pointed guns both out to sea and across the river. As long as Fort Fisher held off the Union forces, blockade runners could continue to run cotton out of Wilmington, returning with vital war supplies.

The Wilmington and Weldon

Did you know? The town of Brunswick, founded in 1726 on the west bank of the Cape Fear, was deserted after being burned by the British in 1776. Later the Confederacy fortified the spot, naming it Fort Anderson, to defend blockade runners entering the river. Today ﴾ **Brunswick Town/Fort Anderson** (910-371-6613; www.nchistoric sites.org) is a North Carolina Historic Site, with a visitor center, trails, and outdoor exhibits. Admission is free.

Railroad carried these supplies to the outskirts of Richmond, supporting General Lee's forces entrenched around the Confederate capital. When Fort Fisher finally fell to a massive combined land and sea assault on January 15, 1865, Richmond—and the Confederate cause—was doomed.

Following the Civil War, Wilmington became an important port for cotton, with steamboats running up the Cape Fear as far as Fayetteville. The excellent supply of lumber and naval stores made Wilmington a natural for the shipbuilding industry. Local boatyards contributed vessels to both the Civil War and World War I, but really came into their own during World War II when more than 200 Liberty ships and numerous other vessels launched down the slipways into the Cape Fear. In 1945 North Carolina designated Wilmington an official state deepwater port (www.ncports.com), making it a destination for huge cargo carriers from around the world.

Cranes at the state port are just one of the sights along the Cape Fear River.

When the Atlantic Coast Line Railroad, Wilmington's major industry in the early 20th century, pulled up stakes and moved its headquarters to Jacksonville, Florida, in 1955, Wilmington reinvented itself once again. Capitalizing on the area's rich history, the genteelly derelict downtown was rescued and renovated, creating a magnet for tourism. This process continues today with a new convention center and the mile-long Riverwalk recently added to the city's attractions.

In the 1980s, Hollywood discovered the charms of the old port city, when Dino De Laurentiis built an enormous studio complex on the edge of downtown. Wilmington residents grew accustomed to sharing their sidewalks with stars of the silver screen and gave their city a new nickname, Wilmywood.

Did you know? Beginning with *Firestarter,* filmed in 1983 at Orton Plantation, Wilmington has provided the location for over 350 films and more than 10 TV series. Among the more notable films made here are *Blue Velvet* (1986), *Teenage Mutant Ninja Turtles* (1990), *The Crow* (1994), *Empire Records* (1995), *Lolita* (1997), *Divine Secrets of the Ya-Ya Sisterhood* (2002), *Loggerheads* (2005), *Nights in Rodanthe* (2008), and *The Secret Life of Bees* (2008). Television shows filmed here include *Matlock,* starring North Carolina native Andy Griffith, six seasons of *Dawson's Creek,* and eight seasons and counting of *One Tree Hill.* Find out where the cameras are turning and what stars may be in town during your visit at the website of the **Wilmington Regional Film Commission** (www.wilmingtonfilm.com).

Quick tips:
• Find out more about life in wartime Wilmington in Wilbur Jones's award-winning books, *Sentimental Journey: Memoirs of a Wartime Boomtown* and *The Journey Continues: The World War II Homefront*. Both are available on the author's website, www.wilburjones.com, and at local bookstores.
• Visit in December for a screening of the great classic *It's a Wonderful Life* on the campus of the University of North Carolina Wilmington (UNCW), a tradition begun by the late Frank Capra Jr., longtime head of EUE/Screen Gems Studios, in honor of his father. Other holiday traditions in Wilmington include the World's Largest Living Christmas Tree, lighted boat parades, and Enchanted Airlie. Trolleys drawn by horses wearing reindeer antlers tour the holiday lights.
• Consult *The Film Junkie's Guide to North Carolina* (www.filmjunkiesguide.com), written by Connie Nelson and Floyd Harris, to find many local spots featured on the big screen.

Wilmington's Beaches: Wrightsville Beach and Pleasure Island

Although Wilmington's attention has always focused on the river, in the first years of the 20th century an electric trolley connected downtown with Lumina Pavilion on Wrightsville Beach, beginning the region's reign as an oceanfront resort. The three-level Lumina entertainment complex, visible for miles thanks to

Wrightsville Beach is just a short drive from downtown Wilmington.

the hundreds of electric lights on its exterior, boasted a ballroom visited by the big bands of the era, a bowling alley, a shooting gallery, and a movie screen set right in the surf. Famous journalist David Brinkley worked there as a boy.

When the Beach Trolley began its run in 1899, there were no stops between downtown and Wrightsville, but stations were added as the city grew, and by 1940, when the trolley ceased operation, there were 20 along the way. Pink and white Dorothy Perkins roses were planted along the rails, climbing up the poles that supported the streetcar wires.

In the years following the Civil War, entrepreneurs began to develop Federal Point, today called Pleasure Island. The first visitors arrived via steamer down the Cape Fear. By the 1950s, when a road and bridge over Snow's Cut connected the island with the mainland, two popular beach resorts, Carolina Beach and Kure Beach, attracted a growing tide of visitors.

Today the EUE/Screen Gems Studios (910-343-3433; www.screengems studios.com/nc) continue to play an important part in the city's economic and cultural life, giving employment to numerous Wilmingtonians, sponsoring film production degrees at local colleges, and spurring an increasing tide of film tourism. Walking tours of the studio itself are available on weekends year-round.

Pick Your Spot

Best places to stay in and around Wilmington

DOWNTOWN

Wilmington is a great walking city, and to take full advantage of that, most visitors choose to stay downtown in the historic district. There you have two major options: modern waterfront hotels or period bed & breakfast inns.

Several high-rise hotels lie along the north end of the Riverwalk with views overlooking the Cape Fear River. The ♿ 🛜 ↻ Best Western Plus Coastline Inn (910-763-2800 or 1-800-617-7732; www.coastlineinn.com) offers river views from all 53 rooms, plus free WiFi, complimentary breakfast, and free parking. From the hotel, guests can access the Riverwalk or a public dock and pier. Many attractions are close by, including the Wilmington Railroad Museum and the Wilmington Convention Center (www.business madecasual.com). Children 17 and under stay free with a paying adult, making this a top choice for families.

If you like this . . . a bit farther south along the Riverwalk, the 🏨 ♿ ♂ 🛜 *Hilton Wilmington Riverside (910-763-5900; www.wilmingtonhilton.com) provides a full-featured hotel experience close to the Market Street action.*

The 🍴 🐾 ♂ 🛜 Wilmingtonian (910-343-1800 or 1-800-525-0909; www.thewilmingtonian.com), located just a block off Market Street and two from the river, offers lodgings in historic surroundings that are an easy walk from all the downtown excitement. Comfortable one-bedroom suites featuring balconies with rocking chairs occupy several buildings, including a former convent and the Cinema House, a favorite with movie folk, where suites are named for famous films and stars. The real stars of this show, however, are the luxury suites in the de Rosset House, a carefully renovated 1841 mansion set amid manicured gardens. Rent the Cupola Suite and climb the spiral staircase to a bird's-nest sitting room for unmatched views over the city's rooftops.

With more than a dozen inns located in the historic district, Wilmington is considered the bed & breakfast capital of the North Carolina coast.

Balconies overlook gardens at the Wilmingtonian.

The Riverwalk is a popular place for jogging.

Visitors can choose to spend the night in an ornate Queen Anne Victorian, an antebellum mansion, a belle epoque showplace, a renovated Catholic school, or even a refurbished Salvation Army building. Many of these establishments occupy the elegant residences of Wilmington movers and shakers from eras past, continuing a long history of hospitality. All of the establishments listed below include breakfast, usually lavish, in the room price. Many, however, require a two-night minimum stay, at least on weekends.

One of the most luxurious, the ♂ (ᵖ) Greystone Inn (910-763-2000 or 1-888-763-4773; www.graystoneinn .com), occupies the 1905 Bridgers Mansion on S. Third Street, just a block off Market. American Historic Inns named it one of the top 10 romantic inns in the United States, and it received a four-diamond rating from AAA.

If you're bringing the children along, check out the child-friendly ♪ Blue Heaven Bed & Breakfast (910-772-9929; www.bbonline.com/nc/blue heaven/) on Orange Street, or the ♪ Taylor House Inn Bed & Breakfast (910-763-7581 or 1-800-382-9982; www.taylorhousebb.com) on N. Seventh Street. Children stay free at the ♪ & (ᵖ) Port City Guest House (910-762-1790 or 1-888-802-6862; www .portcityguesthouse.com), located in the Mansion District a bit farther out Market Street.

Traveling with your pet? Book a room at the ❀ ▼ Camellia Cottage Bed & Breakfast (910-763-9171 or 1-866-728-5272; www.camelliacottage .com), just four blocks from the Riverwalk.

The ❀ & (ᵖ) Front Street Inn (910-762-6442 or 1-800-336-8184; www.frontstreetinn.com) occupies an old Salvation Army building, preserving its thick brick walls, maple floors, and arched windows. And the location, just half a block from Chandler's Wharf and the Riverwalk, can't be beat. The nearby & (ᵖ) Clarendon Inn (910-343-1990 or 1-888-343-1992; www.clarendoninn .com) receives top ratings from guests. Both inns have handicapped-accessible accommodations available.

UNIVERSITY/MIDTOWN

Several dozen hotels, most of them national chains, cluster around the intersection of Market Street (US 17 Business), US 117, and US 74. And no

Quick tip: If you're planning a Wilmington wedding, the 1846 ♂ **St. Thomas Preservation Hall** (910-763-4054; www.saintthomas preservationhall.com), a restored Roman Catholic chapel located adjacent to the Wilmingtonian, is a popular venue for both ceremonies and receptions.

wonder. The Riverwalk is about 4 miles away. Both UNCW and the Wilmington International Airport are close by. I-40 ends at US 117/NC 132 (College Road), which you can follow straight to Carolina and Kure Beaches, while US 74 leads out to Wrightsville Beach.

The full-service & (ꝅ) Ramada Conference Center (1-866-790-8512; www.ramadasoutheast.com), with the Banyan Asian Café and Carolina Lounge on-site, is one of several Wyndham properties located in the area. You should be able to find a hotel belonging to your reward program at whatever price point you're looking for. Several extended-stay establishments offer great rates on weeklong rentals.

MAYFAIRE/LANDFALL /LUMINA

As you head toward Wrightsville Beach on US 74, you'll pass some of the city's finest shopping and dining options. The area makes a good place to rent a room as well, especially if you'll be splitting your time between the beach and the historic attractions downtown.

The ꝅ & (ꝅ) Hilton Garden Inn Mayfaire Town Center (910-509-4046; www.hiltongardeninn.hilton.com), adja-

cent to one of the city's largest shopping centers, is Wilmington's highest-rated hotel, with a swimming pool and restaurant on-site, plus free parking, Internet access, and comfortable Garden Sleep System beds.

MONKEY JUNCTION/MYRTLE GROVE

While most travelers headed south of town choose to stay at the beaches on Pleasure Island, golfers will like the ♂ (ꝅ) Beau Rivage Golf & Resort (910-392-9021 or 1-800-628-7080; www.beaurivagegolf.com). Spacious suites that sleep six surround the challenging golf course, which stretches along the Cape Fear River. Guests enjoy private patios, a pool, and meals at the Veranda Bar & Grill in the columned Southern clubhouse.

Local Flavors

Taste of the town—local cafés, restaurants, bars, bistros, etc.

RESTAURANTS

Wilmington in recent years acquired a reputation as an up-and-coming foodie town. In 2011 this trend solidified in the person of Keith Rhodes, a self-taught chef and local boy from Porter's Neck, just north of town.

After a stellar run as chef at the

popular Deluxe, Rhodes struck out on his own a few of years back, opening ⤖ Catch Modern Seafood (910-799-3847; www.catchwilmington.com), where he showcases local produce from land and sea in his own brilliant preparations. Much like the eclectic menu he designed for Deluxe, the menu at Catch features Asian influences, as well as Southern regional classics, using Snead's Ferry clams; North Carolina shrimp, scallops, and oysters; fish from sustainable fisheries; and pork from local farms. All vegetables and fruits are locally sourced as well.

Chef Rhodes consistently wins best chef awards in local polls, and several times has won the Best Dish in North Carolina contest (www.best dishnc.com), awarded to chefs using local products and ingredients by the North Carolina Department of Agriculture. In 2011 Rhodes moved onto the national stage when the James Beard Foundation nominated him for Best Chef in the Southeast. A must-stop for visiting foodies, Catch is located in the Midtown area, at 6623 Market Street. Reservations are suggested. A second location downtown at 215 Princess Street (910-762-2841) specializes in small plates featuring Southern/Asian fusion cuisine.

If you like this . . . Marc's on Market (910-686-6465; www.marcson market.com), owned and operated by Marc Copenhaver, another award-

winning chef, is noted for its creative cuisine, pleasant atmosphere, and reasonable prices. Located farther out on Market in the Ogden neighborhood, it serves dinner plus Sunday brunch. Reservations suggested.

Unique among Wilmington eateries, Ⓨ Indochine Restaurant (910-251-9229; www.indochinewilmington.com), located just off Market Street at Wayne Drive, east of the historic district, continues to rack up awards in local polls, for both its exceptional cuisine—a blend of healthful Thai and Vietnamese dishes—and its outstanding atmosphere. Restaurant owner, Vietnam native, and war bride Solange Thompson created a museum—or perhaps a shrine—to her native culture, filling her restaurant with Asian artwork and antiques, and outside creating a lush garden with a lotus pond, koi, and Thai huts where patrons can dine or enjoy tropical drinks. Arrive early to avoid a long line or enjoy a cocktail in the Saigon Saigon Martini Lounge while you wait.

Balconies at Riverboat Landing provide a romantic view of the river.

Historic Downtown

Downtown Wilmington has an enormous number of restaurants, nightclubs, and bars, all within just a few blocks. Almost all have happy hours, if you'd like to sample the atmosphere and cuisine before the late-night crowds arrive. Many are well worth a look, occupying historic buildings or offering superb views across the river.

Two restaurants recommended in our 48 Hours section, ⅄ Caprice Bistro (910-815-0810; www.caprice bistro.com) and Riverboat Landing (910-763-7227; www.riverboatlanding .com), are in the first block of Market Street. Two more, Deluxe Café (910-251-0333; www.deluxenc.com) and Dixie Grill (910-762-7280; 116 Market Street), are in the second block of Market. And two more, Front Street Brewery (910-251-1935; www.front streetbrewery.com) and ⅄ Fat Tony's Italian Pub (910-343-8881; www.fat tonysitalianpub.com) are near the corner of Market and N. Front Street. You'll find more options listed below.

After sunset, bar hop down the Riverwalk and check out the restaurants—and the views—along the waterfront. See our section on the Wilmington Waterfront below for suggested stops.

And keep an eye out for celebrities! That may really be John Travolta ducking into the Italian Gourmet Market (910-362-0004; www.thefoods ofitaly.com) for a bottle of virgin olive oil. He's rumored to have a home in the area.

Market and Front

The local foods movement is alive and well in downtown Wilmington. ⅄ ↭ Crow Hill (910-228-5332; www.crow hillnc.com), in one of the city's most prominent spots at the corner of Front and Market, offers a rustic take on American classics made from locally sourced ingredients. While offerings change seasonally, the usually available North Carolina trout with sweet potato hash won a rave review from the *New York Times*. Crow Hill serves dinner, Sunday brunch, and a special late-night menu until 2 AM on Fridays and Saturdays.

Crow Hill took over the spot long occupied by the somewhat legendary ↭ Caffe Phoenix (910-343-1395; www .caffephoenix.com), which moved a few doors down to 35 N. Front. The Phoenix, which hangs a rotation of local art—and doesn't take a commission— serves lunch, dinner, and Sunday brunch, featuring many Mediterranean and vegetarian selections.

*If you like this . . . check out some of downtown Wilmington's other chef-driven venues, including **Caprice Bistro** (910-815-0810; www.caprice bistro.com), operated by Thierry and Patricia Moity, consistently ranked as one of the finest restaurants in the city; and ↭ **Deluxe** (910-251-0333; www .deluxenc.com), where the influence of Chef Keith Rhodes continues in a menu featuring local and organic ingredients. Both restaurants are on Market Street, and both are great spots to watch for celebrities.*

At 123 Princess Street, the trendy Manna (910-763-5252; www.manna avenue.com), helmed by creative Chef Jacob Hilbert, serves American cuisine that's fresh, original, and occasionally humorous, including such dishes as Hot Stone Orange Hen and Drunk Pigs on a Cot.

Expect modest serving sizes and an upscale cocktail scene at ⅄ Circa 1922 (910-762-1922; www.circa1922 .com), located at 8 N. Front. This is at heart a tapas restaurant, so share one of its large regionally themed platters

Caffe Phoenix offers local foods and art-works.

or a selection of items from the inventive international menu that runs from crab cheesecake to sushi. Desserts are huge; split the crepes Grand Marnier or chocolate coconut sushi.

With the ocean so close by, Wilmington can't get enough sushi and sashimi, and the proof lies right in downtown, where two mainly sushi restaurants, both wildly popular, face off across S. Front Street. On the east side of the street, on the second floor of the historic Roudabush store, the pan-Asian ⵗ YoSake Downtown Sushi Lounge (910-763-3172; www.yosake .com) exudes a Tokyo-cool vibe with bold colors, sleek decor, and anime-inspired art. This trendy spot may be as famous for its pomegranate ginger mojito as its artful specialty sushi rolls and huge list of sakes. A late-night menu of snacks fires up the cocktail crowd that hangs till closing at 2 AM.

Across the street, Nikki's Fresh Gourmet & Sushi Bar (910-772-9151; www.nikkissushibar.com) welcomes its many fans from lunchtime through late

night. This location, the first of the Nikki's empire created by brothers Andy and Johnny Chen, natives of Japan, is small, casual, and often very busy. But the sushi and sashimi are the freshest and highest quality around, the lychee sake is deliciously cold, and the prices are reasonable. The menu includes Greek and American items in addition to all the Japanese standards, from tempura to teriyaki, with lots of vegetarian choices.

Wilmington Waterfront

Most of the restaurants along the Riverwalk are south of Market Street. Close to the Market Street corner, Mixto (910-399-4501; www.mixto wilmington.com) is creating a buzz with creative Latin cuisine by award-winning chef Eric Gephart, a popular patio, and great margaritas.

If you're after seafood, fresh and simply prepared, stop at the Dock Street Oyster Bar (910-762-2827; www.dockstreetoysterbar.net). No fried seafood here, just steamed and grilled.

A block farther down the River-walk, The George (910-763-2052; www.thegeorgerestaurant.com) offers a more upscale menu of seafood and steaks as well as a deck that's perfect for a sunset cocktail. If you're arriving by private boat, The George on the

Fast fact: The Roudabush Seed & Feed Store near the corner of Front and Market Streets was a Wilmington landmark from 1917 until 2002, selling plants, flowers, seeds, and farm supplies. Today the third floor, known as the ⵙ **Balcony on Dock** (910-342-0273; www.thebalcony ondock.com), is a popular spot for weddings.

Riverwalk is the only waterfront restaurant offering "dock and dine" facilities.

Keep heading south toward the towering Cape Fear Memorial Bridge, and you'll find Le Catalan French Café and Wine Bar (910-815-0200; www.lecatalan.com), where you can savor a glass of wine and a plate of cheeses and pâtés at a riverfront table.

Next door, enjoy a light lunch or afternoon tea at the Wilmington Tea Room (910-343-1832; www.wilmingtontearoom.com) or select a premium tea to take home.

Anchoring the southern end of the Riverwalk are two restaurants developed as part of the Chandler's Wharf complex, both with deck dining and stunning views. Elijah's Grill and Oyster Bar (910-343-1448; www.elijahs.com), at the end of Ann Street, occupies a building that once housed a maritime museum. Step inside to see the many ship models and nautical artifacts.

Just beyond, the Pilothouse Restaurant (910-343-0200; www.pilothouserest.com) serves contemporary Southern cuisine. Check the walls here for works by local artist Claude Howell (1915–1997). The bar offers a great view of the river.

The Cape Fear River dominates Wilmington's past and present.

Did you know? Steamed seafood is a specialty along the Carolina coast. Steamed oysters may arrive by the bucket for you to open yourself, although most oyster bars have a shucker on hand. Many menus feature a Carolina steam pot filled with a spicy selection of clams, oysters, shrimp, crab legs, sausage, corn on the cob, and new potatoes.

Lumina

Lots of dining options are grouped close to the causeway leading to Wrightsville Beach, with addresses on Eastwood Road, Oleander Drive, Military Cutoff, and Wrightsville Avenue.

Lumina Station (www.luminastation.com), on the south side of Eastwood Drive about a mile west of the Wrightsville Beach drawbridge, houses several fine-dining spots, including the Brasserie du Soleil (910-256-2226; www.brasseriedusoleil.com), a French bistro complete with a traditional zinc bar and an active late-night scene, and the Port Land Grille (910-256-6056; www.portlandgrille.com), serving upscale fare crafted by chef and owner Shawn Wellersdick using heirloom vegetables and fruits, fresh fish from area dayboats, and free range game birds grilled over a wood fire.

Other Lumina Station restaurants include the Stone Crab Oyster Bar (910-256-5464; www.stonecraboysterbar.com), a laid-back spot serving a casual menu of fish tacos, quesadillas, and steam pots created by Chef Sean Newcomer; and the Cameo 1900 Restaurant & Lounge (910-509-2026; www.cameo1900.com), with intriguing tapas-style dishes designed by rising chef Kirsten Mitchell.

Dining options at the nearby Forum Shopping Center (www.shop theforum.com), on Military Cutoff Road, include the Bento Box Sushi Bar & Asian Kitchen (910-509-0774; www.bentoboxsushi.com), where you can sample the sushi creations of chef and owner Lee Grossman, former executive chef at the legendary Break- ers in South Florida. Come at lunch to enjoy your meal in a traditional bento box. And save room for a dessert of chocolate pot stickers or tempura cheesecake.

Other restaurant options at the Forum include Osteria Cicchetti Ristorante and Wine Bar (910-256- 7476; www.osteria-cicchetti.com), one of the city's finest Italian restaurants, with an antipasto bar and gourmet- quality wood-fired pizzas. Its sister restaurant, The Kitchen (910-256- 9133; www.thekitchenwilmington.com), also at the Forum, serves a casual menu of wood-fired and rotisserie meats with farm-fresh Southern sides, accompanied by big lists of wine by the glass and microbrews.

A visit to the Forum isn't complete without a stop at the award-winning NOFO (910-256-5565; www.nofo .com), a combination café, gourmet market, and gift shop housed in a fun, artistic environment. Weekday lunch and weekend brunch feature a 25-item salad bar and Bill Neal's famous shrimp and grits. The adjacent market sells gourmet coffees and teas, locally made pickles and jams, and beer and wine, as well as novelty items such as bacon candy.

Mayfaire Towncenter (www.may fairetown.com), located between East- wood and Military Cutoff Roads, has the city's largest collection of chain eateries, including the Melting Pot, Brixx Wood Fired Pizza, Fox & Hound Pub, ⌁ Mama Fu's Asian, and (((•)))

Panera Bread, with free WiFi. A cou- ple of locally owned spots to look for include the kid-friendly ⌁ Ⲩ Happy Days Diner (910-256-6224; www .happy-days-diner.com), serving break- fast all day, and Yuki Roll & Grill (910- 679-4489), specializing in Korean classics such as *bulgogi*, plus sushi and other Japanese dishes.

Pavilion Place, near the junction of Eastwood Road and Wrightsville Avenue, is home to one of the city's favorite lunch spots, the ⌁ Ⲩ Sweet and Savory Bake Shop and Cafe (910- 256-0115; www.sweetandsavorycafe .com), where breakfasts, daily bar spe- cials, homemade soups, and freshly baked breads, pies, and other confec- tions earn raves. At dinner the café breaks out the white tablecloths and gourmet dishes designed by Chef Josh Petty. Eat indoors or on the patio shaded by live oaks. Live local music begins early most evenings.

Seafood is the order of the day at Boca Bay (910-256-1887; www.boca bayrestaurant.com) on Eastwood Road, where patio dining and evening jazz bands create a special atmosphere.

Several popular local spots lie along Oleander Drive. ⌁ (((•))) Olympia Mediterranean Cuisine (910-796- 9636; www.olympiaofwilmington.com) has introduced generations of Wilm- ington residents to authentic Greek specialties. Just down the road, Flaming Amy's Burrito Barn (910- 799-2919; www.flamingamysburrito barn.com) is a favorite with vegetarians who like the design-your-own burrito menu, the famous pineapple-jalapeño salsa, and absurdly low prices.

Don't expect anything fancy at Casey's Buffet Barbecue & Home Cookin (910-798-2913; 5559 Oleander Drive), just an all-you-can-eat buffet of traditional Southern-style food, including fatback-flavored collards,

Quick tip: For special occasions, make reservations at **Jerry's Food, Wine & Spirits** (910-256-8847; www.jerrysfoodandwine.com), operated by one of the city's top caterers and a local favorite for romantic meals. **Port City Chop House** (910-256-4955; www.chop housesofnc.com) fits the bill for special occasions that require a significant steak or perhaps garlic-roasted whole lobster, a signature dish.

vinegar-spiced North Carolina barbecue, batter-fried chicken, catfish, fruit cobblers, banana pudding, and all the other dishes typical of the South, even chitlins and pig's feet.

Monkey Junction

Numerous eateries, including many chains, cluster near the junction of College and Carolina Beach Roads, the area referred to by locals as Monkey Junction.

The casual ❧ ♈ Fish Bites Seafood Restaurant and Fresh Market (910-791-1117; www.fishbites seafood.com), in Masonboro Landing next to Salt Water Marine on Carolina Beach Road, is one of the region's top-rated restaurants and also a seafood market. Lunch, dinner, and Sunday brunch specials focus on fresh seafood just off the boat. Desserts are homemade, including fine cheesecakes and key lime pie. The Bottoms Up Lounge offers full cocktail service.

Other locally owned spots worth checking out include ❧ Giorgio's Restaurant (910-790-9954; www .giorgios-restaurant.com) on College Road, serving huge portions of classic Italian dishes; and the Cape Fear

Seafood Company (910-799-7077; www.capefearseafoodcompany.com), owned and operated by Chef Evans Trawick, featuring his signature dishes: Cape Fear shrimp and grits and grouper saltimbocca.

For something light in a great environment, visit the 🐾 (📶) Coastal Roaster Coffee House and Café (910-399-4701; www.thecoastalroaster.com) in the Beau Rivage Marketplace on Carolina Beach Road for breakfast burritos, Apple Annie's pastries, soups, panini, and house-made gelato, plus a full bar and espresso service. You can check your e-mail while your coffee beans roast in your individual roaster. Out back, the elevated patio equipped with fans and fire pits is pet friendly.

If you like this . . . (📶) Holy Grounds (910-350-6985; www.holy groundswilmington.com), a coffeehouse at 2841 Carolina Beach Road, next to Calvary Chapel, caters to the teen java crowd, with low-priced espresso and free WiFi. Proceeds fund the church's youth programs.

BAKERIES

Several Wilmington bakeries cater to the new craze for cupcakes. Downtown, look for Coastal Cupcakes (910-251-8844; www.coastalcupcakes.com) at 129 Princess Street or the Hot Pink Cake Stand (910-343-4727; www.hotpinkcake stand.com), also serving coffee and tea from the Old Wilmington Tea Company (www.oldwilmingtontea.com), at 114 N. Front.

Wilmington's favorite bakeries are the locally owned Apple Annie's Bake Shops (www.appleanniesbakeshop.com), with several locations around town. They're known for their wedding and groom cakes, but this Italian family also makes delicious cookies and biscotti.

Dining on the ICW

The ICW runs between Wilmington and Wrightsville Beach. Along its banks, several restaurants provide delightful spots to relax over a plate of seafood and your favorite beverage, listen to music, or just kick back on the deck and watch the boats go by. Most also have their own docks, so you can arrive by boat if you like.

On the Wilmington side of the waterway along Airlie Road, two sister restaurants sit at the foot of the causeway. The *⌀* **Bridge Tender Restaurant** (910-256-4519; www.thebridgetender.com) is the more upscale of the two, adding certified Black Angus steaks to its seafood offerings. A specially priced three-course sunset menu is available 4–6 PM. Next door, the *⌀* **Fish House Grill** (910-256-3693; www.thefishhousegrill.com) is more casual, with extensive outside seating on the waterway and a nice bar menu. Mahi sticks with lemon pepper curly fries and the fish stew are house specialties, and its onion rings earn raves.

A landmark on the ICW for over 25 years, **Dockside Restaurant and Marina** (910-256-2752; www.thedockside.com), a bit farther down Airlie Road, consistently ranks as one of the favorite local spots for outside dining. This is a good place to try a traditional Shrimp-a-Roo, a Lowcountry boil with fresh shrimp, Cajun sausage, corn on the cob, green beans, and new potatoes, seasoned with the Dockside's special seafood spices.

On the Wrightsville Beach side of the ICW, the *⌀* **Bluewater Waterfront Grill** (910-256-8500; www.bluewaterdining.com) on Marina Street captures local hearts with its laid-back vibe, fabulous views, and Sunday afternoon music series on the covered outdoor deck.

If you like this . . . extend your visit to the ICW by renting a boat at one of the nearby marinas to go waterskiing, fishing, or exploring on Masonboro Island. **Entropy Boat Rentals** (910-675-1877; www.entropyboats.com), a family company that makes its own craft, rents fully equipped boats, and will help plan your trip.

BARBECUE

If authentic regional barbecue tops your vacation wish list, Wilmington has two old-fashioned, family spots that serve original eastern North Carolina 'cue with a vinegar-based sauce:

Jackson's Big Oak Barbecue (910-799-1581; 920 S. Kerr Avenue), and Flip's Bar-B-Que House (910-799-6350; www.flips bbq.com) at 5818 Oleander Drive. Don't expect anything fancy, just smoked pork, chopped or sliced, with a spicy tang, pork ribs and BBQ chicken, plus traditional Southern sides such as

Did you know? North Carolina barbecue is traditionally pork, hickory smoked, and served chopped with bits of fat moistening the mix. In eastern North Carolina the sauce, served on the side, consists of vinegar with various additions, usually including flecks of red pepper. Farther west, the BBQ parlors in Lexington, North Carolina, the self-proclaimed barbecue capital, use a sauce with both vinegar and tomato flavors. Wherever they get their barbecue, North Carolina pork connoisseurs place their order for some "outside brown" (the crispy and delicious outer edges of the meat) and top a sandwich with traditional mustard or barbecue slaw.

Pender's Café, where Katharine Hepburn filmed her last scenes, is a stop on the Hollywood Location Walk.

fried okra, collards, candied sweet potatoes, hush puppies, and banana pudding. At Flip's, serving since 1950, you can try the original Flipburger, a fried bologna sandwich popular in the Carolinas.

BREAKFAST & LUNCH

Looking for a casual meal downtown? See the suggestions in our 48 Hours section: the Dixie Grill (910-762-7280; 116 Market Street), The Basics Southern Gourmet (910-343-1050; www.the basicscottonexchange.com), and Press 102 (910-399-4438; www.press102 .com) are all good bets for either breakfast or lunch. The Pink Pig Café (910-399-6096; 124 Princess Street) serves breakfast all day, as well as some good eastern North Carolina–style barbecue.

Farther out on Market Street, toward Ogden, look for the Goody-Goody Omelet House (910-762-0444; www.goodygoodyhouse.com) at 3817 Market, or Leon's Ogden Restaurant (910-686-0228; 7324 Market) in the Big Lots parking lot. Both are long-

time local favorites run by local families, and the prices are from another era. Leon's is known for its handmade salmon patties and Goody-Goody for its Spanish omelet.

In the Lumina area, go for breakfast to Chris' Cosmic Kitchen (910-792-6720; www.cosmickitchenonline .com) at 420 Eastwood Road, where chef and owner Chris Lubben, a Culinary Institute of America grad, and his wife, Kristin, turn out made-from-scratch comfort food, wicked good cheesecake, and plenty of hospitality. Closed evenings and Mondays.

In Monkey Junction, check out the down-home cooking at the Sawmill (910-350-6909; www.thesawmillgrill .com) or the chef-designed fare at Bon Appetit (910-796-0520; www.bon appetitwilmington.com). Both establishments rank among the region's top caterers.

COFFEEHOUSES

Port City Java (www.portcityjava .com), Carolina's answer to Starbucks, began in Wilmington back in 1995. Today its coffee empire extends across three states and several foreign countries. Several dozen of the locations are in Wilmington itself, and you're bound to see one as you travel around the area. The downtown shop at 21 S. Front Street (910-762-5282), as well as locations in Lumina Station, Monkey Junction, and on Eastwood Road, is decorated with unique works by local artists. Stop in for hot and cold drinks made with house-roasted beans and get online with the free WiFi.

Bella's Sweets and Spirits (910-762-2777; www.bellassweetsand spirits.com), located just steps from the river at 14 Market Street, serves organic, fair-trade coffee made of locally roasted beans, as well as ice cream, panini sandwiches, and build-your-own salads. Local bike rides begin here on Sunday evenings.

FAST FOOD

For an expertly constructed deli sandwich in downtown, stop by Chop's Deli: A Boar's Head Delicatessen (910-399-6503; www.chopsdeli.com) at 130 N. Front, or try the internationally inspired menu at the Wayfarer Delicatessen (910-762-4788; www.wayfarerdeli.com), a hole-in-the-wall spot at 110 S. Front, where empanadas share the bill with sandwiches and vegetarian items.

For a quick and inexpensive dog downtown, stop by Louie's Hot Dogs (910-763-8040; www.louieshotdogs.net), two blocks from the river on Princess Street. In business since 1989, its 100 percent all-beef dogs with your choice of toppings cost just $2.25.

Or drop by the downtown Trolley Stop (910-343-2999; www.trollystophotdogs.com) at 121 N.

Port City Java is Wilmington's answer to Starbucks.

Front, serving hot dogs and sausages of all sorts, including vegetarian, plus burgers and grilled pimento cheese sandwiches until 3 AM Thursday–Saturday evenings. Bring Fido along, and he eats free.

All the national chain burger joints are in plentiful supply in Wilmington, but for a more authentic taste of the town, check out some of the local establishments. P. T.'s Olde Fashioned Grille (www.ptsgrille.com), with numerous locations, wins awards for its never-frozen Angus burgers, gardenburgers, and fries dusted with lemon pepper. Most locations have outside patios, where you mark your order on a form and pass it through the service window—fun for kids.

Two Guys Grille (www.twoguysgrille.com) also has several locations with a surfer theme, serving burgers, salads, seafood, and sandwiches, including vegetarian options.

At another locally based chain, Andy's Cheesesteaks & Cheeseburgers (www.andysburgers.net), frozen custard desserts join the menu of burgers, chicken sandwiches, and wings.

NATURAL FOODS

Wilmington has two markets specializing in natural, local, and organic products. Tidal Creek Co-op (910-799-2667; www.tidalcreek.coop), at 5329 Oleander Drive, is open to nonmembers, and offers free lectures and films spotlighting healthy lifestyles. The Co-op's Kitchen stocks deli sandwiches and numerous prepared salads. Lovey's Market (910-509-0331; www.loveysmarket.com), near Wrightsville Beach on Military Cutoff, also features a café and juice bar, plus a hot and cold food bar with organic entrées and salads, to eat in or take out.

WINE & BEER

At Cape Fear Wine and Beer (910-763-3377; www.capefearwineand beer.net), you can sample rare ales, local microbrews, and fine vintages from around the world, then buy some to take home. This spot on N. Front Street downtown is a rare combination—both a bar and a store, and has the best selection of beers in town.

The Fortunate Glass (910-399-4292; www.fortunateglasswinebar.com), on S. Front near the corner of Market, serves some 50 wines by the glass and 30 craft beers, accompanied by small plates of cured meats, cheeses, and antipasti.

Two other spots in the historic district worth seeking out for wine lovers are Le Catalan French Cafe & Wine Bar (910-815-0200; www.lecatalan .com) along the Riverwalk and Wilmington Wine (910-202-4749; www.wilmingtonwinecompany.com) in the Castle Street Art & Antique District, which hosts wine and beer tastings each week.

For beer lovers, a visit to the ✦ ♉ Front Street Brewery (910-251-1935; www.frontstreetbrewery.com) for a free brewery tour and tasting of the microbrews on tap is a must. Tours are offered daily from 3 to 5 PM.

If you like this . . . Wilmington has two boutique wineries bottling their own vintages within the city limits. The Lumina Winery (910-793-5299; www. luminawine.com) makes wines such as pomegranate zinfandel from both local and imported juices, plus small batch varietal beers. Operated by a winemaking Italian American family, Noni Bacca Winery (910-397-7617; www.nbwinery.com) is known for its big Italian reds. The tasting room on Eastwood Road is open daily.

Quick tip: Wilmington residents are crazy for beer, and a year-round schedule of beer festivals keeps the suds flowing. Two of the largest are the **Lighthouse Beer Festival** (www.lighthousebeerfestival.com), held in October at Greenfield Lake, featuring breweries from around the world; and the **Cape Fear Craft Beer Festival** (www.cape fearbeerfest.com), a June event attracting more than three dozen craft breweries.

SPECIALTY MARKETS

For gourmet gifts or meals to go, Wilmington residents head for the Pine Valley Market (910-350-3663; www.pinevalleymarket.com) on S. College Road, stocking a wide variety of wines, deli sandwiches, and prepared foods.

The Wilmington Visitor Booth at the foot of Market Street

Temptations Everyday Gourmet (www.temptationseverydaygourmet .com), with two locations, stocks gourmet goodies, hosts weekly wine tastings, and serves gourmet salads and sandwiches in its on-site café.

The Italian Gourmet Market (910-362-0004; www.thefoodsofitaly .com), on S. Front Street downtown, carries hard-to-find products imported direct from Italy.

One of the benefits of vacationing this close to the ocean is enjoying fresh seafood just off the boat. The Seaview Crab Company (910-793-0404; www.seaviewcrabcompany .com), on Carolina Beach Road, specializes in blue crabs and spots caught in Masonboro Sound, plus other locally sourced seafood, and will ship fresh seafood to your home after vacation is over.

48 Hours

Wilmington's compact historic district, with its many attractions within easy walking distance, makes the perfect destination for a weekend or midweek getaway. Ideal for foodies, history buffs, movie mavens, or river lovers, Wilmington's downtown can easily keep you busy for 48 hours. Find out what will be going on during your visit at www.wilmingtondowntown.com.

ON ARRIVAL

Select a hotel in the heart of the action for easy access to all Wilmington has to offer. Many of the city's attractions are located around the foot of Market Street where it meets the Riverwalk at Water Street.

Several high-rise hotels dot the riverfront. You can check out boat traffic on the river from your windows at the (ᵖ) Best Western Plus Coastline Inn (910-763-2800; www.coastlineinn .com), located adjacent to the new convention center. All rooms here feature a riverfront view, complimentary breakfast, and free WiFi.

If your tastes run to something more atmospheric, check into the 🐾 (ᵖ) ↵ Wilmingtonian (910-343-1800 or 1-800-525-0909; www.thewilmington ian.com) or the ♂ (ᵖ) Hotel Tarrymore (910-763-3806; www. hoteltarry more.com) across the street. Both offer a variety of comfortable suites set in charming historic buildings just two blocks from the river and a block from Market.

Downstairs in the Hotel Tarrymore, one of the city's hottest new restaurants, 🍸 Press 102 (910-399-4438; www.press102.com), a French-style café, serves locally roasted coffees, late-night meals, and breakfast until 2 PM.

Wilmington is a noted destination for fans of both live theater and cinema. Check the schedule at the Thalian Hall Center for the Performing Arts (910-632-2285 or 1-800-523-2820; www.thalianhall.org), a recently restored 1855 opera house. One of the oldest surviving theaters in the country, it hosts more than 400 events a year, including national and international acts, art films, and children's productions.

Passionate about independent film? Plan your visit for the annual Cucalorus Film Festival (www .cucalorus.org) held every November. Selected as one of the top 10 film festivals in the United States, and certainly one of the most fun, the festival includes indies made in the area, shorts

An easy way to get around is the free WAVE trolley (910-343-0106; www.wavetransit.com), which circles the downtown from 7 AM to 9:20 PM Monday through Friday, 11 AM to 9:20 PM Saturdays, and 11 to 6 Sundays.

You can also hail a golf cart. The ⊷ Cartmen (910-264-4442; www.cartmen.org) will hold a parking spot for you, then ferry you to your destination, provide a ride to festivals, or deliver food right to your door via electric car. The company also rents bikes.

DAY 1

Explore Downtown

Start your day with a stroll or jog along the Riverwalk, stretching for more than a mile along the banks of the Cape Fear River in the heart of downtown Wilmington. Along with numerous works of public art, you'll have a great

The Cucalorus Film Festival is named for this kind of lighting effect.

created by local students, mixers with filmmakers, tours of *Blue Velvet* locations, and more.

Theater fans can enjoy a performance at City Stage (910-342-0272; www. citystagenc.com), producing plays in a 100-year-old Masonic Temple building on Front Street renovated by film star Dennis Hopper. Allow time before the show for a cocktail on the rooftop deck overlooking the river.

Horse-drawn carriages are the best way to tour Historic Wilmington.

view of the USS *North Carolina* (910-251-5797; www.battleshipnc.com), berthed just across the river from downtown.

If your visit occurs on a Saturday between April and December, you'll find the Riverfront Farmers' Market (910-538-6223; www.wilmington farmers.com) in full swing along N. Water Street. The city-run market hosts two blocks of booths occupied by local farmers and craft vendors selling everything from goat cheese to seafood.

The center of the Riverwalk at its intersection with Market Street serves as a central clearing house for Wilmington tours. Catch a Horsedrawn Tour (910-251-8889; www.horsedrawn tours.com) in a carriage pulled by magnificent Percherons for a leisurely and informative trip through the historic district. The drivers' stories of scandals, ghosts, and selfless deeds bring the stately mansions that line the streets to life. Reservations are not required.

You can also opt for a wider-ranging tour with the ✐ Wilmington Trolley Company (910-763-4483;

www.wilmingtontrolley.com). Children under 12 ride free with paying adults on these motorized trolleys, departing from the foot of Market Street.

For a more high-tech orientation, contact Cape Fear Segway Tours (910-251-2572; www.capefearsegway .com), offering a variety of trips to historic and film-related locations.

Late Breakfast/Early Lunch

If the line isn't too long outside the hip ✻ Dixie Grill (910-762-7280; 116 Market Street), stop in for one of their legendary Southern-style breakfasts or blue plate specials. Vegetarian items, including sweet potato pancakes and the Dixie Benedict—fried green tomatoes and poached eggs atop a fluffy biscuit—are also available.

If a quick bite is more in order (service at the Dixie is notoriously pokey), several spots along Market Street offer fast ice cream, hot dog, and burger fixes, often at outdoor tables. For pizza, tacos, or salads, stop by ✻ Slice of Life Pub and Pizzeria (910-251-9444; www.grabslice.com). It also serves late night and boasts the largest selection of tequilas in Wilmington.

Quick tip: At the park where Market Street meets the Riverwalk, the **Wilmington/Cape Fear Convention and Visitor Bureau's Riverfront Booth** (910-341-4030 or 877-406-2356; www.capefearcoast .com) offers information and maps from April to October. The Bureau's main office, located at 505 Nutt Street in a renovated railroad freight warehouse close to the new **Wilmington Convention Center** (www.businessmadecasual.com), is open year-round.

MYRTLE BEACH AND SOUTH CAROLINA'S GRAND STRAND

Afternoon Sightseeing

One of Wilmington's nicknames is "The Port City," and no visit is complete without a cruise on the Cape Fear River. See it in style aboard the ♿ 🍸 *Henrietta III* (910-343-1611 or 1-800-676-0162; www.cfrboats.com), an authentic sternwheel riverboat that's one of the most noticeable features on Wilmington's waterfront. Capt. Carl Marshburn narrates the history of the city as the *Henrietta III* passes historic homes, derelict shipbuilding yards, and huge cranes that serve the thriving deepwater port, just downstream.

Many other sightseeing options are available in Wilmington depending on your interests. Foodies will enjoy local food writer Liz Biro's Culinary Adventures (www.lizbiro.com), exploring the city's hottest restaurants and bars. Movie buffs can join the Hollywood Location Walk of Old Wilmington (910-794-1866; www.hollywoodnc.com) to discover local places featured in Wilmywood movies and TV shows.

EUE/Screen Gems is open weekends for tours.

If you like this . . . plan a visit to EUE/Screen Gems Studios *(910-343-3433; www.screengemsstudios.com/nc). Walking tours of the 50-acre lot generally include visits to sets used by the CW series* One Tree Hill *and the new Dream Stage 10, with a 50-foot indoor tank for in-water scenes.*

Quick tips:
• Along the Wilmington waterfront, **Orange Street Landing**, a site on the National Underground Railroad Network to Freedom (www.nps.gov/ugrr), commemorates the 1862 escape of William B. Gould and seven other enslaved people. After his escape, Gould joined the U.S. Navy, serving throughout the war, and kept an eloquent diary of his experiences.
• If you prefer to tour on your own, download a map of African American heritage sites from the virtual exhibits section of the website of the future **African American Heritage Museum of Wilmington** (www.aahfwilmington.org). Or ask for a list at area visitor centers.

Fast fact: In November 1898, white supremacists staged an illegal coup d'état, seizing control of Wilmington and massacring many black citizens. For more information, visit http://core.ecu.edu/umc/wilmington/. The 1898 Memorial Park, dedicated in 2008 at the corner of N. Third and Davis Streets, features a 16-foot bronze monument symbolizing social progress and harmony, created by noted artist Ayokunle Odeleye.

Ghost hunters can find the city's most terrifying locations with Haunted Wilmington (910-794-1866; www .hauntedwilmington.com), offering both a ghost walk, considered one of the best in the country, and a haunted pub crawl. Or meet the ghosts in the haunted Cotton Exchange with Tour Old Wilmington (910-409-4300; http://touroldwilmington.blogspot.com).

Wilmington also has a rich African American history, including the 1898 Racial Massacre and Coup. American Heritage Tours (910-371-2848; www .amhtours.com) offers a bus trip to many sites highlighting African American contributions to Cape Fear history, including the Burnett-Eaton Museum (910-815-1029; 410 N. Seventh Street).

Drinks & Appetizers

Quench your thirst after a busy day of touring at the ☕ ☲ Front Street Brewery (910-251-1935; www.front streetbrewery.com). Free brewery tours and samples of the nine microbrews on tap are offered every day from 3 to 5 PM, followed by a daily happy hour with half-price appetizers 4–7 PM and after 9 PM.

Dinner

Dine along the river with views of both the sunset and the battleship. One popular spot, especially for couples, is Riverboat Landing (910-763-7227; www.riverboatlanding.com), with nine personal balconies just big enough for two. The specialties here are steaks and seafood, and the place is easy to find— it's the sky-blue building at the foot of Market Street. Call ahead to reserve a balcony if you're dining at a busy time.

If you like this . . . continue the romantic mood with chocolate fondue on the back deck at **Little Dipper** *(910-251-0433; www.littledipperfondue .com), close by on S. Front Street.*

Did you know? Download self-guided tours of local sites used in *One Tree Hill* and *Dawson's Creek* from the website of the **Wilmington/Cape Fear Coast Convention and Visitors Bureau** (www.capefearcoast.com), listed in the Press section under "Story Ideas." Printed versions are available at area visitor centers.

Fast fact: In addition to the fresh beers at Front Street Brewery, several microbrews are made locally. Keep an eye out for **Good Vibes Beer** (910-274-2258; www.good vibesbrew.com), available on draft at local restaurants, and bottles of **Wolf Beer** (910-763-8586; www .wolfbeerco.com) at area eateries and retail stores.

Foodies may have a better time at ☲ Caprice Bistro (910-815-0810; www.capricebistro.com) a couple of doors down Market. No view of the river here, but the food is marvelous: authentic dishes from France and Belgium prepared by Chef Thierry Moity, a French native and veteran of restaurants in Europe and New York City. The menu includes crepes and mussels, prepared several delicious ways, plus small plates and classic entrées, such as duck comfit and waterzooi, a traditional Belgian seafood stew. The three-course prix fixe, served nightly, is a bargain at $25. A comfortable sofa lounge serves a reasonably priced bar menu until 2 AM.

After Dinner

Downtown Wilmington boasts lots of nightspots located within a couple of

Party Like a Star

Several nightspots in downtown Wilmington are noted for their movie connections. Some have been used as locations for films. Others are favorite hangouts for movie stars when they hit town.

The sets for *Dawson's Creek* are long gone, but fans still come to Wilmington to see its locations, including the site of "Leery's Fresh Fish" at 5 S. Water Street, currently the hot Latin restaurant Ⴤ **Mixto** (910-399-4501; www.mixtowilmington .com), and Ⴤ **Hell's Kitchen** (910-763-4133; www.hellskitchenbar.com), a temporary set for an episode, now a real nightspot. The decor combines fishing boats with skeletons, an unforgettable ambiance.

Beatle George Harrison filmed a 1987 movie titled *Track 29* at Ⴤ **Blue Post Billiards** (910-343-1141; 15 S. Water Street).

On the corner of Front and Market Streets sits locavore landmark Ⴤ **Crow Hill** (910-228-5332; crowhillnc.com). The build-

Hell's Kitchen, featured in *Dawson's Creek*

ing, formerly the **Caffe Phoenix** (910-343-1395; www.caffephoenix.com, now located at 35 N. Front Street), hosted the *Lolita* wrap party.

Around the corner on Front Street lies Ⴤ **Barbary Coast** (910-762-8996; 116 S. Front Street), Wilmington's oldest bar, and the location used for the brothel in the 1986 classic *Blue Velvet*.

North on Front Street, the Ⴤ **Firebelly Lounge** (910-763-0141; www.facebook .com/FirebellyLounge) gained fame as the spot where Vince Vaughn got into a knife fight with a local tough guy during the filming of *Domestic Disturbance*.

Next door sits one of the city's most evocative spots—**Pender's Café** (910-762-4065; 205 N. Front Street). Here, Katharine Hepburn filmed her last movie appearance, in the TV drama *One Christmas* in 1994.

blocks of the Market Street corridor. Many feature live music, and, with so many actors in town, the open mic, comedy, and karaoke scenes here are way above average. Check the listings in *Encore* magazine (www.encore pub.com), "What's On Wilmington" (www.whatsonwilmington.com), or the entertainment pages of the *Wilmington Star News* (www.starnewsonline.com) for the latest update.

For fun with a view, drop by Ⴤ (((ŋ))) Fat Tony's Italian Pub (910-343-8881; www.fattonysitalianpub.com), at 131 N. Front Street, where a menu of Italian specialties joins a fun bar scene, happy hour, late-night menu, live music, and a resident ghost. More than two dozen beers are on tap, including the house special Haunted Pub Brew. Take a table on the back patio for a fabulous view of the river, and don't miss the meatball sliders.

DAY
2

Breakfast/Early Lunch

Enjoy a superb brunch accompanied by acoustic music at the Deluxe Café (910-251-0333; www.deluxenc.com) at 114 Market Street. The menu here is ever changing and beautifully crafted, ditto the setting filled with original art. If the lobster, mushroom, and Brie omelet is on the menu—don't hesitate. If not, consider the house-smoked salmon with grits and eggs.

The Deluxe serves brunch only on Sunday, so for an early meal every (other) day of the week, check out The Basics Southern Gourmet (910-343-1050; www.thebasicscottonexchange .com) inside the Cotton Exchange on N. Front. This casual café gives Southern soul food a gourmet twist, presenting memorable vegetable plates with fried okra, hoppin' john, and shrimp and grits, plus Southern-style breakfasts piled with biscuits, grits, and smoked ham. Breakfast is served weekdays from 8 AM, followed by lunch and dinner; weekend brunch runs 10 AM–4 PM. Try the classic Coca Cola cake for dessert.

Shopping

Downtown Wilmington makes a wonderful spot to explore, for those looking for something unusual to commemorate their trip. Shops line Front Street from the Cotton Exchange on its north end to Chandler's Wharf on the south. Both complexes bring together a selec-

Fast fact: Many places offer happy hours, usually between the hours of 4 and 7 PM, but in North Carolina, these can only be food specials. Drink specials are permitted, but must be offered for the entire time the establishment is open that day. Last call for alcohol in North Carolina is 2 AM. The drinking age for every adult beverage, including beer, is 21 years old.

Did you know? Hoppin' john, a combo of black-eyed peas and rice, accompanied by collards and smoked ham hocks, is served in many areas of the South every New Year's Day for good luck.

Quick tip: If you enjoy a Bloody Mary or mimosa with your Sunday brunch, plan your meal for after 12 noon. North Carolina law forbids Sunday liquor sales in the morning.

tion of specialty shops, galleries, and boutiques, conveniently located under one roof.

The ↑ Cotton Exchange (910-343-9896; www.shopcottonexchange .com) houses dozens of shops in eight restored buildings, several dating to before the Civil War. As you move through the courtyards and brick walkways, keep an eye out for artifacts from the huge cotton market, once the largest in the South, which thrived here. Among the galleries, Port City Pottery & Fine Crafts (910-763-7111; www.portcitypottery.com) and Crescent Moon Glass & Metal Art (910-762-4207; www.crescentmoonnc.com) both offer works by local artists. Two Sisters Bookery (910-762-4444; www .twosistersbookery.com) specializes in books by local authors, plus local histories and cookbooks.

Refreshments in the Exchange include a Victorian-style pub, Paddy's Hollow Bar & Grille (910-762-4354; www.paddyshollow.com); The Basics, serving Southern soul food (see above); and the German Cafe (910-763-5523), plus a coffee shop and an ice cream parlor. Java Dog (910-343-8890) serves coffee and espresso. The Cotton Exchange, said to be haunted, stretches along the 300 block of N. Front, with a free customer parking lot along Nutt Street on the river side of the complex.

On the southern end of the Riverwalk, Chandler's Wharf (910-762-4106; www.chandlerswharfshops.com) occupies restored historic buildings at the corner of Ann and Water Streets, connected by cobblestone alleys, boardwalks, and oyster shell paths decorated with maritime artifacts. Watch

Fast fact: The **Wilmington Walk of Fame** (www.celebratewilming ton.org), a Hollywood-style series of stars set into the sidewalk, honors local folks who have gone on to national fame, including David Brinkley, Charlie Daniels, Charles Kuralt, Frank Capra Jr., and Roman Gabriel. Find it on the Water Street side of the Cotton Exchange.

Quick tip: If you'd rather sightsee than shop, cruise the **Cape Fear Historic Byway** by automobile or bicycle. Along its route, you'll pass many of Wilmington's historic mansions and public buildings and circle scenic Lake Greenfield. Detailed directions for this North Carolina scenic byway, as well as other scenic drives in the region, can be found at www.ncdot.org/travel /scenic/.

The Cotton Exchange offers a variety of shopping in a historic setting.

clay come to life at Creations by Justine (910-763-4545; www.clay goddess.com), the gallery and studio of Justine Ferreri, a sculptress with an international following. The Barista Cafe and Cape Fear Bakery (910-399-3108; www.thebaristacafebakery.com) serves tasty breakfast and lunch specialties. Special events held at the wharf include Full Moon Saturday celebrations and Fourth Fridays with wine tastings and live music. Free parking is available.

Lunch before You Go
For a lasting memory of Wilmington, enjoy a bucket of steamed oysters and fabulous views on the deck at Elijah's (910-343-1448; www.elijahs.com) on the Riverwalk opposite Chandler's Wharf.

Extend Your Stay

HERITAGE

Third Street near its crossing with Market has been the center of Wilmington civic life since the city's earliest days. Near the south corner of Third and Market stands St. James Episcopal Church (910-762-7537; www.stjamesp.org), the city's oldest, originally built in 1770. The current Early Gothic building, designed by Thomas U. Walter, architect of the cast-iron U.S. Capitol dome, dates to 1839. Its soaring turrets are a Wilmington landmark. Inside, rather miraculously preserved through British and Yankee occupations, hangs a painting of Ecce Homo, seized from an attacking pirate ship in 1748. Behind the church, the Parish Graveyard is the final resting place of many Wilmington residents from the Colonial era, including America's first homegrown playwright, Thomas Godfrey. The church and graveyard are open for self-guided tours daily.

If you like this . . . the Temple of Israel (910-762-0000; www.temple-of-israel.org), North Carolina's oldest Jewish synagogue built in a unique Moorish Revival style, with onion-shaped domes, stands at the corner of S. Fourth and Market Streets. Contact the temple office to request a tour.

Two blocks north of St. James on Third Street, ♿ Thalian Hall (910-632-2285 or 1-800-523-2820; www.thalianhall.org), built in the mid-1850s, combines the functions of city hall and Wilmington's premier performance space, which through the years has hosted such luminaries as Buffalo Bill Cody, Lillian Russell, Maurice Barrymore, and many others. Recently restored, this is one of the oldest surviving theaters in the country, and preserves many original features, including the main curtain, painted in 1858 by William Russell Smith, and the Thunder Run, an original 19th-century sound effect device. Thalian Hall is open during the afternoon for self-guided tours Monday–Saturday. Guided tours, which stop at areas not included in the self-guided tour, are available by reservation only (910-632-2241).

The neighborhoods in the streets surrounding Thalian Hall and east along Market Street contain many historic buildings, some dating to the 1700s, including impressive mansions built before and after the Civil War by members of the wealthy merchant class. Plaques distributed by the Historic Wilmington Foundation (910-762-2511; www.historicwilmington.org) mark buildings over 75 years old. More than 500 of these plaques are scattered around the city.

Most impressive of all is the ⚙ Bellamy Mansion Museum of History and Design Arts (910-251-3700; www.bellamymansion.org), a landmark on Market Street since 1861. Surrounded by broad verandas and tall white columns, the 22-room antebellum mansion contains exhibits on architectural history and historic preservation. Behind the mansion, a two-story brick building is among the best-preserved urban slave quarters still standing in the South.

The antebellum Bellamy Mansion houses a museum devoted to historic preservation

Quick tip: Plan your visit to coincide with the annual **North Carolina Azalea Festival** (www.ncazaleafestival.org), held every April, for tours of the city's historic homes and gorgeous gardens.

Fast fact: The ornate Kenan Fountain, occupying the square in front of the Bellamy Mansion, was designed by Carrère and Hastings, the New York architectural firm that designed the New York Public Library.

If you like this . . . purchase a passport ticket giving discounted admission to three of Wilmington's historic homes. In addition the Bellamy Mansion, the passport includes the **Latimer House** *(910-762-0492; www .hslcf.org), an Italianate mansion at the corner of Third and Orange furnished with originals from the Victorian period, and the* **Burgwin-Wright House and Gardens** *(910-762-0570; www.burgwinwrighthouse.com) at 224 Market Street, used by Lord Cornwallis as his headquarters during his occupation of the city in 1781. Passport tickets are available at each of the house museums.*

For a look at a more rural version of antebellum life, visit ✎ ♂ Poplar Grove Plantation (910-686-9518; www.poplargrove.com), just north of Wilmington along US 17. In operation since the 1760s, this peanut plantation is largely intact with an 1850 Greek Revival manor house, restored tenant house, smokehouse, and an exhibit on peanut agriculture. Other outbuildings house a variety of craft studios, including a basket maker, blacksmith shop, and weaving studio. Children enjoy meeting the many farmyard animals. Pleasant walking trails wind through the grounds, which include display gardens as well as old-growth forest, part of the Abbey Nature Preserve (www.coastallandtrust.org).

Plan your visit to Poplar Grove on a Wednesday morning from April to October when one of the region's best farmer's markets is held from 8 AM to 1 PM under the huge live oak trees on the manor's front lawn.

Explore a different sort of heritage at the USS *North Carolina* (910-251-5797; www.battleshipnc.com). One of the largest and fastest battleships ever built, the "Showboat," as she was nicknamed by her crew, participated in every major World War II battle in the Pacific, earning 15 battle stars. All nine decks, crew quarters, and gun turrets are included in the self-guided tour.

Sailors aboard the USS *North Carolina* nicknamed her the "Showboat."

The USS *North Carolina* was scheduled to be scrapped in 1958 when the citizens of North Carolina mounted the Save Our Ship (SOS) Campaign to bring her back to her namesake state as a memorial to North Carolinians who served in World War II. State schoolchildren played an important part, contributing their pennies to the rescue effort.

If you like this . . . the lobby of the Historic Hannah Block USO (910-341-7860), at 120 S. Second Street downtown, has been restored to its World War II appearance and houses a display of homefront memorabilia.

The ✍ ☂ Cape Fear Museum of History and Science (910-798-4350; www.capefearmuseum.com), in the 800 block of Market Street, provides an overview of the region's history. New exhibits detail the history, natural science, and culture of the region from the Native Americans who first roamed "the Land of the Longleaf Pine" through the 20th century. Kids enjoy the skeleton of a giant ground sloth that roamed the region 1.5 million years ago, as well as the Michael Jordon Discovery Center, an interactive area funded by the basketball legend (a Wilmington native), where they can feed a Venus flytrap and crawl into a beaver lodge.

The Cape Fear Museum of History and Science is North Carolina's oldest history museum, founded in 1898 by the Daughters of the Confederacy to preserve relics of the Civil War.

The Cape Fear Museum is the only place you can buy plans for a Simmons Sea Skiff (www.simmons seaskiff.com), a style of wooden fishing boat produced by Wilmington native T. N. Simmons from the 1940s to the 1970s. The museum displays a Simmons skiff in its lobby and in the outdoor Marine Pavilion.

Housed in an 1883 railroad freight warehouse on the waterfront near the new convention center, the ✍ ☂ ☂ Wilmington Railroad Museum (910-763-2634; www.wrrm.org) explores the importance of railroads to the city's history, from the 1840 Wilmington &

The Wilmington Railroad Museum recalls the city's days as a major rail center.

Weldon, at the time the longest railroad line in the world, through the heyday of the Atlantic Coastline Railroad, headquartered at Wilmington until the 1950s. Exhibits include extensive model train setups that visitors can operate, including a Lionel set with Thomas the Tank in the children's area.

ARTS & CULTURE

Art Museums & Galleries

Wilmington's Cameron Art Museum (910-395-5999; www.cameronartmuseum .com) hangs fascinating exhibits of works from around the world, as well as pieces from its own collection, which includes a complete series of 1881 drypoint etchings by American Impressionist Mary Cassatt; works by local African American folk artist Minnie Evans; and paintings by Claude Howell, a lifelong resident of Wilmington. The Cameron's modernistic new building on Independence Street, the work of architect Charles Gwathmey, designer of the Guggenheim Museum extension in New York, is topped by signature glass pyramids. The surrounding Pyramid Park displays an ever-expanding collection of significant outdoor sculpture.

If you like this . . . explore the Museum of World Cultures (910-962-3276; http://library.uncw.edu/museum/), a "museum without walls" at UNCW featuring African, Latin American, Native American and Pacific artifacts and musical instruments at locations across the campus. A map to the exhibits is available online.

Wilmington nurtures a vibrant arts scene with many galleries and active artists. For a good introduction, visit during Fourth Friday Gallery Nights (www.wilmingtonfourthfridays.com). Held year-round, these free, self-guided events encompass some two dozen galleries, and include restaurants hanging local art, funky shops, and more in downtown. Many of the venues offer complimentary wine and cheese. Maps are available at each location and online.

A number of galleries and eclectic shops cluster in the Castle Street Art & Antique District located between Fourth and Seventh Streets. Among them, the Wilmington Art Gallery (910-343-4370; www.wilmington-art.org) hangs work by members of the Wilmington Art Association.

Select one of the handmade wooden objects on sale at Kids Making It (910-

Did you know? The Cameron's location is also the site of the 1865 Battle of Forks Road, the Confederates' last stand against the Union army advancing on Wilmington. Short trails lead through the longleaf pine forest to Confederate earthworks. The museum hosts a Living History Weekend each year in February. Other Civil War sites in the area include Fort Fisher State Historic Site and Fort Anderson State Historic Site. Visit www.civilwartraveler.com for more information.

Quick tip: After visiting the Cameron, continue your artistic experience by scheduling a meal at nearby **Henry's Restaurant** (910-793-2929; www.henrysrestaurant .com), considered one of the loveliest eateries in the city, with walls and ceiling painted by a local artist, and cocktails served at a 100-year-old tiger oak bar.

763-6001; www.kidsmakingit.org) at 15 S. Water Street, and make a difference in a young life. This award-winning program teaches at-risk youth woodworking and marketing skills. Working with a professional artist, they craft pens, bottle stoppers, salt and pepper grinders, turned bowls, and other one-of-a-kind objects. The young artists receive 100 percent of the profit from every sale.

If you like this . . . check out the gallery operated by Wilmington's public radio station WHQR 91.3 FM (910-343-1640; www.whqr.org), located in the War-wick Building at 254 N. Front Street. The WHQR Gallery is open Monday–Friday, and all sales benefit the station.

Several galleries offer experiences beyond the ordinary. Visit ℣ Bottega Art and Wine (910-763-3737; www.bottega gallery.com) at 208 N. Front Street for an eclectic blend of poetry slams, acoustic music, wine tastings, open-mike nights, and a vegetarian-friendly menu, along with changing exhibits of modern art.

Fast fact: Whistler's mother, the subject of one of the most famous American paintings of all time, was born in Wilmington.

Performing Arts

With the many professional actors—as well as makeup, costume, and scenery design experts—attracted to Wilmington because of the activity at EUE/Screen Gems Studios, it comes as no surprise that the city's local theater scene is particularly vibrant and high quality.

In addition to productions at City Stage (910-342-0272; www. citystagenc .com), suggested in our 48 Hours section, check the schedule at Big Dawg Productions (910-341-7228; www.bigdawgproductions.org), an independent nonprofit group mounting full seasons of comedies and dramas at the Cape Fear Playhouse in Castle Street's Art & Antique District.

The ℣ Brown Coat Pub & Theatre (910-341-0001; www.guerillatheatre.com) presses the theatrical envelop, presenting original works, its own live soap opera, and original films, as well as poetry slams, karaoke, and trivia nights. Several groups call this venue home, including Pineapple Shaped Lamps (www.pineapple shapedlamps.org), presenting monthly shadow-cast performances of the *Rocky Horror Picture Show.*

Thalian Hall is both a theater and city hall.

Several theater groups stage their performances at ♿ Thalian Hall, including the Thalian Association Community Theatre (www. thalian .org), founded in 1788, one of the oldest theatrical groups in the country; and the Opera House Theater Company (www.operahousetheatre company.net). Tickets for both companies are available online or through the Thalian box office: 910-632-2285 or 1-800-523-2820.

Wilmington also has theater for the young (and young at heart). The 🎭 Thalian Association Children's Theater (910-251-1788; www. thalian.org) presents a full season of lighthearted musicals at the Hannah Block Second Street Stage (910-341-7860; www.wilmingtoncac.org), a former World War II USO club. Performance Club Studio Theater (910-338-3378; www.performanceclubkids .com) produces plays and offers a summer camp and parties for young thespians. Stageworks Youth Theater Company (910-538-8378; www.stageworksyouth.org) combines puppets and young actors with spectacular results.

Several of Wilmington's smaller theater groups produce just a few productions a year, but they're well worth watching. The Willis Richardson Players (910-763-1889), named for a Wilmington native who became a founder of the Harlem Renaissance, specializes in works by minority playwrights. The Porch Theatre Company (910-232-6611; www. porchtheatre.com) presents murder mystery dinner shows at Front Street Brewery.

Productions of the Red Barn Studio Theatre (910-762-0955; www.redbarn studiotheatre.com), begun by Tony Award–winning actress (and former star of the sitcom *Alice*) Linda Lavin and her actor husband, Steve Bakunas, garner rave reviews.

If you like this . . . the UNCW Department of Theatre *(910-962-2793; www.uncw.edu/thr/) stages several productions of often challenging plays on campus each semester.*

Wilmington has lots to offer music and dance fans as well. The North Carolina Symphony (www.ncsymphony.org), Chamber Music Wilmington (www.chambermusicwilmington.org), and the Wilmington Symphony Orchestra (www.wilmingtonsymphony.org) present full seasons each year, while the Wilmington Concert Association (www.wilmingtonconcert.com) hosts touring music, opera, and dance companies. Most performances take place at the 1,000-seat Kenan Auditorium and other venues on the UNCW campus (910-962-3500 or 1-800-732-3643; www.uncw.edu/kenan/) or at the several performance venues at Thalian Hall (910-632-2285 or 1-800-523-2820; www.thalianhall.com) downtown. Check their websites for current schedules.

On a smaller scale, the 🎭 Brooklyn Arts Center at St. Andrews (910-538-2939; www.brooklynartsnc.com), a former Presbyterian chapel, hosts intimate concerts and dance performances.

Wilmington also has classical and jazz concerts at museums, mansions, and gardens; chamber music concerts at churches; and much more. Visit the website www.whatsonwilmington.com to keep up with events of every sort in Wilmington, including many free activities.

Quick tips:
• If you come to Wilmington during the month of June, see the Bard for free at the annual **Shakespeare on the Green** series (910-399-2878; www.myspace.com/shake speareonthegreen) at the open-air **Greenfield Lake Amphitheater** (www.greenfieldlakeamphitheater .com). Bring a picnic, a bottle of wine—and plenty of bug spray.
• Visit the website of the **Cape Fear Jazz Society** (www.capefear jazz.com) for concert and club information.

Wilmington's Film Scene

As you'd expect in such a film-oriented city, Wilmington hosts numerous film festivals, and opportunities to view indie films abound. Both UNCW and Cape Fear Community College run burgeoning programs for young filmmakers, and the results can be seen on screens all over the city.

One of the highest-rated festivals in the country, the annual **Cucalorus Film Festival** (910-343-5995; www.cucalorus.org), held every November, also sponsors films the rest of the year at **Jengo's Playhouse** (910-343-5995), a funky yet state-of-the-art microcinema at 815 Princess Street.

Jengo's Playhouse screens cutting-edge films.

The film studies department at UNCW (www. uncw.edu/filmstudies) hosts a busy schedule of films and festivals in its Lumina Film Theater, including an International Cinema Series, lectures by prominent filmmakers, and several film festivals, such as the **Visions Film Festival**, featuring undergraduate films from around the world; and the **Real Teal Film Festival**, screening films by UNCW students in April. Best of all, most of these events are free and open to the public. Call the Lumina movie hotline at 910-962-2900 or check the current schedule at www.uncw.edu/lumina.

Other annual film festivals in Wilmington include the **Cape Fear Independent Film Festival** (www.cfifn.org) at the end of April and the **North Carolina Black Film Festival** (www.blackartsalliance.org) every March.

The **Cinematique Film Series** (910-632-2285 or 1-800-523-2820; www.thalianhall.com) brings notable independent films from around the world to Thalian Hall.

In addition, several Wilmington nightclubs and galleries sponsor film nights showing hard-to-find or local films. Regular screenings take place at the ♉ **Juggling Gypsy Hookah Bar** (910-763-2223; www.jugglinggypsy.com); **Projekte Gallery** (910-763-1197; www.theprojekte.com); ♉ **Arabian Nights Lounge** (910-763-3456; www.arabiannightshookahcafe.com); ♉ **Brown Coat Pub & Theatre** (910-341-0001; www.guerillatheatre.com); and the ♉ **Opera Room Bar & Gallery** (www.facebook.com/picturepitcher).

Local favorite ✆ ☀ ♉ **Satellite Bar and Lounge** (910-399-2796; www.satellitebarandlounge.com), a neighborhood bar near Greenfield Lake, hosts frequent films on its outdoor screen, as well as live music, including Sunday night bluegrass.

From piano bars to hookah lounges, Wilmington has plenty of nightlife to offer. While clubs come and go, here are some that have stood the test of time.

Downtown, the Ⴘ Soapbox Laundro-Lounge (910-251-8500; www.soapboxlaundrolounge.com) on N. Front offers three stories of entertainment, from indie rock bands to the naughty Peepshow Cabaret (www.thepeepshowcabaret.com), plus you can do your laundry while you party. In the basement, the Nutt Street Bar & Comedy Room (910-251-7881; www.nuttstreet.com) hosts the city's only full-time comedy club, with appearances by national stand-up stars.

The Whiskey (910-763-3088; www.myspace.com/wilmingtonwhiskey), at the corner of S. Front and Market, is many locals' choice for nightly live music and hard-core dancing.

Looking for a spot to watch the big game? Two downtown spots with plenty of TVs and game-day specials are Ⴘ Hell's Kitchen (910-763-4133; www.hellskitchen bar.com) on Princess Street and the family-friendly ❧ Ⴘ Copper Penny Pub (910-762-1373; www.copperpennync.com) on Chestnut Street, where kids eat free on Monday nights.

Want to shoot some (historical) pool? You'll find plenty of action downtown at Ⴘ Blue Post Billiards (910-343-1141) at 5 S. Front and Ⴘ Orton's Pool Room and Sports Bar (910-343-8881; www.ortonpoolroom.com) just a few blocks away at 133 N. Front. Established in 1888 and recognized as the oldest surviving pool room in America, Orton's occupies the basement of the old Orton Hotel, which burned down in 1949. Both pool rooms are said to be haunted. In 1958 pocket billiards champion Willie Mosconi set a new world's record at Orton's Pool Hall, pocketing 365 balls. The table he used is still in play.

Fans of the blues will feel right at home at the Ⴘ Rusty Nail (910-251-1888; www.myspace.com/rustynailnc), where the Cape Fear Blues Society (www.capefearblues.org) hosts weekly open jam sessions. A little off the beaten track at 1310 S. Fifth Street, the club exudes a friendly juke joint vibe, with live music several nights a week.

> **Fast fact:** Every Friday night from May to Labor Day, the **Downtown Sundown Concert Series** (www.downtownsundown.com) presents bands at Riverfront Park along the Riverwalk. The free concerts run 6–10 PM with food, wine, and beer available.

> **Quick tip:** Max out your laugh meter at the annual **Cape Fear Comedy Festival** (www.capefear comedyfestival.com) held every May.

George Harrison used Blue Post Billards as the setting for a 1987 movie.

Shanty's II (910-233-3266; www .shantys2.com) down in Carolina Beach is the area's hottest shag club. Check the schedule of the Cape Fear Shag Club (www.capefearshagclub.net) to find out where the cool cats are dancin'.

Not all the nightlife takes place downtown. Along Eastwood Drive, leading to the Wrightsville Beach causeway, Y Kefi (910-256-3558; www.kefilive.com) is a longtime local favorite for get-down live music. Y Fibber's Public House (910-256-0102; www.fibberspublichouse.com) is an Irish pub with pool, pints, and live bands in Pavilion Place off Eastwood Drive.

Lumina Station houses several upscale nightspots, including the classy dance spot Y Dirty Martini (910-256-5514; www.dirtymartiniwb.com), repeatedly voted best martini bar in the city, and the Y Cameo 1900 Lounge (910-509-2026; www .cameo1900.com).

In Midtown, near the university, ✆ Y Katy's Grill & Bar (910-395-5289 or 910-395-6204; www.katysgrillandbar.com) is a favorite with all ages, thanks to the kid-friendly dining room; casual menu served until late night; Ping-Pong on the patio; and some of the city's best karaoke.

FAMILY-FRIENDLY WILMINGTON

Families with kids in tow will find plenty to keep them busy in Wilmington, even when the weather is rainy.

The youngest set will enjoy a day of fun at the ✆ ↑ Children's Museum of Wilmington (910-254-3534; www.playwilmington.org), where the interactive exhibits are designed for ages 1–10.

Kids of all ages love ✆ Jungle Rapids Family Fun Park (910-791-0666; www.junglerapids.com), with its water park featuring a million-gallon wave pool, go-cart track, minigolf course, indoor climbing wall, Alien Invader laser tag, and the best arcade games in the region.

Enjoy a good scare? Take the kids to the ✆ ↑ Cape Fear Serpentarium (910-762-1669; www.capefearserpentarium.com) to meet over 50 varieties of venomous snakes, boa constrictors, crocodiles, and giant lizards. One of the world's foremost reptile collections occupies a former ironworks in the historic downtown, steps from the Riverwalk. The indoor habitats, created by professional film industry set designers, allow visitors to see rarely observed behaviors in complete safety.

For a less heart-stopping reptile encounter, consider a visit to the nature center at ✆ Halyburton Park (910-341-0075; www.halyburtonpark.com), where snake and turtle feedings are designed for the preschool crowd.

Looking for the monkeys at Monkey Junction? Visit ✆ Tregembo Animal Park (910-392-3604; www.tregemboanimalpark.com), a family-owned zoo in operation

Music Festivals in Southeast North Carolina

The **NC Jazz Festival** (www. ncjazzfestival.com), held every February in Wilmington, attracts jazz greats and fans from around the world for a weekend of traditional jazz sounds and all-star jams.

At the **Carolina Beach Music Festival** (www.pleasureislandnc.org), held the first Saturday in June at Carolina Beach, top R & B bands have fans shagging on the sand.

The **Cape Fear Blues Festival** (www.capefearblues.org), held annually in Wilmington toward the end of July, features a blues cruise on the *Henrietta III*, indoor and outdoor concerts, and all-day jams.

The **Southern Coastal Bluegrass Festival** (www.coastalbluegrassfestival.org), held in September in Wilmington, features top bluegrass and gospel groups, plus local cuisine, arts and crafts, storytelling, clogging, and square dancing

The annual **Seafood, Blues & Jazz Festival** (www.pleasureislandnc.org), held the second weekend in October at the Fort Fisher Air Force Recreation Area on Pleasure Island, pairs top blues and jazz performers with fresh seafood from area restaurants.

for over 50 years. Recently updated habitats house animals from around the world, including nine species of monkeys, and kids can feed many of the tamer critters.

Got a budding skateboard or disc golf champion in the family? Greenfield Grind Skatepark (910-362-8222; www.greenfieldgrind.com), a 9,000-square-foot concrete park adjacent to Greenfield Lake, offers day and night skating plus beginners' clinics.

If you like this . . . disc golf courses are free to play at Castle Hayne Park (910-798-7620; www.nhcgov.com), north of downtown, and Joe Eakes Park (910-458-8216; www.townofkurebeach.org) in Kure Beach.

The ⚓ ⛵ Wilmington Ice House (910-686-1987; www.wilmingtonice.com), with public ice skating sessions daily, is a great place to work off extra energy.

⚓ ⛵ 🍴 Break Time Billiards and Ten Pin Alley (910-395-6658; www.breaktimetenpin.com) is a real find for family groups with something for every age including daily bowling specials, the largest pool hall in North Carolina, foosball tournaments, TV screens tuned to sports, daily specials on drinks and food, and a grill serving food until 2 AM every night of the week.

OUTDOOR ADVENTURES

Biking

The flat terrain of the coastal plain makes the region around Wilmington a popular one for biking. Numerous bike paths, both on and off road, snake through the city itself and into the surrounding countryside.

Quick tip: Join the locals for a cruise around Greenfield Lake aboard a paddleboat rented from **Cape Fear River Watch** (910-762-5606; www.cfrw.us), a long-standing tradition in Wilmington.

Some of the most pleasant rides are within city parks. A 5-mile biking and pedestrian path surrounds Greenfield Lake near downtown. Other paved paths circle Hugh McRae and Halyburton Parks.

An ambitious project, the Gary Shell Cross-City Trail (www.crosscitytrail .com), is under way to create a 10-mile bike path from near the UNCW campus to Wrightsville Beach. Many parts of the trail, including the section near the Cameron Art Museum, are already in place. Check the website for the latest developments. More information, including detailed maps, can be found on the websites of Live Fit Cape Fear (www.livefitcapefear.org) and the Wilmington Urban Area Metropolitan Planning Organization (www.wmpo.org/WMBPC).

For the more dedicated cyclist, a number of established bike paths radiate out from Wilmington's downtown in every direction. The most popular is the River to the Sea Bikeway (www.rivertoseabikeway.com), an 11-mile ride from the base of Market Street all the way to the pier in Wrightsville Beach, following the route once taken by the Beach Car trolley line. This is Wilmington Bike Route 1, which has signs throughout its course.

Ports of Call, NC Bike Route 3, another signed route, follows River Road down the Cape Fear River to the ferry landing at Fort Fisher, and across to Southport and Brunswick County. NC Bike Route 5, the Cape Fear Run, also signed, follows the west side of the river for 160 miles, passing battlefields, parks, and other historic sites. A popular loop route follows Bike Route 3 down Pleasure Island and over the Southport Ferry, then returns up the other side of the river along Bike Route 5. Maps for these itineraries, and many others, can be ordered free or downloaded from the North Carolina Department of Transportation website (877-DOT-4YOU; www.ncdot.org/transit/bicycle/).

> **Quick tip:** Plan your visit to coincide with the annual **River to Sea Bike Ride** (910-341-3258; www .rivertoseabikeway.com), held the first Saturday of May. This popular ride is free and no preregistration is necessary.

Cape Fear Cyclists (www.capefearcyclists.org) organizes rides suitable for all abilities almost daily, and visitors are welcome to join in. Visit their website for planned rides and routes.

Single-track mountain biking trails can be found at the Blue Clay Mountain Bike Park. For information on these trails and others in the region, visit www.sir bikesalot.com.

Bike rentals are readily available in the city. In the historic downtown, bikes are available from the Cartmen (910-264-4442; www.cartmen.org) and at Ted's Fun on the River (910-231-3379; www.tedsfun.com), at the end of Castle Street. Bike rentals are also available seasonally in Greenfield Park, near the kayak shed.

In Mayfaire Center about a mile from Wrightsville Beach, Bike Cycles (910-256-2545; www.bikecycleshop.com) rents beach cruisers, tandem bikes, and road bikes for adults and kids, as well as baby jogger strollers. The shop also organizes breakfast rides and guided bike tours of Wilmington neighborhoods.

Birding

The Cape Fear region is a hotspot for bird-watching, with 14 different birding areas designated important by the Audubon Society. Audubon North Carolina

(910-686-7527; nc.audubon.org) and the Cape Fear Audubon Society (www.cape fearaudubon.org) are both active in the area, sponsoring numerous bird walks, field trips, and educational events open to the public, including nature cruises of the undisturbed Black River, home of the oldest trees east of the Rockies, and free weekly guided bird walks during the summer months to see the shore birds nesting at Mason Inlet on Wrightsville Beach.

If you like this . . . the North Carolina Birding Trail identifies numerous sites in Wilmington and along the southern coast where birding is exceptional. Download maps and directions at www.ncbirdingtrail.org or order a copy by calling 1-866-945-3746.

Boating

A cruise on the stately ♿ ♂ *Henrietta III* provides a lounge-chair voyage through Wilmington's history and is one of the don't-miss experiences in the city. But the paddlewheeler is just one of the Cape Fear Riverboats (910-343-1611 or 1-800-676-0162; www.cfrboats.com) plying the river. From Memorial Day to Labor Day, down at the docks at the foot of Market Street, you can hop aboard a water taxi for a quick trip across to the battleship, sign up for an evening cruise of the waterfront, or take a nature cruise aboard the SS *Maffitt* up the unspoiled Black River.

Wilmington Water Tours (910-338-3134; www.wilmingtonwatertours.com) will take you on a sunset cruise around Eagle Island or on a day-long trip down the Cape Fear to Carolina Beach. Or enjoy a relaxing sunset under sail with Sail Wilmington (910-538-8884; www.sailwilmingtonnc.com).

For a more intimate experience with the river, get out on its waters in a canoe or kayak. When the river is calm, you can rent a boat at ♂ 🐾 (((ᵠ))) Ted's Fun on the River (910-231-3379; www.tedsfun.com), a laid-back general store at the bottom of Castle Street, almost under the Cape Fear Memorial Bridge. The public boat launch at Dram Tree Park is right next door.

The Cape Fear region is a terrific one for kayaking, and several outfitters operate tours that take you into the small creeks and offshore islands that can only be explored by boat. Watersmyth Kayaking (910-805-2517; www.watersmyth kayaking.com), The Expedition Organization (910-200-1594; www.expedition organization.com), and Hook, Line & Paddle (910-792-6945 or 877-91-KAYAK; www.hooklineandpaddle.com) all are based in Wilmington.

Cape Fear Expeditions (919-349-8599; www.capefearexpeditions.com) offers similar tours in the comfort of a 22-foot Boston whaler.

If you're an experienced paddler and want to explore on your own, Hook, Line & Paddle will also rent you a kayak, fishing kayak, or stand-up paddleboard, complete with a soft roof rack for transport. The website of the Cape Fear Paddlers (www.capefearpaddlers.org) details numerous trips in the area, complete with suggested routes and maps to put-ins.

If you arrive in Wilmington via your own boat, tie up in the heart of downtown, steps away from the restaurants, museums, and nightlife, at the City Docks (910-520-6875; www.wilmingtonnc.gov/community_services/recreation/), operated by the city of Wilmington.

Another interesting spot for boating is historic Greenfield Lake, surrounded by cypress trees, Spanish moss, and blooming gardens. Cape Fear River Watch

Airlie Gardens are especially lovely during the annual Azalea Festival.

(910-762-5606; www.cfrw.us) rents canoes, kayaks, and paddleboats on the lake, and conducts birding tours aboard its electric launch.

Gardens & Nature Centers

A don't miss for garden lovers, ♿ ♂ Airlie Gardens (910-798-7700; www.airliegardens.org), established over 100 years ago at Wilmington's eastern edge, is magnificent year-round, with dogwoods and azaleas in spring, magnolias and roses during the summer, and 5,000 camellias blooming during the colder months. Over the flower beds and wandering paths tower ancient live oaks, including the nearly 500-year-old Airlie Oak, spreading shade and a sense of timeless calm. Another highlight is the Bottle Chapel, constructed of colorful glass bottles in honor of visionary artist Minnie Evans, once the garden gatekeeper. A tram is available for access to all the garden's features on a limited schedule.

If you like this . . . the ♿ ♂ New Hanover County Extension Arboretum (910-798-7666; www.gardeningnhc.org), located across Bradley Creek from Airlie, includes mature herb and water gardens, a special children's garden, and a lovely streamside Japanese teahouse surrounded by Asian species. Open daily; free.

Oakdale Cemetery (910-762-5682; www.oakdalecemetery.org), a survivor from the Victorian Age and an early member of the rural cemetery movement, is considered one of Wilmington's finest examples of natural beauty. Historical tours, wagon rides, and an annual azalea driving tour are some of the events held amid the live oak trees, gardens, and many beautiful and curious monuments, some considered works of sculptural art. Self-guided tours are available daily.

Quick tip: A map on the Oakdale Cemetery website (www.oakdalecemetery.org) leads to the graves of some of the most famous residents buried here, including a female Confederate spy and newscaster David Brinkley.

Horseback Riding

Hanover Stables (910-675-8923; www.hanoverstables.net) in Castle Hayne and Peterson Stable (910-686-2909; www.freewebs.com/peterson_stables/) offer trail rides and other equine services in the Wilmington area.

Parks

The city of Wilmington (910-341-7852; www.wilmingtonnc.gov/community_services.aspx) maintains many parks with a full array of services. Paved walking paths and nature trails are found at Greenfield Lake, Halyburton, and Empie. At the ♂ ♿ Halyburton Nature Preserve (910-341-0075; www.halyburtonpark.com), trails cross a remnant of longleaf pine savannah, a rare native ecosystem. The Tennis Complex at Empie Park (910-341-4631), named for Althea Gibson, the nation's first great African American female tennis player, has 18 lighted courts available for public play. Empie also has a dog park. Greenfield Lake Park (910-762-5606; www.cfrw.us), about 2 miles south of downtown on S. Third Street, has an amphitheater, paved bike path, boating concessions, playground, tennis courts, and a skate park.

New Hanover County (910-798-7620; www.nhcgov.com) also has an extensive network of public parks, many with specialized facilities. Launch boats and kayaks at River Road Park on the Cape Fear or Trails End Park on the ICW. River Road Park (910-798-7198) also has a ♿ fishing pier; fishing license required. ♂ Hugh McRae Park has a 1.5-mile nature trail around a pond lined with cypress and home to some giant carp—real kid pleasers. Castle Hayne Park has an 18-hole disc golf course.

Located in the heart of the UNCW campus, the Bluethenthal Wildflower Preserve (910-962-3100; www.uncw.edu) offers pleasant, pine-needle covered paths through a variety of native habitats including a pond and a carnivorous plant garden. The trail begins across from the University Union. Dogs and bikes are not permitted.

SHOPPING

In addition to the Cotton Exchange (910-343-9896; www.shopcottonexchange .com) and Chandler's Wharf (910-762-4106; www.chandlerswharfshops.com) described in our 48 Hours section, the city has a number of other retail experiences worth seeking out.

The six blocks that separate the Cotton Exchange and Chandler's Wharf provide a multitude of shopping options. A must-stop for book lovers: Old Books on Front Street (910-762-6657; www.oldbooksonfrontst.com), occupying a 100-year-old building in the 200 block of N. Front, is an award-winning used bookstore, with miles of shelves packed with everything from first editions to children's classics. Sugar (910-254-1110; sugaronfrontst. wordpress.com), a bakery and coffee shop making delicious cookies, muffins, and pies, shares the building.

The Old Wilmington City Market (119 S. Water Street), one of the city's oldest surviving commercial buildings, now houses a variety of shops, includ-

Market Street is lined with fun shops.

Quick tip: The website www
.wilmingtonantiqueshops.com
offers a current listing of antiquing
options in the region, plus a map.

ing 🐾 My Porch Dawg (910-512-2794; www.myporchdawg.com), a local bakery selling all-natural pet treats.

Antiques

Wilmington, an old and wealthy city, makes a great destination for antiquing. Several shops are located in the historic downtown, including J. Robert Warren Antiques (910-762-6077; www.j robertwarrenantiques.com), which occupies a historic house just a block from the river on Orange Street.

Many shops and galleries cluster in the Castle Street Art & Antique District, between Fifth and Seventh Streets south of Market. This is a great destination for browsing, either during the day or during the Fourth Friday Art Crawl. Stop for breakfast or lunch at Jester's Café (910-763-6555; www.jesterscafe.com) at 607 Castle Street, or for a glass of pick-me-up, try Wilmington Wine (910-202-4749; www.wilmingtonwinecompany.com) at 605 Castle.

One don't-miss shopping option for those who love to browse is the 🌳 Ivy Cottage (910-815-0907; www.threecottages.com), located about 3 miles down Market Street from the river, Four buildings stuffed with an ever-changing selection of antiques, furniture, and household consignment items provide hours of exploration.

Get in on the bidding action at Big South Auctions & Antiques (910-251-1038; www.bigsouthauction.com), located at 3911 Market Street. Auctions are held several times a month, preceded by preview sessions open to the public.

Books

In the historic downtown, shop for used books at 🌳 Old Books on Front Street (910-762-6657; www.oldbooksonfrontst.com) and new releases at the 🌳 Two Sisters Bookery (910-762-4444; www.twosistersbookery.com) in the Cotton Exchange.

At 🌳 (📶) Pomegranate Books (910-452-1107; www.pombooks.net), on the corner of Park and Kerr Avenues, browse a selection of new and used books of local interest while enjoying a cup of coffee or tea, along with free WiFi. 🌳 McAllister & Solomon Books (910-350-0189 or 1-888-617-7882; www.mcallisterandsolomon .com), on Wrightsville Avenue, specializes in rare and vintage used books.

Consignment Clothing

Thanks to the many films made in the region, Wilmington hosts a booming vintage and consignment clothing scene. Flashbax (910-547-5567; www.etsy.com/shop /Flashbax), a vintage clothing store at 20 N. Front downtown, provides wardrobes for films and TV shows. You'll find '50s cocktail dresses, western shirts, and velvet smoking jackets on its diverse racks.

If you like this . . . browse the current offerings at the Fairy Circle (910-790-2025; www.fairycircleconsignment.com) in Monkey Junction.

Sales at the several locations of Vintage Values (910-762-7720; www .domesticviolence-wilm.org) benefit the Domestic Violence Shelter and Services of Wilmington.

Gifts

With more than 100 shops under one roof, ↑ Blue Moon Gift Shops (910-799-5793; www.bluemoongiftshops.com), off Eastwood Road, is a local favorite for unusual and one-of-a-kind gifts. Locally produced artwork, crafts, handmade clothing, and food items are featured, and gift wrapping is free.

If it's always Christmas in your heart, visit the ↑ Cape Fear Christmas House (910-796-0222 or 1-800-494-9627; www.christmas-noel.com) on Oleander Drive for an addition to your holiday baubles. Don't miss its collection of rare Nutcracker figures.

SPORTS SCENE

Golf

Located just minutes from the many exceptional courses in Brunswick County, Wilmington makes a great base of operations for golfers. Visitors with a taste for both golf and history will enjoy a round at the city-owned Municipal Course (910-791-0558; www.wilmingtonnc.gov/community_services/recreation.aspx), designed in 1926 by Donald Ross, the legendary creator of Pinehurst's famed No. 2. Recently restored to Ross's original vision, the course offers quality golf at a very reasonable price. You can walk the course or rent a cart.

Several clubs accepting public play are just to the south of the city on the Cape Fear peninsula. Two, Beau Rivage Resort & Golf Club (910-392-9021 or 1-800-628-7080; www.beaurivagegolf.com), a "stay and play" resort, and Echo Farms Golf & Country Club (910-791-9318; www.echofarmsnc.com), lie along the east bank of the Cape Fear River. Just north of Carolina Beach, Masonboro Country Club, (910-397-9162; www.masonborocountryclub.com) a public course recently redesigned by architect Bob Moore of JMP Designs, is considered one of the most challenging in the region.

The Seahawk is the mascot of UNCW collegiate sports.

For a quiet port city, Wilmington has an amazing number of sport leagues, including professional basketball, pro soccer, and all-star college baseball, all with seasons during the summer months.

The Wilmington Sea Dawgs (910-791-6523; www.goseadawgs.com) provide exciting minor league basketball every summer in the Cape Fear Community College's Schwartz Center, located in the historic downtown at 610 N. Front Street.

If you like this . . . the Cape Fear Roller Girls (www.capefearrollergirls .com), with bouts year-round, also compete at the Schwartz Center.

&. Legion Stadium (910-341-4604), a city-owned facility on Carolina Beach Road, hosts the Wilmington Hammerheads (910-777-2111; www.wilmington hammerheads.com), a professional soccer league, and the Wilmington Sharks (910-343-5621; www.wilmingtonsharks.com), a baseball team made up of college all-stars competing in the Coastal Plain League, the hottest summer collegiate baseball league in the country. Both are local favorites and attract large crowds every summer.

UNCW Athletics (www.uncwsports.com) fields men's and women's Seahawk teams competing in a variety of collegiate sport during the school year.

North Carolina's Lowcountry Coast

BEACHES, SEAFOOD, AND FAMILY TRADITIONS

LIVE OAKS DRAPED IN SPANISH MOSS bend low over mysterious blackwater rivers. Great plantation houses doze amid gardens ablaze with azalea and camellia blooms. Seaports, once bustling with blockade runners and diplomats, nap in the backwash of history.

This is the heritage of the North Carolina's Lowcountry, a land of sand beaches and salt marshes, of history and family tradition.

Stretched along the state's southeast coast, a chain of barrier islands stand guard against the Atlantic surf. Generations of summer visitors treasure these beach communities as North Carolina's most family-friendly vacation spots. Today, even after a decade of unprecedented growth, these communities retain a small-town charm that reminds visitors of days gone by.

The region is particularly rich in fishing piers, a rapidly disappearing breed. Nine of North Carolina's 20 surviving piers are located here, offering new generations a chance to cast a line.

FIGURE EIGHT ISLAND

Just north of Wrightsville Beach lies a secluded island, rarely mentioned in the travel press, but well known to the well heeled as an exclusive getaway. Once the home of wild ponies, Figure Eight Island today is accessible only by a gated causeway that connects it with the mainland. If your name is not on the guest or resident list, you'll not get in.

Although the names of residents are highly guarded, celebrities known to have

LEFT: Fourth of July brings out the crowds on Pleasure Island.

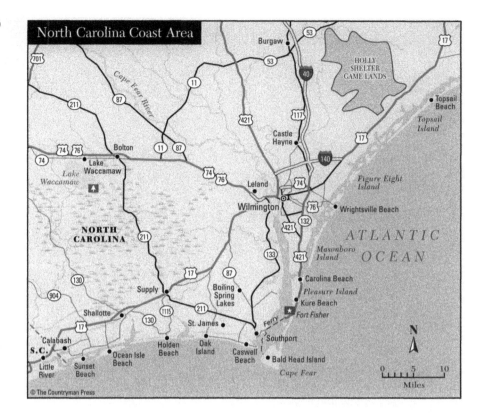

North Carolina Coast Area

© The Countryman Press

vacationed here include John Edwards, Al Gore, and John Travolta. Episodes of the television series *Dawson's Creek* were also filmed here.

About 70 of the 440 cottages are available for rental. If you'd like to join the elite, contact Figure Eight Realty (910-686-4400 or 1-800-279-6085; www.figure 8island.com).

WRIGHTSVILLE BEACH

The history of Wrightsville Beach, originally called Ocean View, is a classic story of the growth of a seaside resort. Originally accessible only by boat, the barrier island began to gain popularity in the years after the Civil War as the American public discovered the health benefits of saltwater bathing. The Shell Road, today's Wrightsville Avenue, was completed to the boat landing in the 1880s. By 1899 a short-line railroad extended all the way to the ocean, spurring the development of hotels and beach cottage communities.

In 1902 the Tidewater Power Company electrified the line, creating the Beach Line Trolley with stops paralleling the beach down today's S. Lumina Avenue. The trolley line ended at the

Quick tip: The **Wrightsville Beach Visitors Center** (910-256-8116 or 1-800-650-9106; www.visitwrightsville.com), located just east of the drawbridge on US 74/Salisbury Street, is open April–September.

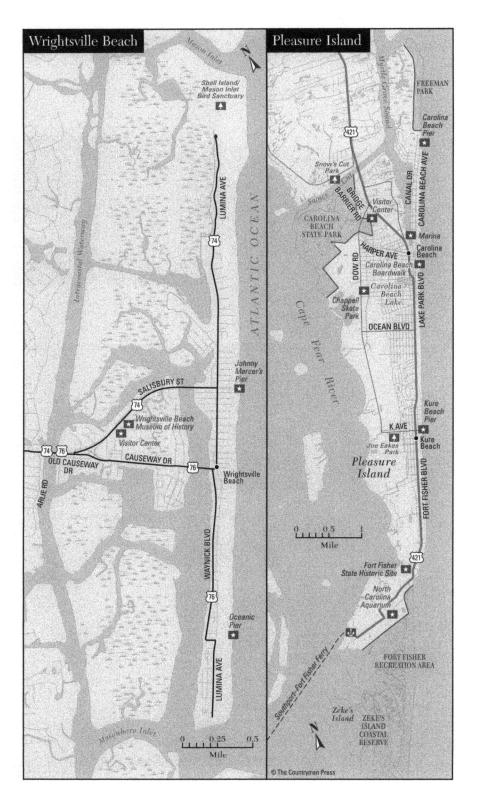

Wrightsville Beach

Mason Inlet

N

Shell Island/
Mason Inlet
Bird Sanctuary

Intracoastal Waterway

LUMINA AVE

74

A T L A N T I C   O C E A N

SALISBURY ST

74

Wrightsville Beach
Museum of History

Visitor Center

74 76

OLD CAUSEWAY
DR

CAUSEWAY DR

76

Wrightsville
Beach

ARLIE RD

WAYNICK BLVD

76

Johnny
Mercer's
Pier

Oceanic
Pier

LUMINA AVE

Masonboro Inlet

0   0.25   0.5
Mile

Pleasure Island

FREEMAN
PARK

Myrtle Grove Sound

Carolina
Beach
Pier

421

Snow's Cut
Park

Snow's Cut

BRIDGE BARRIER RD

CANAL DR

CAROLINA BEACH AVE

Visitor
Center

Marina

CAROLINA
BEACH
STATE PARK

HARPER AVE

DOW RD

Carolina
Beach

Carolina Beach
Boardwalk

LAKE PARK BLVD

Carolina
Beach
Lake

Chappell
Skate
Park

OCEAN BLVD

Cape Fear River

Kure
Beach
Pier

K AVE

Joe Eakes
Park

Kure
Beach

FORT FISHER BLVD

*Pleasure
Island*

0   0.5   1
Mile

421

Fort Fisher
State Historic Site

North
Carolina
Aquarium

FORT FISHER
RECREATION
AREA

Southport–Fort Fisher Ferry

N

*Zeke's
Island*

ZEKE'S
ISLAND
COASTAL
RESERVE

© The Countryman Press

famous Lumina Pavilion, visible for miles up and down the beach and out to sea thanks to the hundreds of electric lights that outlined its exterior.

Automobiles were allowed onto the island in 1935, and the Beach Trolley ceased operation in 1940. The Lumina Pavilion continued to be popular for many years, hosting big band dances, movies in the surf, and summer fun, until it was demolished in 1973.

Today, access to the island follows the historic trolley route over the Intracoastal Waterway (ICW). A drawbridge carries both US 76 and US 74 onto Harbor Island, where they divide, making the jump to Wrightsville Beach by separate routes. US 74 heads north, becoming Salisbury Street, ending at Johnny Mercer's Pier. US 76 heads due

Lifeguards make the North Carolina beaches family friendly.

east as Causeway Drive. Its junction with Lumina Avenue is the island's midpoint and the center of Wrightsville's downtown district.

The charms of Wrightsville Beach remain as they were in the early years of its development—its wide, clean, white sand beach, fishing piers reaching far out to sea, romantic sunsets over the marsh, and fresh sea breezes continue to draw visi-

Did you know?
• The first major building on Wrightsville Beach was the clubhouse of the **Carolina Yacht Club** (910-256-3396; www.carolinayachtclub.org). Founded in 1853, it's one of the oldest such organizations in the country. Still active today, the club sponsors several annual regattas.
• Johnny Mercer's Pier was named for a local businessman, not the famous musician, but no one will mind if you hum "Moon River" as you stroll down the pier on a moonlit night.

Fast facts:
• Today the Oceanic Restaurant occupies the site of the old Lumina Pavilion. To find out more history of this seaside resort, visit the **Wrightsville Beach Museum** (910-256-2569; www.wbmuseum.com).
• The 1996 hurricane season destroyed many wooden piers along this coast, including Johnny Mercer's and the Luna (now the Crystal), with the one-two punch of Hurricanes Bertha and Fran. The Mercer was rebuilt as the concrete giant it now is, able to withstand 200-mile-per-hour winds. The Crystal was not, with just 200 feet of its wooden deck remaining to add to the scenic dining experience at the Oceanic Restaurant.

tors now as then. To those constants, recent years have added a smattering of interesting restaurants and the discovery of a reliable surf break that nurtures a resident surfer culture.

The majority of visitors are families spending their week-long vacation at the shore. Many find the small hot dog stands, ice cream parlors, and seafood joints at Wrightsville the ideal spots for creating family beach traditions and return year after year.

Checking In

Best places to stay in and around Wrightsville Beach

When you arrive on Wrightsville Beach, walk out to the end of Johnny Mercer's Pier (910-256-2743). Turn back and look at the shoreline. You'll see just a few high-rise buildings topping the dune line. Most of the island continues to be residential in nature, with family cottages lining the shore, and many of them are for rent.

Wrightsville does have a few larger resorts. Toward the south end of the island, the ☉ ᚼ ♂ ☿ (ᵠ) ↴ Blockade Runner Resort (910-256-2251 or 1-800-541-1161; www.blockade-runner .com) stretches entirely across, from

the oceanfront to Banks Channel. Guests have the choice of hanging out on the Atlantic, taking surfing lessons or enjoying drinks around the ocean-front pool, or crossing over to the Sunset Beach Club on the west side of the island, where the water is gentler and the views are spectacular. There's a fishing pier here, and you can sign up for a sightseeing cruise or a water taxi ride to uninhabited Masonboro Island or rent a sailboat, kayak, or stand-up paddleboard for fun in the water. Or try kayak fishing with Hook, Line & Paddle (910-685-1983; www.hookline andpaddle.com), one of the area's top outfitters, which has one of its locations here.

Long known as the SunSpree, the ☉ ᚼ ♂ ☿ (ᵠ) Holiday Inn Resort Wrightsville Beach (910-256-2231 or

The Holiday Inn Resort at Wrightsville Beach opens directly onto the sand.

877-330-5050; www.wrightsville.holiday innresorts.com) occupies a prime oceanfront location just to the north of Mercer's Pier. Kids stay and eat free here and can participate in KidSpree Vacation Club activities, making it a top choice for families. Rooms have big balconies overlooking the ocean or the island and come equipped with microwaves and refrigerators. Enormous indoor and outdoor pool areas and wide verandas add to the laid-back vibe. A complimentary shuttle bus takes guests around the island and to the airport. Even if you aren't staying here, drop by to meet the parrot mascots that greet guests in the lobby, or to enjoy live music and cocktails on the oceanfront patio.

For something a bit different, make reservations at the ((ꝙ)) Carolina Temple Apartments Island Inn (910-256-2773; www.carolinatempleisland inn.com), housed in a historic beach house on the sound side of the island. Once Station 6 on the Beach Trolley Line, this charming inn features bal-

conies lined with rocking chairs and hammocks, a private beach and dock on the sound, fully equipped kitchens, and color TVs. Closed during the winter.

The ✍ 🐾 ((ꝙ)) Waterway Lodge (910-256-3771 or 1-800-677-3771; www.waterwaylodge.com), located on the mainland at the base of the drawbridge leading to Wrightsville Beach and across the street from the ICW, is a popular overnight stop for pet owners.

On the beachfront, the ♂ Oceanic Restaurant and Grill (910-256-5551; www.oceanicrestaurant.com) is a must-visit destination. Located on what remains of the Crystal Pier (previously called the Luna), the spacious beach-cottage-style restaurant is a favorite stop for locals who come to share a bowl of she-crab soup, the restaurant's famous hot crab dip, or the Perfect Pier Platter, with enough oysters on the half shell, boiled shrimp, scallops, and flounder for two. Outdoor seating is available on the pier, which hosts frequent live music when the weather cooperates. A public beach access is right next door if you want to stroll the sand.

The wait can be long on summer

Local Flavors

Taste of the town—local cafés, restaurants, bars, bistros, etc.

The Lumina neighborhood in Wilmington, with many of the city's finest restaurants, is just over the bridge from Wrightsville Beach. Also, the restaurants on either bank of the ICW are popular and scenic dining destinations convenient for Wrightsville visitors. See our Wilmington chapter for suggested places to dine, shop, and play on the mainland and along Marina Street, home of the famous ♈ Bluewater Waterfront Grill (910-256-8500; www.bluewaterdining.com) on the ICW.

weekends at the ⌀ Causeway Café (910-256-3730; www.wbcauseway cafe.com), located just east of the drawbridge on Harbor Island, but you can help yourself to complimentary coffee on the front deck while you wait. This friendly attitude is part of what makes the Causeway a local favorite, along with the wide variety of breakfast offerings, plate lunch specials, and homestyle, fresh veggies. Open from 6 AM to 2:30 PM, seven days a week, the café serves breakfast all day, including many local specialties such as grouper, perch, or flounder with your eggs. Check the chalkboards for daily specials. The café accepts cash only.

If you like this . . . stop by the nearby ⌀ Shore Shack Donuts (910-274-1383; 222 Causeway Drive), where surfer turned donut-maker Chris Sullivan serves donuts in a wide variety of flavors, including his signature red velvet cake.

Many of Wrightsville's restaurants cluster around the junction of Causeway Drive and Lumina Avenue, within easy walking distance of many cottages, and close to an ocean access point so you can walk in from the beach.

⌀ Tower 7 Baja Mexican Grill (910-256-8585; www.liveeatsurf.com), at 4 N. Lumina, attracts raves for its freshly prepared Tex-Mex dishes, including many vegetarian options. Tortilla chips and salsa are made in-house daily. Next door, its sister restaurant, Y (((•))) Café Del Mar (910-256-1001), serves breakfast burritos, biscuits, and bagels, along with smoothies, shakes, and shaved ice, starting at 6 AM. Coffee drinks made of locally roasted beans are available all day, and often into the night when the café hosts jam sessions, films, poetry slams, chess tournaments, and more.

A block or so south at 94 S. Lumina, the original ☀ Trolley Stop (910-256-3421; www.trollystophotdogs .com) occupies the first station on Wrightsville's Beach Car Line. A takeout spot that serves only hot dogs, it's a traditional stop for many families. Make your choice from a variety of different dogs, including Sabrett, smoked sausage, fat-free turkey, or vegetarian, then dress it in one of the many cleverly named combinations, such as the Wrightsville Beach (topped with chopped onion and tomato with a secret sauce). This location is open late night and is truly dog friendly. Order a hot dog, and your canine friend gets one, too, for free.

If you like this . . . Trolley Stop has a number of other locations around the region, including in downtown Wilmington, Carolina Beach, and Southport. They all have pretty much the same menu, but not always the free deal for Fido.

Two of Wrightsville Beach's most acclaimed restaurants are also located within the same couple of blocks. The ⌀ Y South Beach Grill (910-256-4646; www.southbeachgrillwb.com), at 100 S. Lumina, is a casual spot across the street from the sound serving lunch and dinner with some nice vegetarian dishes. Score a table on the patio and dive into some seafood nachos for a pleasant afternoon.

A block away on Lumina, Y ⏴ 22 North Dining and Spirits (910-509-0177; www.22north.net), named for its location, attracts the foodie crowd with menus that change nightly to reflect the freshest locally sourced foods and the creative vision of Chef Brent Poteat, a consistent Top Chef finalist in the annual Taste of Wilmington competition. If you're not quite ready to roll the dice on the sometimes pricey blackboard menu, stop by its Twisted Martini lounge for a signature cocktail and a po'boy, hand-patted burger, or Calabash-style catfish. Dinner only; online reservations available.

If you prefer a more entertainment-oriented atmosphere, try the Ⓨ Banks Channel Pub and Grille (910-256-2269; www.bankschannel pub.com) on the causeway. At this fun spot, pool tables, dartboards, and other games combine with sports on TV and a casual bar menu with some twists, such as fries topped with gravy (a Pennsylvania specialty), steamed seafood, and lots of fried green tomatoes. A big selection of draft beers, a late-night menu, happy hour specials, and live entertainment add to the fun.

The first few blocks of N. Lumina make fertile ground for a pub crawl with Ⓨ King Neptune's Pirate Lounge (910-256-2525), featuring rums from around the world; legendary surfer /skater bar Ⓨ Red Dogs (910-256-2776; www.reddogswb.com); and Ⓨ Lager Heads Beach Tavern (910-256-0171; lagerheadswb.com) lining the strip. Over on Salisbury Street near Mercer's Pier, you'll find ⦿ Buddy's Crab and Oyster Bar (910-256-8966; www.buddyscrabhouse.com), and

local favorite, the 🐾 Ⓨ Palm Room (910-509-3040; www.palmroombar .com), about as close to beach bars as Wrightsville gets.

Two spots on the causeway are great places to stock your refrigerator. Motts Channel Seafood (910-256-3474; www.mottschannelseafood.com) buys seafood right off the boats that dock behind the store. Close by, Lighthouse Beer and Wine (910-256-8622; www.lighthousebeerandwine.com) stocks 400 different beers from around the world, plus wine, cigars, specialty foods, and one of North Carolina's largest selections of kegs. The store hosts the Lighthouse Beer Festival (www.lighthousebeerfestival.com) in Wilmington every October.

Extend Your Stay

HISTORY & CULTURE

To really get to know this seaside resort, a visit to the ♿ 🔱 Wrightsville Beach Museum of History (910-256-2569; www.wbmuseum.com) is a must. Housed in the Myers Cottage, a historic building once on the oceanfront, now moved to Salisbury Street/US 74, the exhibits take you on a fun trip back to Wrightsville's Golden Age, when the Lumina Pavilion and Beach Trolley were the talk of the East Coast. A scale model of the island as it was 100 years ago (with working trolley), vintage postcards, and rooms filled with memorabilia bring the beach of yesteryear to life.

If you like this . . . visit the 🐾 🔱 Cape Fear Museum of History and Science (910-798-4350; www.capefearmuseum.com) in Wilmington and the

♂ ☂ *Missiles and More Museum* (910-328-8663; *www.topsailhistoricalsociety.org*) on *Topsail Island for two different takes on local history.*

Wrightsville Beach isn't a hotspot for art galleries, although several restaurants, including Café del Mar and the Oceanic, hang local art. For a look at a monumental work by local artist Claude Howell, visit the ♂ Little Chapel on the Boardwalk (910-256-2819; www.littlechapel.org), off N. Lumina at Fayetteville Street. Howell's triptych *The Miraculous Draft of Fishes*, painted in the early 1950s, depicts Christ and the Apostles catching and eating fresh seafood.

If you like this . . . you can see other works by Claude Howell at the **Cameron Art Museum** (910-395-5999; *www.cameronartmuseum.com*) *and the* **Pilothouse Restaurant** (910-343-0200; *www.pilothouserest.com*), *both in* *Wilmington.*

The Town of Wrightsville Beach (910-256-7925; www.towb.org) sponsors many special events including the Sounds of Summer Concert Series at Wrightsville Beach Park, located on Causeway Drive.

Parking on Wrightsville Beach can be challenging, especially during the summer season. Free parking is available at the Wrightsville Beach Town Hall off Causeway Drive, at the boat ramp beside the drawbridge, and on Old Causeway Drive, but none of these are convenient if you're headed for the beach. Most streets on the island have either meters or paystations. Larger paystation lots are located at the north and south ends of the island and at the intersection of Lumina and Salisbury near Mercer's Pier. Parking at either meters or paystation spaces is $2 per hour. The paystations also sell daily passes for $12 and take credit cards or cash, or you can register to pay by phone. Parking is enforced from 9 AM to 6 PM, March to the end of October. Visit the website of the town parking office (910-256-5453; www.towb.org) for parking locations and current rates.

Fast fact: Annual festivals on Wrightsville Beach include the Surf-Sun-Sand Celebration in June, Bark in the Park in October, and the North Carolina Holiday Flotilla (910-256-2120; www.ncholidayflotilla .org) in November.

OUTDOOR ADVENTURES

At the north end of Wrightsville Beach, beyond the Shell Island Resort (www.shell island.com), lies an undisturbed stretch of sand and mud flat that plays an important part in the survival of several rare shore birds. The Mason Inlet Water Bird Management Area (910-686-7527; www.ncaudubon.org) provides summer nesting sites for black skimmers, various terns, and Wilson's plovers. Audubon North Carolina conducts free tours of the refuge, Friday mornings, April–September. Or you can visit on your own for expansive views of Mason's Inlet and Figure 8 Island.

If you like this . . . another must for birdwatchers is a trip to **Masonboro Island** (252-838-0890; *www.nccoastalreserve.net*), *just to the south of Wrightsville. Accessible only by boat, this bird sanctuary is home to nesting shore birds and sea turtles.*

Many sea turtles nest on Wrightsville, and a vigilant volunteer force works at giving the hatchlings their best chances for survival. Members of the Wrightsville Beach Sea Turtle Project (910-791-4541; www.turtles.wrightsville-beach.info) give Turtle Talks regularly at Wrightsville Beach Park, and also excavate nests after the hatchlings begin to emerge to free any young turtles stuck under sand. The public can attend these excavations and see the tiny turtles head for the sea.

If you like this . . . take an ecocruise. Wrightsville Cruises (910-509-9289; www.wrightsvillecruises.com) uses a classic tugboat for its relaxing trips on the ICW. ❦ Wrightsville Beach Scenic Tours (910-200-4002; www.capefearnaturalist .com) offers birding, shelling, and sunset tours, as well as a Pirate Cruise to Money Island.

One of the qualities that brings visitors back to Wrightsville year after year is its family-friendly beach policies. More than 40 beach accesses line the shore and life guards monitor the beach all summer. Unlike many beaches, you can ride bicycles on the sand. Surfing is permitted all along the oceanfront, except near the piers and jetty, and in front of the lifeguard stands, from Memorial Day to Labor Day.

Recognized as one of the top 10 surf towns in the United States by *Surfer* magazine, Wrightsville Beach nurtures an active surf culture, headed up by the Wrightsville Originals, an informal group of guys and gals who have been catching waves here since the '60s. Hang around the local surf shops and breaks for a while and you'll hear about their exploits, maybe meet them yourself.

Sweetwater Surf Shop (910-256-3821; www.sweetwatersurfshop.com), owned by the family of champion surfer Ben Bourgeois, occupies a prime downtown location at 10 N. Lumina. Red Dogs, the area's top surfer bar, is just across the street; Tower 7, with its famous fish tacos, is next door; and the surf is just a block away.

Quick tip: Joggers and walkers enjoy doing the **Nesbit Loop** (910-256-7925; www.townofwrightsville beach.com), a 2.5-mile route on sidewalks around the central island, following the causeway to N. Lumina to Salisbury back to the US 74/US 76 junction. There's free parking at the town hall on Bob Sawyer Drive.

Did you know? Wrightsville Kayak Company (910-599-0076; www.wrightsvillebeachkayak.com) will deliver a kayak or stand-up paddleboard (SUP) to your Wrightsville beach accommodations. **Wrightsville Beach Jet Ski Rentals** (910-279-3769; www .wrightsvillebeachjetskirentals.com) will do the same with motorized craft.

On Causeway Drive, the Surf City Surf Shop (910-256-2265; gosurfcity.com) is another long time outpost of surfing knowledge and a hotspot for the new sport of stand-up paddleboarding. Chris Curry, son of hall of famer Bill Curry, is a member of the store's SUP team and a top competitor at contests around the world.

Wrightsville has numerous surf schools and surf camps operating during the summer season. Wrightsville Beach Surf Camp (910-256-7873 or 1-866-844-7873; www.wbsurfcamp.com) is the original, offering summer camps and lessons for kids,

Wrightsville Beach is one of the top surfing towns in the United States.

teens, and families, plus women's yoga surf retreats, and weekend classes for adults during the shoulder seasons.

Wrightsville SUP (910-378-WAVE; www.wrightsvillesup.com) is up on the latest trends in stand-up paddleboarding, offering paddle-surfing lessons and excursions to area beaches, plus SUP fitness classes. Soul surfers will want to try SUP yoga, conducted out at sea on boards by instructors from the Wilmington Yoga Center (910-350-0234; www.wilmingtonyogacenter.com).

Did you know? Several world-class surfers developed their style on the Wrightsville Break, including East Coast Surfing Hall of Famers Bill Curry and Will Allison, as well as surfer mag cover boy Ben Bourgeois, currently one of the hottest dudes on the pro circuit. Bill Curry, known as Mr. Iron Man and a local tri-athlete, founded the Wrightsville Beach Longboard Association (www.wblasurf.org).

Quick tip: Check the publications of Slapdash Publishing (www.carolinabeach.net) for more on Wrightsville's surfing history.

Fast fact: Allison Surfboards, shaped by Hall of Famer Will Allison, are works of art decorated with Hawaiian fabrics and his signature seahorse logo. Locally they're sold at **Aussie Island** (910-256-5454; www.aussieisland.com) in Wilmington, and the **Surf House Shop and Café** 910-707-0422; www.surfhousenc.com), formerly The Cove Surf Shop, in Carolina Beach.

Quick tip: Before you fire up the woodie, check the **Wrightsville Beach Surf Report** at 910-256-435 or the live surf cam at **Crystal Pier** (www.surfchex.com). **Wrightsville Beach Live Surf** (www.wblivesurf.com) has cams at Mercer's Pier and C Street behind the Sweetwater Surf Shop.

Did you know? Wrightsville Beach is a hotspot for triathlon training thanks to the convenient combination of swimming, running, and biking opportunities. **Two Wheeler Dealer** (910-799-6444; bikesarefun.com), on Wrightsville Avenue in Wilmington, provides an information clearinghouse for the triathlete community, and the Blockade Runner Resort offers "Tri Paradise" specials. Several triathlons, biathlons, marathons, and paddle races are held locally every year.

MASONBORO ISLAND

A trip to Masonboro Island is a voyage back in time. This barrier island looks as much like all the islands along this coast once looked before the development of beach resorts and cottage communities changed their faces. Uninhabited except by birds, the 8.4-mile island consists of white sandy beaches on the oceanfront backed by deep saltwater marshes and tidal flats where herons and egrets wade about looking for dinner. Dolphins are frequently spotted in the offshore waters, and sea turtles come on shore to nest.

The island is protected as the Masonboro Island National Estuarine Research Reserve (252-838-0890; www.nccoastalreserve.net). Black skimmers, Wilson's plovers, and least terns, as well as loggerhead and green turtles, nest on the island, and the foredunes are covered with endangered sea amaranth.

Visiting Masonboro for a day of shelling and sunning, surfing, or fishing is a cherished Carolina tradition for folks who grew up in the region or visit every summer. Overnight primitive camping is permitted, as long as you respect the endangered species of animals and plants that live here. The reserve's website has camping guidelines. There are no restrooms or drinking water available, and you must pack out all trash.

Access to the island is by boat only. Local kayak companies lead group tours, or you can rent a watercraft and come on your own. A shuttle skiff (910-200-4002; www.capefearnaturalist.com) leaves from the Blockade Runner Resort during the summer season. Entropy Boat Rentals (910-675-1877; www.entropyboats.com) and Reliant Marine (910-256-0638; www.reliantmarine.com), located in marinas near the Wrightsville drawbridge, rent a variety of boats.

If you have your own craft, there are several launch sites and boat ramps convenient to Masonboro Island. Closest, and most laid-back, is Trails End Park (910-798-7620; www.nhcgov.com /Parks/), off the Masonboro Loop Road in Wilmington on the way to Carolina

Fast fact: Masonboro Island gets its name from a community of Masons who established the region's first Masonic lodge near Masonboro Inlet in 1735.

Beach. On Wrightsville Beach, a popular public boat ramp is located just north of the drawbridge.

Most boaters come ashore on the sound side of the island at the northern or southern ends, where trails lead over the dunes to the oceanfront.

While Masonboro is typically a quiet getaway, the island is also a traditional place for rowdy parties, especially on summer holiday weekends. Families should avoid visiting on Memorial Day, Fourth of July, and Labor Day.

PLEASURE ISLAND: CAROLINA BEACH, KURE BEACH & FORT FISHER

Pleasure Island, the modern name of the peninsula between the ocean and the mouth of the Cape Fear River, became an official island in 1931 with the completion of Snow's Cut, a canal about 1.75 miles long that forms part of the Atlantic Intracoastal Waterway (ICW). Carolina Beach Road/US 421 runs over the highrise Snow's Cut Bridge, becoming Lake Park Boulevard, then passes through the oceanfront communities of Carolina Beach and Kure Beach, down to the southern point of the island at Fort Fisher, a distance of just under 10 miles.

Much of the land around the point is administered by the state, including the Fort Fisher State Historic Site, Fort Fisher State Recreation Area, the North Carolina Aquarium, and Zeke's Island Coastal Reserve. From here a state-operated ferry makes the trip to Southport.

Pleasure Island was originally called Federal Point. To find out more about the history of the area, visit the Federal Point History Center (910-458-0502; www.federalpointhistory.org) located next to the Chamber's welcome center. The museum is free, but hours are limited.

> **Quick tip:** The **Pleasure Island Chamber of Commerce** (910-458-8434; www.pleasureislandnc.org) operates a welcome center on the south side of the Snow's Cut Bridge at 1121 N. Lake Park Boulevard.

Carolina Beach

A classic Southern beach town, Carolina Beach packs many attractions into a compact, easily walkable area. The boardwalk, with traditional attractions such as arcades, ice cream and souvenir shops, bingo parlors, bumper cars, even a puppet show, is just a short walk from the marina where fishing and sightseeing boats tie

Top 5 Don't Miss: Pleasure Island

- Explore the Carolina Beach Boardwalk and savor a Britt's doughnut.
- Enjoy the view from the Carolina Beach Pier House lounge.
- Walk or take a boat around Carolina Beach Lake.
- See what's biting on the Kure Beach Pier.
- Learn about blockade runners at Fort Fisher State Historic Site.

up. A few blocks the other way, Carolina Beach Lake Park provides a wonderful community gathering spot, with outdoor movies, concerts, and special events all summer.

Once known as a rowdy party spot for GIs and college kids, Carolina Beach has cleaned up its act, revitalizing its downtown and boardwalk to offer a more family-friendly experience, while at the same time preserving its nostalgic appeal. Still a place for all ages to have fun, this community offers the most concentrated traditional beach experience on the North Carolina coast.

The Carolina Beach Boardwalk lies along the oceanfront from Harper Avenue to Cape Fear Boulevard, ending at the beachfront ♿ ⧉ Courtyard by Marriott (910-458-2030; www.courtyardcarolinabeach.com). The blocks

Wide white-sand beaches are the norm along the Carolina coast.

between the ocean and Lake Park Drive/US 421 house numerous old-style beach attractions, including a summer amusement park (www.facebook.com/carolinabeachcarnival) with a merry-go-round, Ferris wheel, tilt-a-whirl, and many other classic rides and games. Weekly fireworks displays make the summer season along the boardwalk memorable for all.

Wandering through the maze of shops, restaurants, and bars reveals a number of hidden treasures. Carolina Beach Avenue continues as a pedestrian street where you'll find spots like the Fudgeboat (910-458-5823; www.fudgeboat.com), where an actual fishing boat serves as the counter, and the Island Ice Factory (910-707-0366; www.theislandicefactory.com), serving homemade gelato and Italian ice.

Keep an eye out for the Agape Inn Puppet Shows, sponsored by St. Paul's United Methodist Church (910-458-5310; www.stpaulscb.org).

Places geared to the adult crowd include Ⓨ Charlie's Boardwalk Subs (910-458-5502; www.charliesboardwalksubs.com), with a late-night menu and a hot wing challenge; and long-time bars, the Ⓨ Silver Dollar (910-458-0977), serving steamed seafood, sandwiches, and beer on the boardwalk since 1956, and Ⓨ Loretta's Surfside Bar and Lounge (910-458-8242), with walls covered in Carolina Beach memorabilia.

Fast fact: For more information on the transformation of the Carolina Beach Boardwalk and a full listing of the special events there, visit www.boardwalkmakeover.org.

Did you know? The town of Carolina Beach (www.carolinabeach.org) has bought many properties downtown, where it plans to build a North Carolina Aquarium Pier like the one in Nags Head as part of a park that would extend to the marina.

The boardwalk's most famous and beloved landmark is Britt's Donut Shop (www.facebook.com/BrittsDonut Shop). Established in 1939, this icon hasn't changed much since those days—it stills serves just one kind of doughnut, a glazed beauty that melts in the mouth, handmade on-site from the same secret recipe developed back before World War II. Fans insist this is the best doughnut in the country and warn that you can't eat just one. Britt's back door is on Canal Drive in case you want to make a direct approach by car.

During the off-season the Carolina Beach Boardwalk winds down. The rides are gone, and many of the attractions close for the winter, but the fun continues on a more laid-back level at several local hangouts. You'll find many of them clustered around the corner of Lake Park and Cape Fear Boulevards.

Shuckin' Shack Oyster Bar (910-458-7380; www.pleasureislandoysterbar .com), at 6 N. Lake Park Boulevard, carries on through the winter, serving steam pots and enormous platters of seafood. Combine yours with a serving of jumbo wings for a fast surf and turf. The bartenders will open your oysters for a small additional fee.

Next door the ☙ Ÿ Dive Food & Spirits (910-458-8282; www.thedivefoodand spirits.com), founded by a local scuba diver, serves famous crab balls, fish tacos, burgers, and seafood baskets, along with live music and plenty of local flavor.

If you like this . . . the Ÿ Fat Pelican (910-458-4016; www.thefatpelican .com), Carolina Beach's most notable dive, is just down the street at 8 S. Lake Park Boulevard, serving a huge selection of beers to take out or to enjoy on the funky backyard patio.

Carolina Beach Avenue runs along the oceanfront north from the boardwalk. At its end, the Carolina Beach Fishing Pier (910-458-5518) is a must-stop whether you fish or not. In addition to a tackle shop, the three-story pier house has a snack bar and grill, and, on the top floor, the Ÿ High Tide Lounge (910-458-0807), a local favorite with full ABC permit, frequent live music, and an outdoor deck with stupendous views of the pier and ocean. The pier is open 24 hours a day, April–November.

Just north of the pier lies another local favorite, 🐾 Freeman Park Recreation Area, where, for a fee, you can drive your four-wheel-drive vehicle onto the beach for a day of sunning, swimming, surf fishing, or crabbing among undeveloped dunes and marshland. Daily and weekend passes are available at the gate at the end of Canal Drive. Contact the town of Carolina Beach (910-458-4614; www.carolinabeach.org) for current fees and regulations.

Did you know? Carolina Beach Lake Park hosts a number of events during the year, including free outdoor movies in the summer, and the Light Up the Lake celebration, which features a walk-through display of Christmas lights, part of the annual **Island of Lights Festival** (910-458-5507; www.islandoflights.org). Other events during the holiday season include a Christmas parade, lighted flotilla, tour of homes, and the family-friendly New Year's Eve countdown to the dropping of a lighted beach ball at midnight.

Quick tip: Wheel Fun Rentals (910-458-4545; 107 Carolina Beach Avenue North) has a second location on the boardwalk where it rents surreys, bikes, surfboards, and other equipment to optimize your day at the beach.

In addition to these classic beach attractions, Carolina Beach has something most other shore communities lack: a freshwater lake in its midst. Just a few blocks south of the boardwalk, the 11-acre Carolina Beach Lake is in the midst of a park featuring a paved walking trail with four gazebos, plus restrooms, a playground, and a picnic area. Swimming is not permitted, but boating is. You can launch your own kayak or canoe or rent a pedal boat or kayak from Wheel Fun Rentals (910-617-9792; www.wheelfunrentals.com) on the north side of the lake.

Lifeguards patrol the many miles of Pleasure Island beaches.

Pick Your Spot

Best places to stay in and around Pleasure Island

Although many visitors come to Carolina Beach for the day, Pleasure Island has many different kinds of accommodations, including a number of low-rise family-owned motels along the oceanfront, available at reasonable rates. Only a few high-rise hotels and condominium projects have reached this coast.

The websites of the Cape Fear Convention and Visitors Bureau (www.capefearcoast.com), the Pleasure Island Chamber of Commerce (www.pleasureislandnc.org), and Carolina Beach Getaway (www.carolinabeachgetaway.com) have many suggestions for lodgings and special packages, as well as attractions, dining, and activities for every taste.

The ♂ ⚅ ♈ Golden Sands Motel (910-458-8334; www.goldensandscarolinabeach.com), at 1211 S. Lake Park Boulevard, occupying an uncrowded stretch of beach, makes a good choice for families, with inside and outside pools, rooms

Piers are where the action is along the North Carolina coast

Quick tip: Even if you aren't staying at the Golden Sands, drop by the Ocean Grill's downstairs bar for a trendy cocktail and the O.G.'s creative appetizers. Or head out onto the remnants of Center Pier, destroyed in 1994 by Hurricane Fran, for a drink at the tiki bar. Open seasonally, this colorful spot serves up a limited menu plus frequent live music.

with microwaves and refrigerators, and the Ocean Grill (910-458-2000; www.oceangrilltiki.com), an on-site restaurant owned and operated by Chef David Sinclair.

Another favorite for families and people traveling with their pets is the ♂ 🐾 ♿ ⑂ (⑈) Drifters Reef Motel (910-458-5414; www.driftersreefmotel carolinabeach.com), just north of the Boardwalk at 701 N. Lake Park Boulevard. The Slickers Raceway next door is a natural for kid's parties, and the Lazy Pirate Sports Bar & Grille, with daily specials, live music, and a big outdoor deck, keeps the grown-ups happy.

For a more romantic time, check into the ♂ (⑈) Beacon House Inn Bed & Breakfast (910-458-6244; www.beaconhouseinnb-b.com), located in an old beach house facing the ocean, with front and back verandas and individually decorated rooms for two. Traveling with children under 12 or with your pets? Ask about the Beacon's nearby family- and pet-friendly beach cottages.

Many families and snowbirds stay at area campgrounds. 🐾 (⑈) Winners RV Park (910-458-1098; www.winners rvpark.com) is close to the boardwalk action. 🐾 Carolina Beach Family Campground (910-392-3322; www.carolinabeachfamilycampground.com) is closest to downtown Wilmington and is open all year. The campground at the 🐾 ♿ Carolina Beach State Park (910-458-8206; www.ncparks.gov) has no hookups but does have a dump station where you can empty your tanks.

Local Flavors

Taste of the town—local cafés, restaurants, bars, bistros, etc.

Carolina Beach offers a wide selection of restaurants and bars, with many different cuisines represented. Within a few blocks you'll find Thai, Mediterranean, Mexican, Irish, and Caribbean restaurants, as well as the more familiar seafood, steak, and breakfast joints.

The hottest dining spot in Carolina Beach is also a surf shop. The ⑂ ⊖ Surf House Cafe & Shop (910-707-0422; www.surfhousenc.com), at 604 N. Lake Park Boulevard, appeals to all ages with cool surfer attire and paddleboard demos, surf films, green policies, and fresh, creative cuisine with a laidback California surfer shack vibe.

Breakfast sandwiches, salads, seviche, and tacos feature organic local produce and hormone-free meats, with many vegetarian options. If the weather is on the chilly side, stop by for one of the gourmet hot chocolate drinks offered at the bar.

If you like this . . . the (ᵞ) *Treehouse Bistro (910-458-6033; www .treehousebistronc.com), also known as The Grind coffeehouse, located near the Lake Park, makes a pleasant stop for coffee and e-mail in the mornings. Later on the menu shifts to tapas and flatbreads created by owner and chef Shawn Underwood with wines available by the bottle or glass.*

For dining with a water view, Harbor Masters (910-458-2800; www .harbormastersrestaurant.com) enjoys a great location at 315 Canal Drive overlooking the marina, with seating on the floating dock. The restaurant serves a wide range of food for breakfast, lunch, and dinner, including sushi, steaks, and a popular shrimp boil, or you can bring in the fish you catch and the chefs will prepare it for you.

For a home-cooked meal at reasonable prices, visit the ✂ Gulf Stream Restaurant (910-458-8774; www.gulf streamrestaurantnc.com), across from the city marina on Myrtle Avenue. This local favorite, run for many years by a Greek family, serves breakfast, plate lunches, and seafood platters in a diner setting.

Snow's Cut Café (910-707-0550; www.snowscutcafe.com), across from the Chamber's welcome center, serves breakfast all day at prices that are easy on the wallet, plus plate lunches with lots of veggie options, until 2 PM.

Another local favorite, the ✂ (ᵞ) Deck House (910-458-1026; 205 Charlotte Avenue), is hard to miss—it occupies a former church with a bright red lobster painted on the roof. Noted for its fresh local seafood and hand-cut steaks, the Deck House is best known for its popular nightly specials, includ-

In Search of Chowder

Carolina Beach hosts an annual chowder cook-off at the Lake Park every April. If you don't happen to be in town that weekend and it's chowder weather, plan your own competition to find your favorite. Along the way, you'll visit the top seafood restaurants and nightspots in the region. (We suggest spreading this quest out over several nights and ordering your bowl at the bar, where you can quiz the locals for more suggestions.) First stop: ✂ **Michael's Seafood Restaurant** (910-458-7761; www.michaelscfood.com), one of the region's most renowned seafood spots, to sample Chef Michael McGowan's award-winning Capt. M's Chowder, winner for two consecutive years at the Great Chowder Cook-Off in Newport, Rhode Island. Next, head to ✂ **Havanna's Seafood** (910-458-2822; www.havanas restaurant.com) for a cup of the chowder that won the 2011 Pleasure Island Chowder Cook-Off. Other contenders: the **Tangerine Caribbean Bar and Grill** (910-707-0202; www.tangerinegrille.com); **Olde Salty's** (910-458-8090) on the boardwalk; the **Seaside Grill** (910-458-2030) in the Courtyard Marriott; two-time winner **Lazy Pirate** (910-458-5414) in the Drifters Reef Motel; **Jack Mackerel's** (910-458-7668) in Kure Beach; and **Fish Bites** (910-791-1117; www.fishbites seafood.com) in Monkey Junction. And don't forget to try the excellent grouper chowder at the **Deck House** (910-458-1026).

ing live Maine lobsters on Thursdays.

For a real taste of the beach, pick
up a plate of whitefish fillets, coleslaw,
potato salad, and hush puppies, washed
down with sweet or "Yankee" tea, at
the fish fry held the first Friday of
every month at American Legion Post
129 (910-458-4253) situated at the
dead-end of Bridge Barrier Road on
Snow's Cut. Legion members make
their own breading and sauces, and
their wives cook up delicious desserts.
On the Wilmington side of Snow's Cut,
American Legion Post 10 (910-799-
3806) at 702 Pine Grove Drive holds
its monthly fish fry on the same day.
If breakfast rocks your world, stop by
the pancake breakfast at the Katie B.
Hines Senior Center (910-458-6609;
308 Cape Fear Boulevard), held on the
first Saturday morning of every month.
Kids under nine eat free.

Some Carolina Beach spots are
best known to locals as places to party,
with live music, sports-friendly bars,
karaoke, and/or dancing. The Y Sea
Witch Cafe & Tiki Bar (910-707-0533;
www.seawitchcafeandtikibar.com), next
to the SeaWitch Motel on Carolina
Beach Avenue, is one of these, with a
friendly bar and live music on the outdoor patio.

Shaggers and those curious about
the rhythm and blues sounds called
beach music should stop by ♂
Shanty's II Beach and Blues Club
(910-233-3266; www.shantys2.com),
where a big wooden dance floor and
top beach DJs keep the shuffle moving.
Lessons are offered several nights a
week, and there's no cover on those
nights if you'd like to come by and
watch. Shanty's is in the center of Carolina Beach at 103 N. Lake Park
Boulevard.

If shagging on the sand fills your
winter dreams, plan your trip to coincide with the annual Carolina Beach
Music Festival (910-458-8434; www
.pleasureislandnc.org), held the first
Saturday in June.

Long-time residents claim Carolina Beach gave birth to the shag after
a local guy named Chicken Hicks visited the town of Seabreeze, an African
American beach community just up the
coast, and brought back some R & B
records to jazz up the jukebox at the
Tijuana Inn, a boardwalk dance hall of
the day.

Extend Your Stay

The Carolina Beach Boat Basin
reaches deep into the center of town,
bringing water activities front and center. If you're arriving by boat, the Public Day Docks on Carl Winner Drive
offer three hours of free docking for transients. Harbor Masters Restaurant also
offers free docking for guests.

The ⚓ ♂ Winner Party Boat Fleet (910-458-3474; www.winnerboats.com)

sets sail from the Municipal Docks on a variety of fishing trips priced per person, including an all-day trip out to the Gulf Stream aboard a high-speed catamaran. Other boats in their fleet offer moonlight and sunset cruises, dinner and dance cruises, and sightseeing up and down the Cape Fear coast.

The Winner family, once one of the major landowners in Carolina Beach, lent its name to many streets and businesses. Pioneers of Gulf Steam fishing as early as the 1880s, this family of sea captains operates the town's largest fleet of pleasure craft and party fishing boats.

Many charter fishing captains work out of the Carolina Beach Boat Basin. Visit the website of Carolina Beach Getaway (www.carolinabeachgetaway.com) for a full listing.

If you'd like to explore the world of surf fishing, Capt. Walter White and his guides at Whitewater Surf Fishing Charters (910-616-4609; www.whitewatersurf fishingcharters.com) will give you an expert introduction to the sport.

The waters off the Carolina coast are also popular for SCUBA diving, with many wrecks and a fossil ledge where huge teeth from megalodon sharks are found. The Cape Fear Dive Center (910-458-7390; www.capefeardivecenter.com) offers scheduled dive trips, classes, gear rentals, and more from the Municipal Docks.

The 🐾 🐶 ♿ Carolina Beach State Park (910-458-8206; www.ncparks.gov), set at the junction of Snow's Cut and the Cape Fear River, is a natural treasure with numerous opportunities to learn more about the local environment. Six miles of trails cross several different habitats, from longleaf pine forest to riverside marshes. A site on the North Carolina Birding Trail (www.ncbirdingtrail.org), the park hosts nesting songbirds in summer; brown pelicans, shorebirds, and woodpeckers year-round; and warblers, orioles, and raptors during migrations. The park's marina, with two boat ramps and transient slips, is a popular stop on the ICW. You can fish from the riverbank or a wheelchair-accessible fishing deck and park your RV in the campground, although there are no hookups available. The park is open all year and admission is free.

Quick tip: Hike the half-mile Flytrap Trail at Carolina Beach State Park to see Venus fly-traps and native orchids in their natural setting.

Carolina Beach has some excellent shopping opportunities. Visit the Artful Living Group (910-458-7822; www.artfullivinggroup.com) at 112 Cape Fear Boulevard near the boardwalk to see the works of local artists or to take a class.

Another good shopping stop in downtown will please the whole family. 🍦 Squigley's Ice Cream Parlor (910-458-8779; www.squigleysicecream.com), in a historic beach house on S. Lake Park Boulevard, serves thousands of different flavors of homemade ice cream. The kids can relax with a cone on the front porch while Mom explores the unique gift gallery upstairs, featuring handmade arts and crafts.

If you like this . . . stop by the Checkered Church Gift Shop (910-458-0211; www.checkeredchurch.com) at 800 St. Joseph Street to browse a wide selection of local art, collectibles, and gifts.

Another must-stop is the Island Book Shop (910-707-0504; www.snowscut .com/bookstore.html) at 100 N. Lake Park Boulevard, where you'll find every local

Family Fun on Pleasure Island

Lifeguards patrol Carolina Beach, Kure Beach, and the Fort Fisher State Recreation Area from Memorial Day to Labor Day, making Pleasure Island a safe place for families to play in the water.

Loggerhead sea turtles nest all along the Pleasure Island beaches. Contact the **Pleasure Island Sea Turtle Project** (1-888-290-1065; www.seaturtleproject.org) to find out about their educational (and free) Turtle Talks.

Biking is a favorite family activity, and the town of Carolina Beach is upgrading many of its streets to increase bike safety. The roads within Carolina Beach State Park are popular for biking, as is a bike path along Snow's Cut. Plans are in the works for an **Island Greenway** (www.islandgreenway.org), providing an off-road multiuse path all the way from the Snow's Cut Bridge to the tip of the peninsula beyond Fort Fisher. Additional bike paths are found around the fort and the aquarium.

The **Carolina Beach Skate Park** (910-458-2977; www.carolinabeach.org) in Mike Chappell Park, off Dow Road running down the west side of the island, is free to use and stays open until about 9 PM.

Pleasure Island has a free disc golf course as well, 18 holes shaded by old oaks at **Joe Eakes Park** (910-458-8216; www.townofkurebeach.org), on K Avenue in Kure Beach.

Kayak Carolina (910-458-9171; www.kayakcarolina.com) offers tours for all ages exploring uninhabited islands, searching for shark teeth and shells, and observing birds and sealife. The company also delivers rental kayaks for free to locations on Pleasure Island.

history book in print, plus new and used books for all ages. It's the only bookstore on Pleasure Island.

Pleasure Island hosts farmer's markets on Saturday mornings almost all year. During the summer months (May–September), the Carolina Beach Farmer's Market (910-431-8122; www.facebook.com/CarolinaBeachFarmersMarket) takes place on the shores of Carolina Beach Lake. In spring (March–May) and fall (September–December), the Pleasure Island Fresh Market (910-960-7436; www .pleasureislandfreshmarket.com) is held at the Carolina Beach Municipal Marina (300 Canal Drive) next to the boat basin.

Kure Beach

The action in Kure Beach, known as the beach town with "one pier, one stop light, no worries," centers on the Kure Beach Fishing Pier (910-458-5524; www.kurebeachfishingpier.com), the oldest surviving pier on the East Coast. It opened in 1923 for the first time and, though swept away by storms several times since, has always been

Fast fact: Kure (pronounced CURE-ee) Beach is named for Hans Kure, a Danish sea captain, who bought most of the property within the current town boundaries in 1900 and began to develop it as a beach resort. In 1923 his son built the Kure Beach Pier, one of the first in the state. Members of the family still operate the pier today.

rebuilt to serve as the heart of this community. The pier enjoys an international reputation among fishermen as one of the best places to pier fish for king mackerel, Spanish mackerel, sheepshead, flounder, and blues.

The Kure Beach Fishing Pier has one of the lowest per pole rates on the coast. You can fish 24 hours a day here from April 1 to November 30. King fishing and shark fishing are available for additional fees. No alcohol is allowed on the pier, but it costs nothing to walk on if you aren't planning to fish.

Despite rising property values and the devastation of several powerful hurricanes, Kure Beach remains today much as it was in the past—a residential resort with cottages, motels, and a few restaurants clustered around K Avenue, the street that leads down to the pier (and the location of that one stoplight).

Most piers, including the famous Kure Pier, stay open all night during fishing season.

The town of Kure Beach (910-458-8216; www.townofkurebeach.org) is committed both to preserving this small-town atmosphere and improving the quality of life for both residents and visitors. A new oceanfront park just north of the pier, now under way, will provide a pavilion for summer concerts, plus restrooms, a playground, and a boardwalk, with walk-overs to the beach.

For more suggestions on things to see and do in Kure Beach, check out its official tourism website: www.visitkure.com.

There are no big high-rise hotels or condominiums in Kure Beach and never will be, thanks to a town ordinance that limits the height of new buildings. A cottage or motel close to the pier is the most convenient, letting you walk to K Avenue without worrying about parking.

The ♂ & (ᵞᵖ) Seven Seas Inn (910-458-8122 or 1-866-773-2746; www.seven seasinn.com), just steps from both ocean and pier, offers a range of accommodations, from hotel rooms to two-room efficiency suites, all with refrigerators, coffeemakers, and HD plasma TVs. Balconies and gazebos offer views of the ocean and the nicely landscaped grounds where adult and children's pools are set amid palms and mature agave plants.

Kure Beach's bed & breakfast inn, (ᵞᵖ) Darlings By the Sea (910-458-1429 or 1-800-383-8111; www.darlingsbythesea.com), is perfect for a romantic getaway. Five suites equipped with whirlpools for two and luxurious bedding occupy an oceanfront building with a lighthouse motif and private porches open to the sea breeze.

Perhaps nothing demonstrates the small-town atmosphere of Kure better than the fact that the town has just a half-dozen restaurants—and they're all located within a block of each other around the junction of K Avenue and US 421, here called Ft. Fisher Boulevard.

The 🏊 🐾 Old Pier House Restaurant (910-458-8616; www.old pierhouserestaurant.com), open seven days a week, all year, sits just across from the pier at the foot of K Avenue and is much beloved by locals for its homestyle breakfasts, daily specials, fresh fried or broiled flounder, and fabulous key lime pie in a chocolaty nut crust. The walls are decorated with pictures of damage from hurricanes past, a real tribute to the town's resilience.

🏊 🍸 Jack Mackerel's Island Grill (910-458-7668), at the corner of K and US 421, goes for a Bahamas vibe with bright colors and a menu spiced with tropical flavors. The cozy bar is a refuge during stormy weather, and the upstairs deck is fun when the moon is out.

Located between Jack Mackerel's and the Old Pier House, 🏊 Freddie's Restaurante (910-458-5979; www.freddieskurebeach.com) serves homemade Italian fare in huge portions, plus steaks, veal, and a long list of pork chops with fruit toppings. Dinner only, all year.

Occupying another corner at K and US 421 since 1970, 🏊 ♿ 🍸 Big Daddy's Restaurant (910-458-8622; www.bigdaddysofkurebeach.com) recently spruced up its act with an outdoor patio and tiki bar, where you can enjoy lunch specials or cocktails. Seafood dominates the menu, along with steaks and an all-you-can-eat salad bar.

During the summer, visitors line up at the colorful little shack called Beach House Burgers (910-458-8586) for breakfast, burgers, hot dogs, and fried bologna sandwiches to go.

> **Quick tip:** Follow K Avenue west to Dow Road, the local's favorite "back road," for a quick alternative to US 421. Dow rejoins US 421 near the Snow's Cut Bridge in Carolina Beach.

> **Fast fact:** Dow Road is named for the Ethyl-Dow Chemical Company plant that produced bromine from seawater here for use in aviation fuel during World War II. On the night of July 24, 1943, a German U-boat shelled the plant, but missed. Remnants of the plant can still be seen.

Burger shacks are popular dining choices at many beaches.

🏊 Joe Eakes Park (910-458-8216; www.townofkurebeach.org), a town park a few blocks down K Avenue, has tennis courts, a bike trail, playground, picnic area with grills, a dog park where your dog can run free, and Pleasure Island's only disc golf course.

Fort Fisher
The end of Pleasure Island, also known as Federal Point, packs lots of attractions into a compact area. History buffs, surf fishers, beach lovers, kayakers, and the curious of all ages find something here for them.

Just outside of Kure Beach, the Fort Fisher Air Force Recreation Area

(910-458-6549; www.ftfishermilrec.com) provides accommodations and a campground for authorized Department of Defense personnel. Also located here, the North Carolina Military History Museum (910-251-7325; www.ncmhs.net) has indoor and outdoor exhibits of military vehicles and artifacts from past wars. The museum is free, and open limited weekend hours all year.

The annual Seafood, Blues & Jazz Festival is held on the grounds of the Fort Fisher Air Force Recreation Area every October.

Artifacts recovered from a sunken blockade runner at the Underwater Archaeology Center

Proceeding south on US 421, you come to the Fort Fisher State Historic Site (910-458-5538; www.nchistoricsites.org), where exhibits provide a fascinating glimpse into a vital battle that sealed the fate of the Confederacy at the end of the Civil War, as well as the blockade runners who kept the South alive for so long. An interpretive trail circles the remains of the fort, passing a rebuilt battery and gun emplacement on a tall dune. Guided tours are available, and admission is free.

If you like this . . . *cross to Southport on the state ferry for a visit to the* ***North Carolina Maritime Museum at Southport*** *(910-457-0003; www.ncmaritimemuseum.org) with special exhibits on blockade runners; and the* ***Brunswick Town/Fort Anderson Historic Site*** *(910-371-6613; www.nchistoricsites.org), another Confederate fort that defended Wilmington during the war.*

At the other end of the Fort Fisher parking lot, the North Carolina Underwater Archaeology Center (910-458-9042; www.archaeology.ncdcr.gov) contains many sunken treasures retrieved from colonial schooners, Civil War ironclads, and steamships that once traveled the Cape Fear River. Free.

The rebuilt Civil War fortifications at Fort Fisher

Just past Battle Acre, Loggerhead Road turns off to the east, leading to two more Federal Point attractions. The first parking lot on the left belongs to the Fort Fisher State Recreation Area, (910-458-5798; www.ncparks.gov) providing year-round access to miles of undeveloped shoreline. From Memorial Day to Labor Day, lifeguards are on duty at the designated swimming area, and rangers offer free nature programs through the fall. The

Quick tip: Across the street from the Fort Fisher Visitor Center, a paved path runs along the ocean through twisted live oaks to the monument at Battle Acre. Beach accesses are located at either end. Swimming is not allowed in this area due to strong rip currents, but the tide pools provide excellent shelling.

visitor center has restrooms, outdoor showers, picnic areas, and seasonal concessions, plus natural history displays of seashells and mounted birds. Purchase a beach access pass here for your registered four-wheel-drive vehicle (no ATVs), allowing you to drive down the beach on marked routes. The mile-long Basin Trail leads through the marsh to an overlook with good birding. Along the way, the trail passes the World War II bunker where the Fort Fisher Hermit spent his final years.

The Hermit of Fort Fisher, Robert E. Harrill, lived for 17 years in an abandoned World War II bunker near the tip of Federal Point, surviving on sassafras tea, oysters, and fish he gathered from the marsh and surrounding waters. Thousands of visitors came each year to meet him and hear his mantra of common sense: "Simplify. Simplify. Simplify." The Hermit died under mysterious circumstances in 1972, but his life continues to fascinate. A film, *The Fort Fisher Hermit* (www.thefortfisherhermit.com), documents his life, and is frequently screened at the Fort Fisher Historic Site. The North Carolina Aquarium at Fort Fisher conducts an environmental education program called "The Fort Fisher Hermit's School of Common Sense." Several books have been written as well, including *The Life and Times of the Fort Fisher Hermit* (www.thehermitbook.com), with text and photos by Fred Pickler, who counts himself among Harrill's closest friends.

Continue down Loggerhead Road to the 🐾 ♿ 🚻 North Carolina Aquarium at Fort Fisher (910-458-8257; www.ncaquariums.com), which follows the course of the Cape Fear River, beginning with freshwater fishes, snakes, turtles, and alligators, then moving downstream into the ocean with exhibits on humpback whales, sea turtles, and hurricanes, plus tanks filled with moray eels, jellyfishes, seahorses,

Unspoiled beaches, once the home of the Hermit, stretch many miles at the Fort Fisher State Recreation Area.

and many local fishes. A touch tank and new interactive megalodon giant shark exhibit are kid favorites. The paved Aquarium Trail visits a pond that attracts wintering waterfowl.

Follow US 421 past the ferry terminal, all the way to the southern tip of Federal Point, where you'll find a boat ramp that's a popular launch spot for kayakers heading out to explore the Zeke's Island Estuarine Reserve (910-962-2998; www.nccoastalreserve.net). The lagoon here was created by a man-made breakwater, called The Rocks, a good spot for fishing and crabbing in calm weather. Close by, a trail leads to the top of what remains of Battery Buchanan, one of Fort Fisher's largest fortifications.

A breakwater, known locally as the Rocks, stretches far out into the Zeke's Island Reserve.

The 🐾 ♿ Fort Fisher–Southport Ferry (910-457-6942; www.ncferry.org) operates seasonally. Fares are $5 for automobiles; $1 for pedestrians; $2 for bikes. The trip takes about 35 minutes each way.

SOUTHPORT & NORTH CAROLINA'S BRUNSWICK ISLES

The southernmost county on the North Carolina coast hosts a string of islands caught between sea and marsh. Dubbed the Brunswick Isles, they're a favorite for family getaways, and an increasingly popular destination for golfers, ecotourists, and history buffs.

For information on touring Brunswick and its islands, contact the Brunswick County Tourism Development Authority (910-755-5517; www.ncbrunswick.com). Other sources of information include the Brunswick County Chamber of Commerce (910-754-6644; www.brunswick countychamber.org) and the North Brunswick Chamber of Commerce (910-383-0553; www.nbchamberof commerce.com).

Quick tip: Much of Federal Point is included in the **North Carolina Birding Trail** (www.ncbirdingtrail .org) thanks to its strategic position along the migration routes for many species.

Southport

At the mouth of the Cape Fear River, the tiny village of Southport reminds many visitors of Beaufort, South Carolina, a couple of decades ago, before Oprah rented a house on the waterfront and development got out of hand. Here old live oaks still shade streets lined with antique stores, curio shops, art galleries, and inns housed in fanciful Victorian mansions. A branch of the North Carolina Maritime Museum tells the town's history, while harborside restaurants serve fish just snatched from the sea.

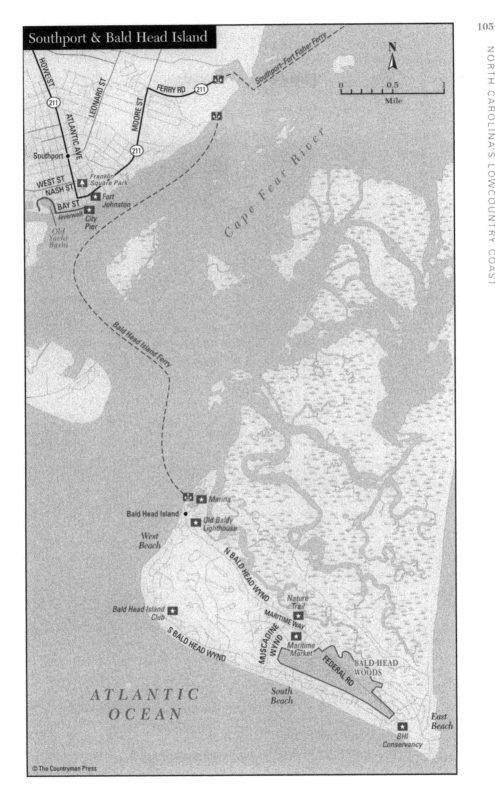

Southport & Bald Head Island

HOWE ST

LEONARD ST

MOORE ST

FERRY RD

211

211

ATLANTIC AVE

Southport

211

Southport–Fort Fisher Ferry

N

0   0.5   1
Mile

Cape Fear River

WEST ST

NASH ST

Franklin Square Park

BAY ST

Fort Johnston

Riverwalk

City Pier

Old Yacht Basin

Bald Head Island Ferry

Marina

Bald Head Island

Old Baldy Lighthouse

West Beach

N BALD HEAD WYND

Nature Trail

MARITIME WAY

Bald Head Island Club

MUSCADINE WYND

Maritime Market

S BALD HEAD WYND

FEDERAL RD

BALD HEAD WOODS

ATLANTIC OCEAN

South Beach

East Beach

BHI Conservancy

© The Countryman Press

From the boardwalk along the river, you can see two lighthouses: the Oak Island Light, newest in the state, and "Old Baldie," the state's oldest, on Bald Head Island. A constant parade of boats, large and small, make their way through the mouth of the Cape Fear River, providing lazy entertainment for visitors relaxing on balconies and waterfront patios.

Pelicans share the waterfront with visitors at Southport's harbor.

One of North Carolina's oldest towns, Southport is a charming, quiet village, still retaining some of the old sand streets that were once common along this coast. The compact historic district provides a wonderful place for a leisurely stroll. Southport's Waterfront Park has a public pier famous as a hotspot for flounder fishing.

Make your first stop the Southport Visitor Center (910-457-7927; www.south porthistoricalsociety.org) on W. Moore Street, next to the famous 400–800-year-old Indian Trail Tree, to pick up a map of the Historic Southport Trail, a self-guided walking tour put together by the Southport Historical Society. Along the way you'll pass the Old Smithville Burying Ground, the site where pirate Stede Bonnet was captured, and the Oak Grove of 200-year-old trees, while learning the history of this riverfront town.

If you like this . . . follow the 0.7-mile historic river walk from Waterfront Park to a scenic gazebo for views of the marsh, ships and boats making their way from river to ocean, and the distant spires of Old Baldy and the Oak Island Light. This is a stop on the North Carolina Birding Trail (www.nc birdingtrail.org); expect to see numerous wading birds and waterfowl, perhaps even the rare white pelican.

Fast fact: Southport, originally called Smithville after a Revolutionary War general, was established around Fort Johnston, built by the British in 1748, and decommissioned in 2006 as the oldest active-duty fort in the United States. Now owned by the city of Southport, the Garrison Building on Bay Street is slated to house a new Southport Visitor Center.

Did you know? Filmmakers are as charmed by Southport as ordinary visitors. Scenes from several movies, including *Nights in Rodanthe*, *A Walk to Remember*, *The Secret Life of Bees*, and *Crimes of the Heart*, were shot here.

You can approach Southport from either land or sea. From Fort Fisher and Kure Beach, take the Fort Fisher–Southport Ferry (910-457-6942; www.ncferry.org) across the Cape Fear River. Follow NC 211 to Howe Street and the downtown waterfront.

As you arrive in Southport via ferry, go to the top deck and look to the north as you enter the harbor to see the area's third historic lighthouse, the Price Creek Light (www.carolina lights.com), last survivor of eight harbor beacons built before the Civil War along the Cape Fear. Located on private property, the lighthouse is closed to the public.

Alternatively, follow the scenic River Road, NC 133, along the west bank of the Cape Fear River from Wilmington. Along the way you'll pass the & Brunswick Town/Fort Anderson Historic Site (910-371-6613; www.nchistoricsites.org), encompassing the ruins of the original 1725 settlement in the area and a Civil War fort; and Orton Plantation and Gardens (www.ortonplantation.com), famous as the location of the movie *Firestarter*. Orton was sold recently and is currently closed for renovations and restoration. Check its website for upcoming opportunities to visit.

Pick Your Spot

Best places to stay in and around Southport

Southport is a favorite day-trip destination for people staying on the Brunswick Islands and in the golf plantations scattered discreetly across Brunswick County, however the town does have several bed & breakfast inns if you chose to stay in the historic district.

🖉 ♂ Lois Jane's Riverview Inn (910-457-6701; www.loisjanes.com), occupying a Victorian cottage still operated by the same family that built it back in the 1890s, sits on the waterfront in the heart of Southport, along with the associated Riverside Motel across the street. Both are smoke-free.

Other B&Bs in the historic district include the waterfront Brunswick Inn Bed & Breakfast (910-457-5278; www .brunswickinn.com), reputedly haunted by Tony the Ghost, an Italian harpist who drowned while out sailing; and the Robert Ruark Inn Bed & Breakfast (910-363-4169; www.robertruarkinn .com), named for Southport's most famous native son, a best-selling journalist and novelist.

If you have a pet with you, make reservations at the 🐾 📶 Inn at River Oaks (910-457-1100; www.theinnat

riveroaks.com), a family-owned spot that played a cameo in the John Travolta film *Domestic Disturbance*.

For the ultimate getaway, book a stay at the Frying Pan Shoals Light Station (704-237-0399; www.fptower .com), located just offshore in one of the region's most treacherous stretches of ocean. It's being restored as a bed & breakfast inn with seven rooms, each offering magnificent water views.

Southport is home to a year-round schedule of family-friendly festivals. Christmas by the Sea (www.christmas bysea.com), held every December, is one of the state's best, with parades, a lighted boat flotilla, a tree lighting on Oak Island, special activities for children, and numerous open houses at area stores. The Southport Wooden Boat Show (www.southportwooden boatshow.com), held the final Saturday in September, brings a wide variety of wooden vessels to the Yacht Basin. Other popular events are the Southport Pirate Fest, in October, and four days of festivities around the North Carolina Fourth of July Festival (www.nc4thofjuly.com) every year.

Fast fact: Robert Ruark's most popular book, *The Old Man and the Boy*, is based on his childhood memories of growing up in Southport.

Local Flavors

Taste of the town—local cafés, restaurants, bars, bistros, etc.

A meal on the waterfront is a South-port dining experience not to be missed. Make your way to the western end of downtown, where you'll find several restaurants lining the wharves of the Yacht Basin.

The most iconic eatery in town, and the most evocative of the region's past, is the Yacht Basin Provision Company (910-457-0654; www .provisioncompany.com). This ram-shackle little spot on the docks, with seating mostly on screened porches and decks overlooking the boat basin, serves seafood pure and simple (and inexpensive). Make your choice from the chalkboard outside, place your order at the counter, help yourself to beverages, and take a seat with a view. Regulars (and there are plenty) swear by the conch fritters, grouper salad, juicy hamburgers, and grilled yellowfin tuna, but follow the crowd and order Thee Special, a half pound of steamed

Restaurants along Southport's harbor may look ramshackle but serve great seafood.

shrimp, a crabcake, and a side of cucumber salad. Provisions is open for lunch and dinner all year; hours are shorter in the off-season, but so are the lines. Drop by to warm up with a bowl of seafood chowder.

If you like this . . . the ☙ ☙ Fishy Fishy Café (910-457-1881; www.fishyfishycafe.com) shares the same great view over the Yacht Basin but offers a more upscale menu and sit-down service. The menu features local seafood, produce, and microbrews.

Most of Southport's restaurants and shops can be found along N. Howe Street, also NC 211, and the town's "main drag."

For the best fine-dining experi-ence in the historic district, seek out the award-winning Live Oak Café (910-454-4360; www.liveoakcafenc .com), occupying a historic house tucked under a huge, old tree at 614 N. Howe. With just a dozen tables, dining here is intimate, with each dish crafted from fresh ingredients by owner and chef Sean Mundy. There's a wine garden out back that makes a pleasant place to wait for your table or just to relax with a glass of vino and the much-praised crab dip.

If you like this . . . Mr. P's Bistro (910-457-0801; www.mrpsbistro.com), at 309 N. Howe, is another chef-run enterprise, with a menu featuring Low-country classics, plus prime rib and steamed oysters. Reservations are highly recommended.

For breakfast or a casual lunch, stop by ☙ Taylor Cuisine Cafe & Catering (910-454-0088; www.taylor cuisinecatering.com) at 731 N. Howe. Owner and chef Karen Taylor is noted for her creative take on Southern stan-dards, and fans rave about her fried chicken, country-fried steak, "Taylor

Made" fried green beans and crab cakes, sweet potato pancakes, and sausage gravy biscuits. Dinner is served some nights, with brunch on Sundays.

If you like this . . . ✿ Local's Family Diner (910-457-0444; www .localsfamilydiner.com), at 832 N. Howe, popular for its daily specials, low prices, friendly staff, and senior meals, serves breakfast, lunch, and dinner seven days a week.

If you're of the locavore persuasion, or just like to support local busi-

nesses, two programs can help you choose your restaurant. Feast Down East (www.feastdowneast.org) brings local farmers and restaurants together. Brunswick Catch (www.brunswick catch.com) sustains and promotes the Brunswick County seafood industry. The Southport Waterfront Market (910-279-4616), with local produce, baked goods, handcrafted items, and entertainment, takes place on the Fort Johnston Garrison Lawn on Bay Street every Wednesday morning, May–October.

Extend Your Stay

HISTORY & CULTURE

Before there was a town of Smithville, later renamed Southport, a great grove of live oaks lined the shore near the mouth of the Cape Fear River, providing shade and shelter for the Native American tribes who came here to fish. Today the oaks, estimated to be between 400 and 800 years old, lend a Lowcountry ambiance to the town. Draped in Spanish moss, with roots digging deep into the sandy soil, they're a natural treasure evoking a different, slower-paced world.

The old oaks line the streets of the historic district, but they cluster most thickly in The Grove, a space set aside for public use in the first town plan. Franklin Square Park occupies the heart of the Grove at the corner of N. Howe and E. West Streets. Stop by to relax and have a sip of water from the old well.

Set amid the live oaks, Franklin Square Gallery (910-457-5450; www .franklinsquaregallery.com), formerly an imposing city hall, features exhibits of local art by members of the Associated Artists of Southport, including juried competitions, photography, and an annual quilt show.

If you like this . . . several galleries line the main drag , including the Ricky Evans Gallery (910-457-1129; www.rickyevansgallery.com), at 211 N. Howe, specializing in images of lighthouses; and the ArtShak Gallery and Sculpture Garden (910-457-1757), at 822 N. Howe.

Many of the oaks lining the streets of Southport predate the town.

The free, state-operated ♂ ⅃ ⓣ North Carolina Maritime Museum at Southport (910-457-0003; www.ncmaritimemuseum.org) recently moved into the former barracks of Fort Johnston, with room for expanded exhibits stretching from Native American days to today's shrimping fleet. A special section details the role of blockade runners in the Civil War.

The 1904 Old Brunswick County Jail (910-457-0579; www.southporthistorical society.org), at the corner of Nash and Rhett Streets, retains its cells and prisoner graffiti and houses a display of memorabilia from the filming of *Crimes of the Heart*. Now the headquarters of the Southport Historical Society, the jail is open several days a week. Across the street, the Old Smithville Burial Ground contains gravestones, many with interesting inscriptions, dating back to Colonial times.

The interesting architecture at the 1843 ♂ Chapel of the Cross at St. Philip's (910-457-5643; www.stphilips church.org), at E. Moore and Dry Streets, combines Carpenter, Greek Revival, and English Gothic elements. The chapel is open daily for meditation and makes a restful stop on the historic walking tour.

> **Did you know?** The Southport–Oak Island Area Chamber of Commerce sponsors **Shop to the Beat** (910-457-6964; www.southport-oak island.com) in Southport, with live entertainment, games, and special deals at participating shops and restaurants. The events run from 4 to 6 PM on the first and third Thursdays of the month, from May to November.

If you don't want to hoof it around town, you can catch a narrated carriage ride down at the foot of Howe Street, with the Old South Tour and Carriage Company (910-713-2072; www.old southtourcompany.com). Its costumed guides also offer lantern-lit ghost walks.

Southport sponsors summer concerts and a film series at the Fort Johnston Garrison House (910-457-7945; www.townofsouthportnc.com) on the waterfront. St. Philip's Episcopal Church (910-457-5643; www.stphilipschurch.org) also hosts a free summer concert series.

The intimate, 80-seat Playhouse 211 Theater (910-200-7785; www.playhouse 211.com) presents plays, concerts, films, and the popular Brouhaha Revue. Beer and wine are available.

If you like this . . . check the schedule at Brunswick Community College's Odell Williamson Auditorium (910-755-7416; www.bccowa.com). Located a short distance up NC 211 in the town of Supply, it hosts a performing arts series, as well as performances of the Brunswick Little Theatre (910-368-6261; www.brunswick littletheatre.com).

The (ⓦ) ⓔ Lockwood Folly Marketplace (910-754-5445; www.lockwoodfolly marketplace.com), a general store established back in 1943 on the banks of the Lockwood Folly River, is worth a stop for locally grown, naturally raised food products such as milk in glass bottles, free-range meats and eggs, and organic veggies, plus gifts created by local artists. A deli on-site serves daily lunch specials. Take NC 211 from Southport toward Supply and turn right at the light on Stone Chimney Road.

Top 5 Don't Miss: Southport and Oak Island

- Walk the Historic Southport Trail under 400-year-old live oaks.
- Take the passenger ferry to Bald Head Island for a day of nature and history.
- Eat lunch or dinner along the Southport waterfront or have breakfast on a fishing pier.
- Visit the Oak Island Lighthouse.
- Ride the state ferry to Historic Fort Fisher and the North Carolina Aquarium.

OUTDOOR ADVENTURES

Down at the Yacht Basin, you can set sail for a sunset cruise or a longer trip with Kelly Allen Cruises (910-524-7245; www.sailkellyallen.com) or Priority Sailing (910-454-4479; www.prioritysailing.com). North Carolina Boat Rentals (910-279-2355; www.ncboatrentals.com) will rent you a Boston Whaler powerboat to explore on your own.

History buffs will enjoy a leisurely narrated cruise with Capt. Bert Felton, formerly on the staff of North Carolina's Historic Sites, aboard his restored 1938 North Carolina workboat, the *Solomon T* (910-457-5302; www.solomontsouth port.com).

The Adventure Kayak Company (910-464-0607; www.theadventurecompany .net) offers kayak trips to both the saltwater marshes and the blackwater rivers of the region, as well as sunset and full-moon paddles and overnight trips to offshore islands. They offer bicycle tours of Southport as well, or they'll rent you a kayak or bicycle so you can explore on your own.

The Scuba South Diving Company (910-457-5201; www.scubasouthdiving .com) takes divers on explorations of the many wrecks on the bottom at Frying Pan Shoals, just offshore, including the famous *City of Houston* steamer. Or try your hand at capturing lobsters. Rental equipment and snorkeling are also available.

The closest golf courses to the town of Southport are the excellent links at St. James Plantation (1-800-245-3871; www.stjamesplantation.com), one of the top golf villages along the coast. St. James boasts four 18-hole courses plus a 9, designed by the likes of P. B. Dye, Tim Cate, Hale Irwin, and Michael Nicklaus. Unaccompanied guest play is sometimes available. Contact the Clubs at St. James (910-253-9500; www.theclubsatstjames.com) for details.

BALD HEAD ISLAND

Two miles off the coast of Southport lies an island paradise, largely unspoiled by modern development. Accessible only by boat, Bald Head Island (often abbreviated as BHI) has no automobiles, few shops and restaurants, and a tiny year-round population. Residents and visitors alike get around on golf carts or bikes or, during the summer months, take the shuttle.

Just 3 miles long, and less than a mile wide, Bald Head nevertheless has 14 miles of untouched beaches, home only to numerous lady sea turtles that come ashore to lay their eggs. Behind the beach dunes lie nearly 200 acres of rare maritime forest and some 10,000 acres of salt marsh, a kayaker's paradise.

For many years, the only permanent residents of the island were the keepers of Old Baldy (910-457-7481; www.oldbaldy.org), North Carolina's oldest surviving lighthouse. Built in 1817 to mark the mouth of the Cape Fear River, the 110-foot lighthouse,

today a colorful patchwork of stucco over brick, was deactivated in 1935 and is preserved by a dedicated group of volunteers. Their efforts have restored the interior of the tower, making the 108 steps to the top safe. Beside the lighthouse, the Smith Island Museum of History preserves artifacts from around the island, and a gift shop stocks lighthouse memorabilia. There's a small charge to climb Old Baldy ($5 for adults; $3 for children 3–12). Proceeds go toward upkeep for the nearly 200–year-old landmark.

While the island is a popular place for family reunions, weddings, and weeklong vacations, many visitors come just for the day, taking the ferry over from Southport to visit the old lighthouse, walk the pristine beaches, and explore nature trails through the maritime forest.

Passenger ferries leave on the hour from Southport's Deep Point Marina, starting at 7 AM, with ferries returning on the half hour until 10:30 PM. Off-season schedules vary. Rates also vary somewhat, but expect to pay about $23 for an adult round-trip ticket. Children 3–12 sail for $12; kids under 3 are free. You can take your pet along, also your bike or kayak, although you'll need a separate cargo ticket for those. A new ferry terminal offers a snack bar, restrooms, and great views from the waiting area and outside deck. The journey takes about 20 minutes. Contact the Bald Head Island Ferry (910-457-5003; www.baldheadisland.com) for reservations and more information.

The passenger ferry to Bald Head Island leaves from Southport.

Deep Point Marina is located off NC 211, just before the Fort Fisher–Southport Ferry terminal. Be sure to have breakfast at Taylor Cuisine (910-454-0088; www.taylorcuisinecatering .com) in the terminal, and consider ordering a lunch for later.

For the easiest way to see Bald Head, sign up for one of the all-inclusive guided tours. The $55 fee ($45 for kids 3–12) includes your ferry ride; a narrated historic tour of the island with tales of pirates, Confederates, and shipwrecks; entrance to the lighthouse; a $10 voucher for Mojo's restaurant; and all transfers. Reservations are required; call 910-457-5003.

A less expensive day package is available at the terminal that includes admission to the lighthouse and your ferry ride at a discounted price. Contact the Old Baldy Foundation (910-457-7481; www.oldbaldy.org) for more information.

Did you know? While the tour packages are convenient, Bald Head also welcomes do-it-yourself visitors. You can hike, rent a bike or golf cart, or take the summer shuttle (910-457-4944; www.riversideadventure.com) from the marina to East Beach, Old Baldy, and the nature trails in Bald Head Woods.

In addition to Old Baldy, the greatest resource of the island is Bald Head Woods and the land protected by the Bald Head Island Conservancy (910-338-0911 or 910-457-0089; www.bhic.org). To introduce visitors to the unique ecology of this barrier island, the conservancy offers a wide range of programs for all ages, including kayak tours, birding expeditions, geocaching, turtle walks, nighttime nature tours, and more. Visit the Fleming Discovery Center in the BHI Conservancy campus at the east end of the island for more information.

A mature maritime forest with a canopy of old live oaks and laurels, Bald Head Woods (252-838-0890; www.nccoastalreserve.net), located along Federal Road, is part of the North Carolina Coastal Reserve, and a site on the North Carolina Birding Trail (www.ncbirdingtrail.org). Several walking paths lace the woods, including the interpreted ⅄ Kent Mitchell Nature Trail, a good spot to see painted buntings in early summer. Other good birding locales include East Beach with its wintering shore birds and Old Baldy, where flocks of warblers gather in the surrounding oak trees during the spring and fall migrations.

Thanks to its miles of undeveloped beaches, Bald Head is a favorite spot for sea turtles to come ashore and lay their eggs. In fact, more than half of all sea turtle nests in North Carolina are found here. Most belong to loggerheads, with a scattering of green turtle nests, and even a few of the very endangered leatherback. Visit ⅃ Turtle Central (910-457-0917), the gift shop of the Bald Head Island Conservancy, for more information. Sales support the conservation efforts.

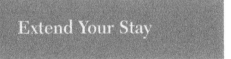

Extend Your Stay

Although most visitors come to Bald Head for just a day, the island makes a great destination for a longer stay. Several rental companies offer vacation cottages, including the 🎨 ⅄ Bald Head Island Company (910-457-5003; www.baldheadisland.com), the developer of most of the resort. An advantage to renting from it is that you receive a temporary membership to the ⅄ ⅃ Bald Head Island Club (910-457-7300; www.bhiclub.net), which includes many dining and recreation options with your rental. Golf privileges on the club's George Cobb championship course, spectacularly sited on dunes and freshwater lagoons, may or may not be included. Be sure to ask, if you enjoy golf.

If you prefer a more hotel-like atmosphere, make reservations at the ⅄ Marsh Harbour Inn (910-454-0451; www.marshharbourinn.com), where spacious balconies and porches offer views of the marina. Accommodations come with continental breakfast and use of a golf cart.

Dining options on Bald Head are rather limited, especially for day visitors and those who don't have access to the Club. MoJo's on the Harbor (910-457-7217;

www.mojoontheharbor.com), in the former Eb & Flo's location, offers lunch, dinner, and drinks along with magnificent waterfront views. The Ÿ River Pilot Café and Lounge (910-457-7390) serves Lowcountry and Creole specialties such as deviled eggs, crawfish beignets, and pan-seared grouper, at dinner only. The adjoining lounge offers cocktails and a late-night menu. Both restaurants are located in the marina complex, where you'll also find Will O' the Wisp Beer & Wine (910-457-6844), a pleasant spot for a drop of refreshment while waiting for the ferry.

The Maritime Market Cafe (910-457-7450), in Maritime Village near the center of the island, makes a great stop for a fast breakfast, lunch, or slice of pizza.

Did you know? Bald Head Island hosts many festivals, featuring live entertainment, oyster roasts, and special menus. Annual events include the Beach Music Extravaganza on Labor Day weekend, the North Carolina Wine & Food Weekend in October, the Golf Cart Parade on the Fourth of July, the Americana Music Festival on Memorial Day weekend, plus fishing tournaments and monthly Howl at the Moon parties. The Bald Head Island Pirate Weekend, evoking the spirit of the gentleman pirate, Stede Bonnet, is held every August and benefits Old Baldy.

Also in Maritime Village, the Woods Gallery (910-454-4892; www.baldhead island.com) is a must-stop for art lovers. Works in many media feature the natural beauty of Bald Head, representing the vision of over 80 artists, including members of the No Boundaries International Art Colony (www.nbiac.org), held on the island every other year.

A couple of outfitters make the natural attractions of Bald Head more accessible for visitors. Riverside Adventure Co. (www.riversideadventure.com), a family-run company that has been on the island since its earliest days, has two locations in the marina area, providing a wide variety of rentals and tours. For getting around, the Rental Shop (910-457-4944) has a stable of golf carts, electric bicycles, beach cruisers, even tandem bikes. You can also rent a GPS system for geocaching. The Kayak Shack (910-457-6844) rents canoes, kayaks, and surfboards, and offers sailing lessons and leisure sails. Other programs include boat and kayak tours of the surrounding islands, surf fishing, GPS scavenger hunts, and a nightly ghost tour.

Another outfitter, Coastal Urge (1-800-383-4443; www.coastalurge.com), specializes in stand-up paddleboard rentals and tours. It also rents bikes and offers lessons in standup paddlesurfing and kiteboarding on BHI beaches. Call to see if you can join one of its bike rides around the island.

Riverside Adventure (www.riversideadventure.com) runs the East Beach Shuttle (910-457-4944) that circles the island from Memorial Day to Labor Day. An all-day pass is $10. If you miss the shuttle, or are visiting in the off-season, Island Time Taxi (910-599-0707) will get you where you need to go.

OAK ISLAND & CASWELL BEACH

With 14 miles of white sand beaches, Oak Island richly deserved its earlier name of Long Beach. Because of the configuration of the coast on this side of Cape Fear, this barrier island faces south, with warmer waters and milder surf perfect for family vacations.

Named for the numerous live oaks that provide a shady canopy over most of the island, this is largely a residential resort with many cottages but few hotels or high-rise buildings. The emphasis remains on creating memorable and relaxing family vacations, featuring fishing, seafood feasting, and plenty of beach time.

Pick up area information at the Southport-Oak Island Chamber of Commerce Welcome Center (910-457-6964 or 1-800-457-6964; www.southport-oakisland .com), on Long Beach Road/NC 133.

Several communities grew up on Oak Island: Long Beach occupied the western end, Yaupon Beach the center; and Caswell Beach the far eastern end. In 1999 Long Beach and Yaupon Beach combined to form the town of Oak Island. Caswell Beach remains independent and unincorporated.

The Intracoastal Waterway (ICW), here a narrow canal through marsh, separates Oak Island from the mainland. Another arm of marsh, Davis Creek, invades the island from the western end, creating more waterfront property but splitting the beachfront from the rest of the island.

For a quick circle tour of Oak Island, take NC 133/Longbeach Road, off NC 211, from the Southport area. After crossing to the island, NC 133 curves around the Oak Island Golf Club before merging into Caswell Beach Road, which will lead you to the Oak Island Lighthouse. As you return, turn west off NC 133 on Oak Island Drive, the island's "main drag," which will take you to the western end of the island. At Middleton Avenue (the center of the street numbering system), you can turn right to go over the new Midway Road Bridge, returning to NC 211. But first, turn left on Middleton and go down to the ocean. If you turn right at the water, Beach Drive will take you all the way to the island's western end. Turn left and you'll find the Ocean Crest Pier just ahead.

Visitors often have the North Carolina beaches all to themselves.

The Oak Island Lighthouse (www.oakislandlighthouse.org) on Caswell Beach Road brings most day trippers to the island. The newest lighthouse in North Carolina, built in 1958, faces the state's oldest, Old Baldy, across the mouth of the Cape Fear River. The Oak Island Light, striped gray, white, and black, stands 169 feet above the water, and its light can be seen far out to sea. A volunteer group conducts free tours of the lighthouse. Regular tours go just to the second level. Special tours go all the way to the top and outside balcony, but you must make reservations online two weeks in advance. Unlike most lighthouses, the Oak Island Light doesn't have a spiral staircase. Instead, you climb a series of very steep, open ladders. It's a total of 131 steps to the top,

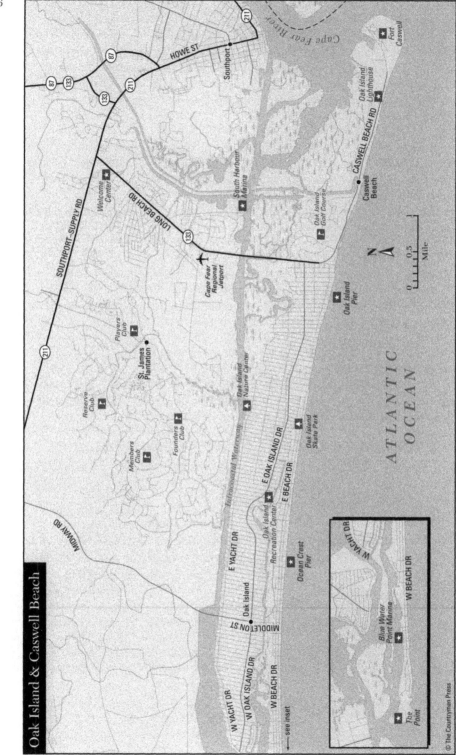

Oak Island & Caswell Beach

Cape Fear River

Fort Caswell

211

HOWE ST

Southport

87

133

87

211

133

211

Oak Island Lighthouse

CASWELL BEACH RD

Caswell Beach

SOUTHPORT–SUPPLY RD

Welcome Center

LONG BEACH RD

South Harbour Marina

133

Oak Island Golf Course

Cape Fear Regional Jetport

Oak Island Pier

Players Club

St. James Plantation

Reserve Club

Oak Island Nature Center

ATLANTIC OCEAN

Members Club

Founders Club

Oak Island Skate Park

MIDWAY RD

Intracoastal Waterway

E OAK ISLAND DR

E BEACH DR

E YACHT DR

Oak Island Recreation Center

Ocean Crest Pier

W YACHT DR

W OAK ISLAND DR

W BEACH DR

Oak Island

MIDDLETON ST

← see inset

Blue Water Point Marina

W BEACH DR

W YACHT DR

The Point

N

0   0.5
Mile

© The Countryman Press

Fast fact: Construction on **Fort Caswell** (910-278-9501; www.fort caswell.com), at the extreme eastern end of Oak Island, began in 1825, and the fort saw service during the Civil War and Spanish-American War, as well as both world wars. In 1946, the government sold the fort to the Baptist State Convention of North Carolina, which continues to use it as a conference center and retreat today. It's not currently open to the public.

Did you know? George Cobb, the legendary designer of the Par 3 course at Augusta National, began his career as a golf course architect while serving in the U.S. Marines.

a trip not for the out of shape or those afraid of heights. Across the street from the lighthouse a boardwalk leads over the dunes to the beach.

Caswell Beach has just a single road with cottages along either side, making this one of the least-visited beaches in the region. The Oak Island Golf Club (910-278-5275; www.oak islandgolf.com) is the only commercial enterprise in Caswell. Its George Cobb–designed, ocean-side course is well worth a day trip, but even if you don't play golf, stop for refreshment in ♂ Duffer's Pub & Grill, an excellent "19th hole" with terrific views of both ocean and fairways from the second floor of the clubhouse.

Oak Island is also a popular destination for those who love to fish. Surf fishing is popular along Caswell Beach, but many come to cast a line from one of the island's two ocean piers. The area is noted for the wide range of saltwater fish caught in its waters, and especially as a great spot for hooking king mackerel. The fishing season runs from April through December.

The family owned, 893-foot ♂ ♿ Ocean Crest Pier (910-278-6674; www .oceancrestpiernc.com), located near 14th Place East, has a special, shaded T-shaped section and a live bait tank at the far end for king fishing. Rod rentals are available in the full-service tackle shop. Next door, the ♂ Island Way Restaurant and Bar (910-278-7770; www.islandwayres.com) serves steaks and seafood in an upscale setting overlooking the ocean. If your budget isn't up to the $20-plus dinner menu, stop in for lunch or the early evening menu served until 6 PM.

Previously known as the Yaupon Pier, ♂ ♈ Oak Island Pier (910-278-6464; www.oakislandpier.com) was renamed after the city bought it to ensure the future of family fishing. It's a hotspot for kings, trout, and flounder. Equipment rentals are available; kids under 10 fish free with an adult. This pier hosts city events and has a restaurant and tiki bar. It's located in the Yaupon section at 705 Ocean Drive near Womble Street.

Pier fishing is a cherished family activity along the North Carolina coast.

Pick Your Spot

Best places to stay in and around Oak Island

Although the majority of accommodations on the island are vacation cottages, a few resorts also offer rooms by the night, including the Blue Water Point Motel and Marina (910-278-1230; www.bluewaterpointmotel.com), located at the western end of the island at 57th Place West. Oak Island is very narrow here, giving the resort both oceanfront and sound side options. From the marina on the sound you can catch a party boat for a day of deep sea fishing, take a sunset sail, and rent Jet Skis, kayaks, or paddleboats. The resort's popular ✿ Fish House Restaurant and Bulkhead Lounge (910-278-6012; www.bluewaterpointmotel.com/html/restaurant1.html) are noted for their fresh seafood and marvelous sunset views over the marsh. Try the award-winning seafood chowder, a creamy blend of clams, shrimp, and scallops.

If your canine pal is on vacation with you, make reservations at the ✿ ♂ (ᵒ) Island Resort (910-278-5644; www.islandresortandinn.com), on the beach near the Oak Island Fishing Pier.

Fast fact: Sunday morning worship services are held on Ocean Crest Pier beginning at 8 AM.

Did you know? Oak Island and Caswell are two of the most pet-friendly beaches in North Carolina. Dogs on leashes are allowed on the beach and other public walkways and trails year-round. Other dog-friendly beaches along this coast include Bald Head Island, Fort Fisher State Park in Kure Beach, and Freeman Park in Carolina Beach. Check for local regulations as they vary considerably.

Quick tip: Only a few roads make the crossing from E. Oak Island Drive to Beach Drive, among them Middleton Avenue and SE 40th, 49th, and 58th Streets.

Guests enjoy free pier passes and private beach access.

Many of the vacation cottages on Oak Island are pet friendly. Check the listings at ✿ Oak Island Accommodations (1-800-243-8132; www.oakisland pets.com) for a variety of options.

Local Flavors

Taste of the town—local cafés, restaurants, bars, bistros, etc.

Several popular restaurants are located along Oak Island Drive, east of Middleton Avenue.

✿ ♈ Shagger Jacks (910-933-4103; www.shaggerjacksoki.com), at 8004 E. Oak Island Drive, attracts the most praise with a menu full of eclectic dishes, from shrimp burgers and beef skewers to lobster corndogs and tuna tacos. Special Sunday brunch and late-night menus hold some surprises, and the selection of beer is one of the largest on the island. Entertainment, including a weekly shag night, draws locals and visitors alike.

You can join the Society of Brunswick Shaggers (www.societyof brunswickshaggers.com) for their local dances, held several times a month.

Another very popular restaurant

The coast's salt marshes provide a refuge for many different birds.

on E. Oak Island Drive is the 🐖 Bar-B-Que House (910-201-1001; www.best bbqonthebeach.com), where you can get hickory-smoked pulled pork, ribs, or chicken; homemade Brunswick stew; banana pudding; and a variety of Southern sides to eat in or take out.

But at the beach, what you really want to eat is seafood, and for the freshest and most local available, you can't do better than Pelican Seafood (www.pelicanseafood.com), part fish market, part restaurant, and completely delicious. Home of award-winning crab- cakes and chowder, Pelican will sell you fresh local fish to cook yourself, or prepare your choice on-site to your personal specifications, whether fried, grilled over a wood fire, or steamed. Pelican Seafood has two locations. The sit-down restaurant (910-454-8477), with a menu of inexpensive specials, is

on the mainland side of Oak Island on Long Beach Road near the airport. Pelican II (910-933-4564), at 6235 E. Oak Island Drive, is takeout only, with a drive-through window and a variety of groceries, beer, and wine. Don't miss Chef Tony Wehbe's unique fried flounder preparation that lets you dive right into a plate of this local specialty.

Two very popular spots serving breakfast all day sit practically next door to each other along E. Oak Island Drive at 58th and 59th Streets. Beana's Kitchen (910-278-7209) and Russell's Place (910-278-3070) serve family-style menus at wallet-friendly prices. Both are open for just breakfast and lunch, closing up at about 2 PM, but serve seven days a week all year.

If you just need a cup of coffee and to check your e-mail, proceed on down the street to the ((ŋ)) Flying Pig Coffee House (910-278-5929; www .flyingpig.us) at E. Oak Island and 60th, which offers coffees, teas, pastries, and a wide variety of pig-themed merchandise. Open until 2 PM.

For a quick and inexpensive lunch, Bob's Dogs (910-278-3456; www.bobs dogsoki.com), at 8903 E. Oak Island Drive, fits the bill. You can design your own dog, try one of Bob's specials, or grab a sandwich to take to the beach.

For relaxation and refreshment later in the day into evening, visit the 49th Street Station and Bar (910-278-9811; www.facebook.com/49thStation), a local hangout in an old gas station on E. Oak Island Drive.

Extend Your Stay

Oak Island nurtures an active colony of artists, most members of the Oak Island Art Guild (910-278-6101; www .oakislandartguild.com). Works by guild artists hang in the Oak Island Recreation Center (910-278-5518) at 3003 E. Oak Island Drive, with a smaller exhibit at the ((ŋ)) G. V. Barbee Sr. Library (910-278-4283; library.brunsco.net) at

E. Oak Island Drive and 82nd.

The Oak Island Art Guild sponsors several art shows each year, including the OIAG Arts and Crafts Festival, held the last Saturday before Labor Day, and the three-day Arts by the Shore in November.

If you're on the island on the second Friday of the month, drop by the free workshops offered by the Art Guild from 9:30 AM to 1 PM at the Oak Island Recreation Center.

If you like this . . . stop by the Oak Island Senior Citizens Craft and Gift Store (910-278-5224; www.oak islandseniorcraftstore.org) to see the wide variety of crafts, including paintings, stained glass, basketry, and photography, produced by local senior citizens. Classes are open to the public.

On the Fourth of July, piers up and down the coast take turns shooting off fireworks.

In keeping with the island's family-friendly philosophy, the Oak Island Parks and Recreation Department (910-278-5518; www.oakislandnc.com/Recreation/) provides a number of different facilities aimed at all age groups. More than 60 public access points lead down to the sandy white beaches. Other docks, piers, and boardwalks provide access to the ICW and Davis Creek for kayakers and fishers.

The largest parks and rec complex stretches from E. Oak Island Drive to the oceanfront between SE 46th and SE 49th Streets. The complex includes six tennis courts, a large playground, restrooms, picnic tables, a gazebo hosting summer concerts, and the ♿ Cabana, a handicapped-accessible beach. On 49th Street, you'll find the Oak Island Skate Park (910-278-4747; www.oakislandnc.com/Recreation), designed by and for skateboard and in-line skaters, and the 🎣 🐢 Oak Island Ocean Education Center (910-278-4747; www.oakisland nc.com/Recreation/), with exhibits and information about sea turtles and other marine life.

> **Fast fact:** Handicapped-accessible parks, piers, and beach access points are located all over Oak Island. For a complete list, contact Oak Island Parks and Recreation (910-278-5518; www.oakislandnc .com/Recreation/).

The Oak Island Skate Park rents helmets and pads. Nonresidents pay $5 to skate.

Another major complex surrounds the Oak Island Recreation Center (910-278-5518), at E. Oak Island Drive and SE 30th Street. Inside, a weight and cardio fitness facility plus a variety of classes are open to residents and visitors alike. Walking, biking, and paddling trail maps for the island can be picked up here.

Behind the center, the Dot Kelly Memorial Butterfly and Hummingbird

Quick tip: Finding your way around on Oak Island can be challenging at times until you get the hang of the street-numbering system. GPS systems tend to gag on it. To get the lay of the land, consider an ultralight flight with **Oak Island Sports Planes** (910-278-9604; www.oak islandsportplanes.com).

Garden has landscaped paths and birdwatching platforms. Next door, at the end of SE 31st Street, Tidalwaves Park and Canoe Dock provides access to Davis Creek. The Environmental Overlook Trail, beginning here, crosses Davis Creek to a boardwalk running down an island in the marsh before continuing on to 29th Place East on the beach side.

Several other scenic walkways cross Davis Creek, providing exceptional views of the marsh and birding opportunities, as well as convenient paths to the beach for bikes and pedestrians. The one at SE 20th Street crosses to the large beach access at 19th Place East. Another, with a canoe dock and beach access, crosses from SE 9th Street to 9th Place East. Parking lots are located at both ends of these boardwalks.

Another complex of parks and rec facilities, &. Malcolm Register Park, at the end of NE 52nd Street on the ICW, is home to the seasonal 🐾 Oak Island Nature Center (910-278-4747; www.oakislandnc.com/Recreation/), with live animal exhibits, and the Talking Tree Walking Trail that introduces local fauna, as well as a fishing dock, a floating dock for kayak launches, and a picnic area.

Another interesting place to visit is &. The Point, a park at the far western end of Beach Drive, where you'll find covered platforms on the beach, interpretive trails, and environmental overlooks.

The town of Oak Island continues onto the mainland and several parks are located there along Fish Factory Road off Long Beach Road. William "Bill" Smith Park has sports fields, plus a nature trail and a heavily wooded nine-hole disc golf course. Just beyond, Dutchman Creek Park has a public boat ramp, a floating dock for fishing and launching kayaks, and a nature trail, plus restrooms, a playground, and a picnic area. Across the street, the city-owned Oak Island Par 3 at South Harbour (910-454-0905; www.oakislandnc.com/Recreation/golfcourse.htm) offers an executive-style 18 holes with club and cart rentals. Walking the course is allowed.

A day at the beach begins.

If you like this . . . after your round of golf (disc or traditional) or a day of fishing, head on down to te end of Fish Factory Road at South Harbour Village for a refreshing beverage and views of the ICW at the **Dead End Saloon and Fish Factory Grille** *(910-454-4002; www.thedeadendsaloon.com). Hang around long enough and the live music will start up.*

A single road leads to the island of Holden Beach, NC 130, which cuts off from US 17 in the town of Shallotte. Officially named the Holden Beach Road, locals call its final mile the causeway. It runs a curvy course

Quick tip: The beach at the end of McCray Street at the east end of Holden Island is a favorite spot for shelling and surf fishing.

through forest and marsh, ending at a high-rise bridge over the ICW. At 65 feet, this bridge is the highest point in Holden Beach and provides a splendid view of the island.

As you make your way onto Holden Beach, you can almost feel time slow down. With a single road on and off the island, this remains a family-oriented beach where the primary activities are walking the sand, collecting seashells, fishing from the pier, and watching the sun rise and set in its majestic rhythm.

Holden Island has belonged to the same family since 1756 when Benjamin Holden bought it from the royal governor for 50 shillings. For more information on the history and early days of the island, visit the website of descendant Alan Holden, now a real estate broker, at www.holden-beach.com.

The unspoiled beaches of Holden are favorites of sea turtles who come ashore to nest during the summer months. The ✍ Holden Beach Turtle Watch Project (910-754-0766; www.hbturtlewatch.org) conducts educational turtle talks, with videos and turtle artifacts. The programs, held at the Holden Beach Town Hall under the water tower, are free to the public.

The town of Holden Beach (910-842-6488; www.hbtownhall.com) also sponsors a summer series of concerts, held at the town pavilion at the end of Jordon Boulevard, next to the ICW almost under the bridge. Visit the town website for the current schedule.

The Holden Town Pavilion complex at the end of Jordon Boulevard also has a fishing dock and public boat ramp on the waterway.

A biscuit stuffed with bacon personifies the Southern breakfasts served at North Carolina fishing piers.

Holden Beach hosts two big annual events, and both are free: Day at the Docks in May, sponsored by the Greater Holden Beach Merchants Association (www.hbmerch .com), and the North Carolina Festival By the Sea in late October, with a parade across the causeway bridge. Both festivals take place under the bridge.

Commercial development is almost nonexistent on the island. Besides a general store and ice cream shop near the fishing pier, and Sandman's Candyland (910-842-6322; 109 Jordan Boulevard) near the bridge, you won't find many spots to spend your vacation dollars. For any serious shopping,

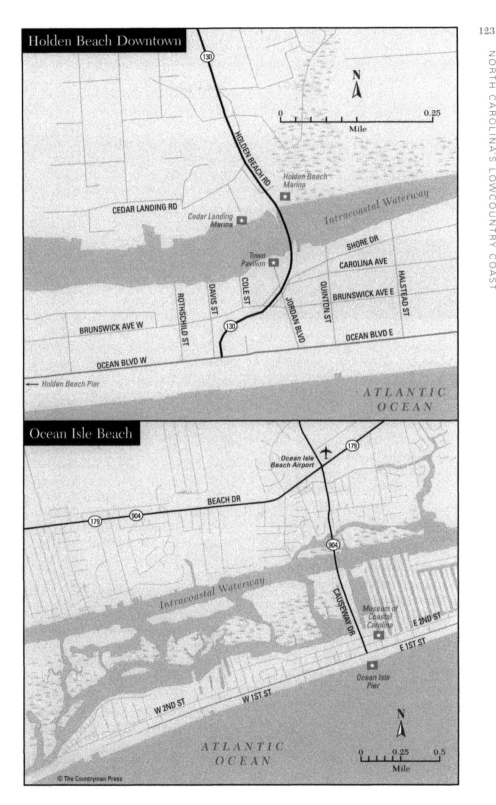

Holden Beach Downtown

N

0   0.25
Mile

130

HOLDEN BEACH RD

Holden Beach
Marina

Intracoastal Waterway

CEDAR LANDING RD

Cedar Landing
Marina

SHORE DR

CAROLINA AVE

Town
Pavilion

COLE ST

DAVIS ST

ROTHSCHILD ST

QUINTON ST

BRUNSWICK AVE E

HALSTEAD ST

130

JORDAN BLVD

BRUNSWICK AVE W

OCEAN BLVD E

OCEAN BLVD W

Holden Beach Pier

ATLANTIC
OCEAN

Ocean Isle Beach

179

Ocean Isle
Beach Airport

BEACH DR

179

904

904

Intracoastal Waterway

CAUSEWAY DR

Museum of
Coastal
Carolina

E 2ND ST

E 1ST ST

Ocean Isle
Pier

W 2ND ST

W 1ST ST

N

0   0.25   0.5
Mile

ATLANTIC
OCEAN

© The Countryman Press

grocery or otherwise, you have to cross the causeway to Shallotte, about 10 minutes away. The causeway itself is lined with shops and restaurants, plus a number of family attractions, including minigolf courses, a water slide, a go-cart track, and bumper boats.

The Holden Beach Fishing Pier (910-842-6483; www.holdenbeachpier.com) sits in the heart of the island. More than just a fishing destination, this is also your best bet for oceanfront motel rooms and RV campsites. A grill serves breakfast, hot dogs, burgers, fried flounder, and barbecue—but no alcohol—on the pier.

Most accommodations on Holden Beach are cottages designed for family vacations. Coastal Vacation Resorts (1-800-252-7000; www.coastalvacation resorts.com) represents over 300 properties from beachfront to the waterway, including some that are pet friendly.

Local Flavors

Taste of the town—local cafés, restaurants, bars, bistros, etc.

Full service dining options are extremely limited on Holden Beach. One of the few spots with an ocean view is also one of the best: Castaways Raw Bar and Grill (910-842-5743; www.castawayshb.com), located at 112 Ocean Boulevard West, just east of the bridge expressway. The screened dining porch and open-air decks let you enjoy the ocean breezes along with your steamed bucket of seafood, sandwich, or pasta dish. Several big screen TVs in the bar area stay tuned to sports, and Castaways hosts live entertainment in season. There's a public beach access across the street if you need to walk off your meal.

If you like this . . . just a block away, the Paradise Cafe (910-842-4999; www.paradisehb.com) serves an eclectic menu of Caribbean and Greek dishes, plus seafood sandwiches and plates, in a fun, tropical environment. A low-priced breakfast buffet is offered daily during the summer season.

Captain Pete's Seafood Restaurant (910-846-9988; www.captpeteshb.com),

on S. Shore Drive next to the high-rise bridge, is a must-stop in the late afternoon to watch the sun go down over the ICW. Shrimp boats tie up nearby, adding to the scenic view. The downstairs bar is a local favorite. Next door, at Capt'n Pete's Seafood Market (910-842-6675), stock up on fresh local seafood to prepare at your vacation cottage.

If you like this . . . several other seafood companies in the area offer fresh locally sourced fish and shellfish, including Cedar Landing Seafood (910-842-8448) at the Cedar Landing Marina on the ICW; Holden Beach Seafood (910-842-6276; www.holden beachseafood.com); and Old Ferry Seafood (910-842-6278) at the end of Old Ferry Road. Check with Brunswick Catch (www.brunswick catch.com) for more options.

Restaurants line the mainland side of the waterway. The best of them is the Provision Company (910-842-7205; www.procohb.com) on Cedar Landing Road. It's the sister restaurant of the famous Provisions (www.provisioncompany.com) on the waterfront at Southport and offers many of the same menu items and much of the same "organized chaos" style of service. Wait on the pleasant

Quick tip: If you're celebrating a special event during your vacation, order a cake worthy of the name "edible art" from the **Salt Aire Bakery** (910-846-2253; www.salt aireliving.com).

waterside deck for a table to become available or visit the downstairs bar. This is another great place to watch the sunset.

The restaurant garnering most praise from diners is ✆ Boone Docks (910-842-5515; www.facebook.com /boonedockshb), located on the mainland at 3386 Holden Beach Road. While the regular menu offers meat lover options, as well as the requisite fried seafood platters, the daily seafood specials designed by owner and chef Scotty Anderson are the items creating waves in the Holden Beach dining universe. Using the freshest local catch, Anderson prepares fish and shellfish simply but deliciously with many Asian touches, such as ginger and plum glazes or spicy Thai curry.

OUTDOOR ADVENTURES

Located on the island, Beach Fun Rentals (910-842-9600; www.beachfunrentals .com) carries a wide variety of sports and beach equipment for your vacation, including kayaks, bikes, and surfboards. Best of all they deliver free on the island.

Two marinas with Jet Ski rentals bracket the high-rise bridge on the mainland side. The Holden Beach Marina (910-842-7222; www.holdenbeachmarina.com) also offers Carolina skiff rentals and fishing charters. At Cedar Landing Marina, you can sign up for rides aboard the red-white-and-blue Sea Thriller (910-842-7000; www.seathriller.com), a speedboat offering dolphin, sunset, and dinner cruises. You can also rent Carolina skiffs and pontoon boats from FantaSea Rentals (910-842-8484; www.holdenrentals.com) based here.

For a relaxed family day on the water, contact ✆ 🐾 Windy Point Nautical Adventures and Water Taxi (910-616-8467; www.wpnadv.com) and spend time tubing, crabbing, shelling, fishing, kayaking the Shallotte River, or just sightseeing along the ICW. The water taxi will take you to your choice of restaurants for a very reasonable fee, with beverages on board included.

For a bird's-eye view of Holden Beach or Oak Island, contact Sharky's Watersports (910-228-7100; www.sharkyswatersportsnc.com) for a parasailing adventure. It also can arrange banana boat rides and pontoon and Jet Ski rentals.

The Lockwood Folly Country Club (910-842-5666; www.lockwoodfolly.com) is the closest golf course to Holden Beach, and it's a great one. Designed by Willard Byrd on the grounds of a 100-year-old hunting preserve, this semiprivate course is legendary for its beauty and a favorite with both golfers and the golf press.

BRUNSWICK COUNTY: NORTH CAROLINA'S GOLF COAST

Between the bridge over the Cape Fear River in Wilmington and the South Carolina state line, US 17 passes more than 30 golf courses. In fact, most of the land not in nature preserves in Brunswick County now hosts greens and fairways.

Golf draws the majority of the visitors that come to Brunswick County every year. Many golfers come in the fall, winter, and spring, adding a much needed

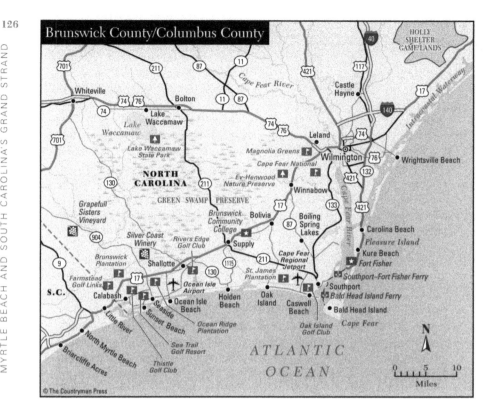

Brunswick County/Columbus County

year-round boost to the formerly summer tourism–based economy. Many local resorts and hotels offer great deals on off-season lodging and golf packages.

Brunswick County is the home of the golf resort, a self-sufficient community with accommodations, dining, entertainment, and family activities, in addition to full-service golf. Most of these communities keep a low profile—you may not notice them as you drive by—and tend to be ecologically sensitive.

♦ ♂ ♈ Sea Trail Golf Resort & Convention Center (910-287-1100 or 1-866-368-6642; www.seatrail.com), close to the causeway to Sunset Beach, is one of the largest and most comprehensive with three championship courses designed by Dan Maples, Rees Jones, and Willard Byrd, plus 400 villa-style accommodations, two restaurants,

Even a foggy morning doesn't discourage avid golfers.

Did you know? Brunswick County, nicknamed **N.C.'s Golf Coast**, has a special website for visiting golfers (www.ncbrunswickgolf.com) with descriptions of all the courses in the region, plus suggestions for places to stay. The **Brunswick Isles Golf Trail** (1-888-477-4407; www.brunswickislesgolftrail.com) includes specials and packages at courses from Little River, South Carolina, to Wilmington, North Carolina.

children's pool and activities, indoor and outdoor adult pools and whirlpools, and a free beach shuttle in season.

Many of the region's other courses are located in the Sunset Beach area, convenient for the golfers who flock to the Grand Strand, just over the state line, every year. The Big Cats at Ocean Ridge Plantation (1-800-233-1801; www.big-cats.com) are award-winning courses with evocative names—Lion's Paw, Tiger's Eye, Panther's Run, Leopard's Chase, and the still-in-progress Jaguar's Lair. These are big courses, carved from pristine forests and marshlands, and rank very high in *Golf Digest* and other publications. Lion's Paw is considered William Byrd's finest work, while Tiger's Eye, designed by Tim Cate to take full advantage of the unique landscape, includes a waterfall on the 18th hole. *Golf Digest* ranks it among America's 100 greatest public courses.

Also among *Golf Digest's* top 100, the Rivers Edge Golf Club (910-755-3434; www.river18.com), the only Arnold Palmer course in the county, occupies a stunning location atop bluffs along the Shallotte River.

Other courses with public play in the Sunset Beach area include the two courses at the Pearl Golf Links (910-579-8132; www.thepearlgolf.com), both designed by Dan Maples in a marshland setting. Maples also designed the courses at the Sandpiper Bay Golf & Country Club (1-800-356-5827; www.sandpiperbaygolf.com) where Piper's Bar and Grill (910-579-9120) is considered one of the top "19th holes" in the region.

Meadowlands Golf Club (910-287-7529; www.meadowlandsgolf.com), a William Byrd course in Calabash, is among *Golf for Women's* top women-friendly courses.

An alligator may be one of the hazards golfers encounter on Brunswick County courses.

Near the South Carolina border, 🐾 Brunswick Plantation and Golf Resort (910-845-6935; www.brunswickvillas.com) offers 27 holes of Willard Byrd-designed golf, plus a full slate of amenities and pet-friendly accommodations.

If you like this . . . Magnolia Greens (910-383-0999; www.magnolia-greens.com) is another golf plantation combining accommodations with a 4.5-star course designed by Tom Jackson.

Designer Tim Cate has done some of his finest work in Brunswick County. The Thistle Golf Club (910-575-8700 or 1-800-571-6710; www.thistlegolf .com), in Sunset Beach, evokes the spirit of Scotland with hillsides covered in heather and an authentic Scottish pub for after the round. One of Cate's newest courses, Cape Fear National at Brunswick Forest (910-383-3283; www.capefearnational.com), just five minutes from downtown Wilmington, was named one of the best new courses for 2010 by both *GOLF* magazine and *Golfweek* magazine.

Fast fact: The 18th hole at **Farmstead Golf Links** (910-575-7999; www.farmsteadgolflinks.com) is the region's only par 6. You tee off in South Carolina, and putt out across the border in North Carolina. *Golf Digest* named it one of the top 18 most fun holes in America.

OCEAN ISLE BEACH

Although actually smaller than Holden Beach next door, Ocean Isle is a livelier place. While Holden remains largely a summer family destination, its neighbor enjoys an injection of money and fun in winter and the shoulder seasons when the golfers come to town.

Ocean Isle Beach (often abbreviated OIB) is located along NC 904, which becomes Causeway Drive. Part of the town, including the Ocean Isle Beach Airport, lies on the mainland side of the bridge that leads to the island. Shallotte, with its numerous shopping options, is just a few minutes away on NC 179. Twenty golf courses are located within 8 miles of Ocean Isle.

Although the majority of the accommodations on OIB remain vacation cottages, the island also has several year-round resorts located on the beach, equipped with indoor pools, hot tubs, and plenty of oceanfront balconies. There's some hot nightlife as well, with lots of live entertainment, even in the off-season.

One of the nicest year-round resorts is the ✈ 🍽 ♿ ⛳ (ᵖ) Winds Resort Beach Club (1-800-334-3581; www.thewinds.com), a family-owned spot with lush landscaping and a tropical vibe. Here you can have your choice of hotel rooms, suites, or private cottages set in a garden atmosphere amid banana trees, palms, and tropical flowers. The wide white beach is just outside your door. Rates include a hot Southern breakfast buffet and complimentary bikes. Children 14 and under stay free.

The ♿ ⛳ (ᵖ) Ocean Isle Inn (910-579-0750 or 1-800-352-5988; www.ocean isleinn.com) is another year-round resort with indoor pool and spa, balconies with views over the ocean or marsh, complimentary continental breakfast, and a beachfront location. It's close to the end of the causeway, near the Ocean Isle Fishing Pier.

Ocean Isle is home to a nudist resort, Whispering Pines (910-287-6404; www.whisperingpinesnudist resort.com), offering rental RV park models and a full-service campground.

At the ✈ Ocean Isle Fishing Pier

Quick tip: If you visit the Winds Resort during the summer, ask about free summer golf at the area's top courses. In winter, check out the great all-inclusive deals.

Game arcades at fishing piers make them great family destinations.

(910-579-3095; www.oibpier.com), located on the ocean at the end of NC 904/Causeway Drive, you can fish, no license required, or walk down the pier to see what's biting. The Pier House rents fishing gear, golf carts, bikes, and surfboards, and there's a minigolf course across the street. An arcade makes this a great spot for kids and the Pier Grill serves breakfast and casual burgers and dogs. This is about the only breakfast available on the island if your hotel doesn't offer one.

*If you like this . . . cast a line into the ICW at the public fishing pier in **Ferry Landing Park** (910-579-2166; www.oibgov.com) on Shallotte Boulevard at the eastern end of the island. A North Carolina fishing license is required.*

 🐟 ♿ ℧ Sharky's Restaurant and Marina (910-579-9177; www.sharkysocean isle.com), on the island side of the causeway, is a landmark to look for whether you're arriving by land or sea. Enjoy cocktails and a fun menu filled with seafood, sandwiches, and pizza on the large screened deck overlooking the waterway, or stay up late for live entertainment. Guests who arrive by boat can overnight at Sharky's dock with water and electric hookups.

*If you like this . . . the 🐟 ℧ **Giggling Mackerel Seafood Grille** (910-575-0902; www.gigglingmackerel.com) is right next door to Sharky's, offering a similar mix of open-air dining, surf and turf specials, cocktails, and live music.*

Also on the causeway, the 🐟 Ocean Isle Fishing Center (910-575-3474; www .oifc.com) has offshore and inshore fishing charters, including a special kids' introduction to fishing, plus adult lessons in the special methods used to catch various kinds of fish such as king mackerel, grouper, and the big fish of the Gulf Stream.

If you're looking for dining with an ocean view, your choices are few. You can either go super casual with a hot dog on the pier, or visit the upscale 🐟 Isles Restaurant & Tiki Bar (910-575-5988; www.islesrestaurant.com) in the 🐧 Islander Beach Club (www.islanderresort.com) at the western end of the island, where you'll dine on Lowcountry classics, prime rib, steaks, and locally sourced seafood on wide decks overlooking the beach. During the summer you can lunch on a more casual, and less expensive, menu at the outdoor tiki bar.

You can almost see the ocean from the deck at the 🐟 ℧ Second Street Bar & Grill (910-579-0102; www .secondstreetbarandgrill.com), a casual spot a block or so from the pier serving lunch and dinner. With a full bar and plenty of TVs, it's a favorite watering hole for local surfers and fishers.

Quick tip: Consult our section on Holden Beach for additional water-sports options and an inexpensive water taxi that will shuttle you to area restaurants.

With such limited dining options on the island itself, crossing over to the mainland in search of food and fun is almost inevitable. The place with the biggest buzz is the ⅋ Sugar Shack (910-579-3844; 1609 Hale Beach Road SW), a reggae-fueled Jamaican joint off Beach Drive near the airport. The creative chef here has developed his own sweet style of jerk seasoning, resulting in legendary ribs and coconut shrimp, as well as Caribbean classics such as stamp and go (spicy cod fritters). You'll need reservations for dinner during the summer season. Live bands entertain some nights.

Casual spots for a meal on the mainland include the Dawg House (910-579-8834; 6415 Beach Drive SW), serving breakfast as well as hot dogs, burgers, and barbecue; and Joey O's Pizzeria (910-575-3233; www.facebook.com/JoeyOsPizza), with New York–style pizzas and other Italian specialties for eat in, take out, or delivery.

For a really special experience, seek out the ⅋ ⅋ ⅋ Inlet View Bar & Grill (910-754-6233; www.inletview.com), a family-run spot at the mouth of the Shallotte River where it meets the ICW, serving breakfast, lunch, and dinner daily. It's a little hard to find, but the great views from the second floor decks and the fresh seafood straight off the owner's fishing boat make the trip worthwhile. It's easily reached by water taxi or boat from either Holden Beach or OIB. Beach music bands play on the weekends, and an elevator takes you to the upper decks.

If you like this . . . contact the **Coastal Shag Club** *(www.coastalshagclub .org) for more opportunities to dance to beach music.*

Wine lovers must make an excursion to the ⅋ Silver Coast Winery (910-287-2800; www.silvercoastwinery.com), just off NC 904 on the west side of US 17. This working vineyard offers tours of its wine-making facilities, tastings of award-winning wines, works by local artists, and great spots for picnicking. You can also pick muscadine grapes in season.

If you like this . . . continue west on NC 904 to the ⅋ **Grapefull Sisters Vineyard** *(910-653-2944; www.grape fullsistersvineyard.com). See our Grand Strand chapter for a complete wine tour of the region.*

Brunswick County has two events perfect for foodie vacations. The Brunswick Stew & Que, sponsored by the Brunswick County Chamber of Commerce (910-754-6644; www .brunswickcountychamber.org), offers tastings of the local classic made by regional experts, plus barbecue, live bluegrass music, kids games, and pony rides. It's held at Planet Fun (910-755-2286; www.planetfuncenter.com), a large bowling and arcade facility in Shallotte, so the event runs rain or

Biking is a year-round activity on the Carolina coast.

shine. In October the North Carolina Oyster Festival (910-754-6644; www.nc oysterfestival.com) takes over Ocean Isle with oyster-shucking competitions, an oyster stew cook-off, and food booths offering local specialties, plus surfing competitions, live entertainment, a road race, and more.

Near the end of the Ocean Isle causeway sits the island's main attraction, the ∂ ⊤ Museum of Coastal Carolina (910-579-1016; www.museumplanetarium.org), housing exhibits focused on the natural and cultural history of the area. Favorite features for kids include the shark teeth sandpit, the Litterbug Hall of Shame, a touch tank with live animals, and the Legend of the Loggerhead with a sea turtle nest. The museum offers special programs and activities for all ages year-round, although winter hours are limited.

Next door to the museum, a large playground operated by the town is open all year. During the summer, special activities for kids 3–10, including programs on turtles and pirates, are offered daily at the ∂ ⊤ ♂ Ocean Isle Beach Community Center (910-579-2166; www.oibgov.com) at 44 E. First Street.

*If you like this . . . to find out more about the sea turtles that nest on OIB, contact the **Ocean Isle Beach Sea Turtle Protection Organization** (910-231-8539 or 910-231-3139; www.oibseaturtles.org) or the **OIB Turtle Patrol** (910-754-9513 or 910-232-7232; www.oibturtlepatrol.com).*

Ocean Isle, with its steady, gentle waves coming in off Long Bay, is an easy spot to learn how to surf. Surfing is permitted on OIB in the areas east of Monroe Street and west of Oxford Street. Salty's Surf Shop (910-579-6223; www.saltyssurf shopoib.com), on the oceanfront near the OIB Pier, is the spot to hang with the board rider crowd. It rents boards, bikes, and kayaks and offers surf lessons.

Rather shop than surf? The ⊤ Fancy Flea Antique Mall (910-755-6665; www.fancyfleaantique.com) on US 17 in Shallotte offers 15,000 square feet of browsing fun.

*If you like this . . . stop by the **Collector's Corner Art Gallery** (910-754-6199; www.collectorscornergallery.com), on Shallotte's Main Street, to see works created by local artists.*

SUNSET BEACH

A tiny island, just 3 miles long, Sunset Beach has the one of the largest year-round populations of any of the Brunswick Isles, but the least-commercial development on the island itself. Most restaurants, services, and shopping are located in the mainland part of the town along Sunset Boulevard, a continuation of Beach Drive from the Ocean Isle area.

Long connected with the mainland via an old-fashioned swing bridge that caused lengthy traffic backups during the summer season, Sunset Boulevard now passes over a new high-rise bridge and runs straight down to the ocean. At its end, a public parking lot, beach access, and gazebo next to the Sunset Beach Fishing Pier make a great first destination on the island.

An exceptionally wide dune system protects Sunset Island from the waves, so most oceanfront rentals don't have their own beach access ramps. Instead, the town maintains many boardwalks over the dunes for public use. You'll find them,

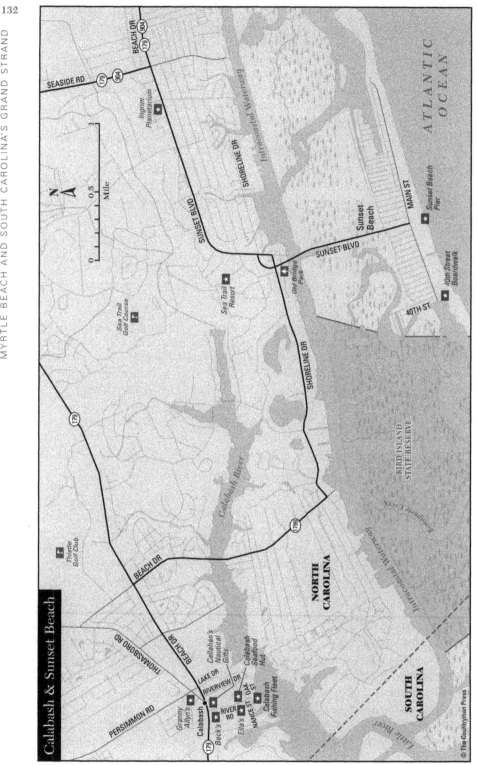

Calabash & Sunset Beach

© The Countryman Press

Did you know? The residents of Sunset Beach were determined to save the beloved old swing bridge, for so many years a local landmark on the ICW. Although it no longer crosses water, you can still visit the bridge and learn about its history. It's been moved to a shady grove of live oaks on the west side of the new high rise bridge on land donated by Ronnie and Clarice Holden, owners of Twin Lakes Restaurant and Island Breeze boutique (910-579-4125; www.island breezeclothing.com), both located nearby. **The Old Bridge Preservation Society** (910-579-9021; www.oldbridgepreservationsociety.org) hosts summer programs at the bridge and fundraisers year-round. Its plans include turning the historic Tender House on the bridge into an interpretive center.

The old swing bridge to Sunset Beach has been moved onshore to become a museum.

along with limited parking, at most cross streets running down to the ocean.

Most accommodations on the island are private vacation rentals, except for the ♂ (ᵞ) Sunset Inn, (910-575-1000; www.thesunsetinn.net) a bed & breakfast recently built next to the spot where the Sunset Boulevard causeway reaches the island. Each of the 14 rooms has a private screened porch overlooking the salt marsh. The inn is open all year.

On the Mainland
If you prefer a complete resort experience, or plan to make golf the centerpiece of your vacation, make reservations at the enormous ♂ ♂ Sea Trail Golf Resort (910-287-1100 or 1-866-368-6642; www.seatrail.com) running along the north side of Sunset Boulevard on the mainland. Sea Trail boasts three championship courses designed by golf's top architects: the Dan Maples Course, the Rees Jones Course, and the Willard Byrd Course. Beautifully maintained, the courses are complemented by two clubhouses complete with golf shops, lounges, and putting greens; a driving range; and a PGA-sanctioned golf learning center. Accommodations at the resort include 400 spacious suites with one to four bedrooms, full kitchens, and screened porches with views of the golf courses, scattered amid nearly 2,000 acres of coastal forest. Other amenities include the Village Activity Center with fitness classes and equipment, bike rentals, indoor and outdoor pools and whirlpools, and a day spa. During the summer a free shuttle takes visitors down to the ocean at Sunset Beach. The Magnolias Lounge (910-287-1119) in the Jones/Byrd Clubhouse provides gourmet meals for breakfast, lunch, and dinner; Brassie's Pub in the Maples Clubhouse serves more casual fare.

The ⚓ Twin Lakes Seafood Restaurant and Lounge (910-579-6373; www .twinlakesseafood.com), next to the former swing bridge location on Old Sunset Boulevard, features a panoramic view from the upstairs dining room over the salt-marsh and ICW with the new high-rise bridge framing the scene. The menu features a wide variety of seafood, with a lower-priced seniors menu available.

If you like this . . . local favorite ⚓ ℆ Crabby Oddwaters (910-579-6372; crabbyoddwaters.com), just a few blocks up Sunset, specializes in buckets of steamed local seafood. Located on an inlet, this 1981 spot is a casual classic with waterfront views and law-mandated plastic cutlery. Bill's Seafood, next door, sells steamed-to-go local shrimp, fish straight off the boat, and homemade key lime pies. Open seasonally.

For breakfast and lunch, Sarah's Kitchen (910-575-3777; www.sarahsatsunset .com), in Pelican Square near the junction of Seaside Drive and Sunset Boulevard, serves freshly baked biscuits, omelets, burgers, and sandwiches, all very reasonably priced, until 2 PM.

Need to check your e-mail? The (((·))) Sunset Beach Gourmet Deli (910-575-6759; www.sunsetgourmet.com), open until midafternoon in the Village of Sunset Beach complex across from the Ingram Planetarium, offers a full coffee bar, outdoor patio, and free WiFi. A couple of doors down, stop at the Blue Heron Gallery (910-575-5088; www.blueherongallery-nc.com) to browse the works of over 200 artists and craftspeople from across the country.

Also in the Village, ℆ (((·))) Fibber McGee's Irish Pub (910-575-2271; www .fibbermcgeesnc.com) offers a full bar to go along with free WiFi. Open from noon to midnight seven nights a week, Fibber McGee's has live music on weekends and a reasonably priced pub menu.

The ⚓ ☥ Ingram Planetarium (910-575-0033; www.museumplanetarium.org) is located off Sunset Boulevard near the Sea Trail Resort. Sky shows, family activities, and laser light shows are offered year-round.

The Ingram Planetarium in Sunset Beach and the Museum of Coastal Carolina in Ocean Isle Beach are sister establishments with the same founder, Stuart Ingram, and are located just 4 miles apart. Both are open on Fridays and Saturdays only, from Labor Day to Memorial Day. Summer hours and days vary.

> **Quick tip:** To get to know the local Sunset Beach residents, visit during the annual **Sunset at Sunset Community Block Party** (www .sunsetatsunset.com) scheduled for early October.

On the Island

There isn't much to do on Sunset Beach itself besides the classics: sunning, swimming in the surf, fishing from the pier, biking or walking on the beach, and kayaking in the marsh.

The best place to drop a line is the ⚓ ♿ Sunset Beach Fishing Pier (910-579-6630; www.sunsetbeachpier.com), at the end of Sunset Boulevard where it meets the ocean. It houses a grill serving breakfast and burgers (the only restaurant on the island), and a game room, as well as a tackle shop offering equipment rentals and an ATM. The pier's 9south00-foot length makes it a favorite with fishers angling for kings.

Complimentary electric scooters are available for guests who have trouble walking the length of the Sunset Beach Pier.

Julie's Rentals & Sweet Shop (910-579-1211; www.juliesrentals.com), just steps from the pier at 2 W. Main Street, rents all kinds of things to make your stay more fun, from bikes and banana peels to kayaks and boogie boards, as well as convenience items such as roll-away beds, cribs, gas grills, and beach umbrellas. Cooter Creek Paddlesports, headquartered at Julie's, leads kayak journeys through the salt marsh and to serene Bird Island.

Part of the North Carolina Coastal Reserve, **Bird Island** (910-962-2998; www.nccoastalreserve.net) can be reached by kayak, foot, or bike. Until recently, Bird Island was only accessible by boat or by wading, but sandbars now join it to Sunset Beach along the oceanfront. To reach it by foot or bike, go to the western end of Main Street where it dead-ends at 40th Street, and take the 40th Street boardwalk to the beach. Head right (southwest) and you'll immediately be on a pristine stretch of shore, one that will never be developed. Keep walking for a mile or so and you'll enter South Carolina.

One landmark to watch for among the dunes is the Kindred Spirit mailbox, filled with notebooks recording visitors' thoughts and feelings about this unique spot. Stop for a moment and add your own reflections.

Birds may be your only companions on Sunset Island's pier.

Dawn is a favorite time for a walk on the beach.

Most people make the trip to Calabash, a small fishing village at the southern edge of North Carolina, for one reason—to eat. Known as the Seafood Capital of the World, this tiny spot has some 30 restaurants, most of them serving the local specialty, Calabash-style seafood.

So great has the fame of this town become that restaurants far and wide advertise Calabash-style seafood on their menus.

The village's cooking reputation began before World War II, when the ladies of Calabash would clean and cook pots of seafood down by the docks as the boats operated by their husbands, brothers, and fathers brought in the day's catch. Shrimp was the major event, along with oysters steamed open on a grate over the fire.

Did you know? Sunset Beach is a noted birding destination, part of the **North Carolina Birding Trail** (www.ncbirdingtrail.org). Wood storks are often seen in the marsh along the causeway from spring to fall. Shore birds and waders frequent the mud flats, and waterfowl winter on the beach. Bird Island is a refuge for Wilson's plover, least tern, and the rare purple sandpiper. Sea turtles also nest along the Bird Island beach. Check with the **Sunset Beach Turtle Watch** (910-579-5862; www.sunsetbeachturtles.org) for current sightings and educational opportunities.

By 1940 enough hungry folk were gathering to eat seafood that two restaurants were established in town. Sisters Ruth Beck and Lucy Coleman were the female forces behind these first two eateries, and so began the friendly argument that continues to the present day about who has the "original" Calabash seafood.

Begin your tour of Calabash down at the docks to see what the fleet brings in, chat with the locals, and enjoy great views of the Calabash River. Many people who stop at the restaurants out on Beach Drive/NC 179 never realize they're eating in a fishing village. To find the docks, turn east off Beach Drive at the light onto River Road, next to Callahan's Nautical Gifts.

The restaurants founded by the sisters are still are in operation today and continue to be run by family members. Their brother, Lawrence High, and his wife, Ella, started their own restaurant, naming it Ella's, in 1950, with the help of his mother, Amanda High, the clan matriarch, and arguably the originator of the Calabash style. Many of the other families in town are related to this High clan, either by blood or marriage.

🖋 Beck's Restaurant (910-579-6776; www.becksrestaurant.com) and 🖋 🍸 Ella's of Calabash (910-579-6728; www.ellasofcalabash.com) are now operated by the same group of descendants, and have very similar menus, with a few differences. Beck's serves beer and wine only, while Ella's has a full ABC license. Beck's is known for its all-you-can-eat Alaskan crab legs, while Ella's offers oyster roasts in season. Both are known for their huge servings and inexpensive lunch specials; both are located on River Road leading down to the docks.

Coleman's Original Calabash Seafood Restaurant (910-579-6875; www.facebook.com/originalcalabash) is located down on the waterfront on Nance Street. The Calabash Seafood Hut (910-579-6723; 1125 River Road), also owned by Coleman family members, received a shout-out from *Coastal Living* in 2010 as one of the best fish houses on the East Coast.

Shrimp boats bring their catch into Calabash and other Carolina ports.

Several large restaurants are located along the waterfront with views of the docks. Capt. Nance's Seafood (910-579-2574) on Nance Street serves shrimp and fish brought in daily by boats owned by the Nance brothers.

Typically, restaurants in Calabash are casual and maybe a bit old fashioned. Local shrimp, caught by the fishing fleet docked in the inlet, is the most common menu item, served boiled or fried. Oysters are served "roasted" or raw as a "cocktail" on lettuce. Local flounder is abundant, often stuffed with crabmeat. Deviled crabs, a sort of spicy crabcake stuffed into a crab shell, are a local specialty.

Fast fact: Jimmy Durante helped make Calabash a household name with his signature sign-off: "Good night, Mrs. Calabash, wherever you are!" Local lore claims that Durante came to town back in 1940 and coined this phrase as he bid farewell to Lucy Coleman after eating at her family's restaurant. Durante himself said the sign-off was directed to his wife in California. Perhaps both stories are true.

These days, most restaurants offer their seafood grilled and sautéed as well as fried, and huge combo platters are the norm with prices typically topping out at about $15. Steaks and burgers are also available on most menus for those who don't eat seafood.

For a more upscale dining experience, try the Boundary House (910-579-8888; www.boundaryhouserestaurant.com) next to Callahan's Gifts. The contemporary interior houses a large bar where you can enjoy seafood along with a Guinness draft, and the menu includes many nonseafood items.

Next door to the Boundary House, Callahan's Nautical Gifts of Calabash (910-579-2611; www.callahansgifts.com), prominently located at the corner of Beach Drive and River Road, is a shopping destination not to be missed. Growing steadily since 1978, it offers 35,000 square feet of browsing nirvana. Home decor, beach wear, jewelry, and stationery line the aisles, but the biggest draw is St. Nick Nacks, a Christmas shop gone global with 100 decorated trees, 3 million ornaments, and decorations for every holiday in the year from Valentine's Day to Halloween.

For a homestyle meal, mingle with the locals at Granny Allyn's Country Kitchen (910-579-8989) at 1530 Thomasboro Road in front of the firehouse. This longtime favorite serves made-from-scratch breakfasts, fresh homegrown veggies, and meat-and-three plate lunches at incredibly reasonable prices.

Did you know? The shrimp season runs from June to the end of November in these waters and many Calabash restaurants close for the season when fresh local shrimp is no longer available. Always call to make sure the spot you're heading for is open, and to make reservations, always a good idea and essential during the high summer season.

If you like this . . . enjoy a family breakfast at the locally owned **Sunrise Pancake House** *(910-575-1001; www.sunrisepancakehouse.com) on Beach Drive.*

For something entirely different, plan a tea party at the ✍ ♂ Calabash Garden Tea Room (910-579-9500; www.calabashgardentearoom.com), a unique Victorian experience on Beach Drive.

If you should decide to extend your visit to Calabash, you have a lodging option besides the many golf resorts. The ⟨ᵞ⟩ Rose Bed & Breakfast (1-866-340-0139; www.therosebandb.com), a charming farmhouse just off US 17, is conveniently located to all the area's attractions.

Besides eating, the other main reason to come to Calabash is to board a boat for a day of inshore or offshore fishing, a sunset cruise, or a dolphin-watch adventure.

Boating on the ICW leads to unihabited islands.

What Exactly Is Calabash-Style Seafood?

A lot of ink has been spilled over the years trying to resolve this issue. Some writers refer to lightly battered, fried seafood as Calabash-style. Others say it's a general term that refers to really fresh, right-out-of-the-water seafood, served in huge quantities, at reasonable prices.

Every restaurant in Calabash has its own "secret" recipe, but in fact most of them have little to do with batter, especially when the seafood in question is shrimp. Local recipes call for shrimp to be soaked in milk, buttermilk, or evaporated milk, before being dipped in a dry mixture of cornmeal and flour or breadcrumbs, with various seasonings, usually pepper and paprika, added. The shrimp is then flash fried in peanut oil and ideally arrives piping hot at the table with an almost transparent coating that lets the pink of the shrimp show through.

One thing is certain. If you ask the residents of the town what makes the famous local style of seafood cooking distinctive, they'll agree on one thing: It's cooked in Calabash.

The ✎ Calabash Fishing Fleet (910-570-0017 or 1-866-575-0017; www
.calabashfishingfleet.com) offers party boat trips, with reasonable per-person rates, including 12-hour trips out to the Gulf Stream and summer night shark fishing, plus dolphin cruises with guaranteed sightings.

If you like this . . . the Hurricane Fleet Fishing Center (1-800-373-2004; www.hurricanefleet.com) also schedules several charter boat excursions, plus trips angling for sharks and tuna. A special cruise takes a close-up look at a shrimp boat in action.

The ✎ Super Voyager III and Voyager Fishing Charters (910-575-0111 or 843-626-9500; www.supervoyagerdeepseafishing.com), also based in Calabash, operate some of the largest party boats on the coast, making 12 to 24 hour fishing trips out to the Gulf Stream, as well as dolphin adventure cruises for all ages.

From Calabash, it's a short drive over the border to the many attractions of the Grand Strand in South Carolina.

The Grand Strand
& Myrtle Beach

FOR GENERATIONS, THE BEACH VACATION has been a treasured tradition and a chance to get back to basics. Soak up the sun. Play in the surf. Stroll the strand. Eat fresh seafood. And nowhere does this formula come together better than the 60 miles of beaches along the South Carolina shore known as the Grand Strand.

Consistently ranked one of the top family beach destinations in the country by everyone from the Travel Channel to AAA, the Grand Strand attracts more than 14 million people every year, drawn by the wide variety of offerings packed into this compact stretch of coast. The readers of *Southern Living* magazine rate it one of the top two beaches in the South.

Centered on Myrtle Beach, the Grand Strand's 60 miles of white sand sweep past a varied collection of oceanfront villages and towns, from the laid-back "shabby arrogance" of Pawleys Island in the south to the hot nightlife of Ocean Drive in the north.

There is something along the Grand Strand to entertain every age group and income level, from luxurious resorts laced with golf courses to ecotours along blackwater rivers; from high-flying parasailing to kid-pleasing carrousels.

Over 100 golf courses designed by the sport's top stars make this the Seaside Golf Capital of the world. In a single weekend, a golfer can play courses designed by Arnold Palmer, Jack Nicklaus, Robert Trent Jones, and Greg Norman. Nearly a dozen courses here have been included in *Golf Digest*'s top 100 courses in America, more than any other destination.

Amusement parks, roller coasters, and water parks line the Strand. More than 50 miniature golf courses welcome players day and night. Beachfront options range from kiteboarding to sea kayaking. Or you can hang up your GONE FISHIN' sign and cast a line from beach, pier, or charter boat.

LEFT: Little River and Murrells Inlet both offer dining with a view.

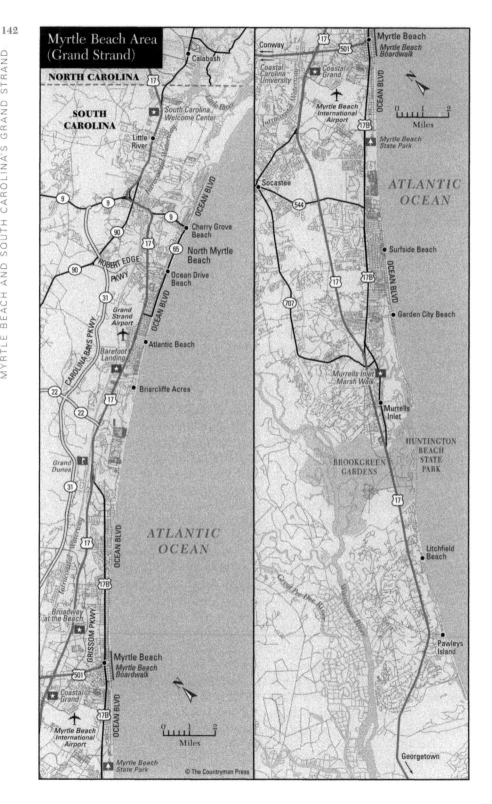

Myrtle Beach Area
(Grand Strand)

NORTH CAROLINA

SOUTH
CAROLINA

South Carolina
Welcome Center

Little
River

Cherry Grove
Beach

North Myrtle
Beach

Ocean Drive
Beach

ROBERT EDGE
PKWY

Grand
Strand
Airport

Barefoot
Landing

Atlantic Beach

Briarcliffe Acres

CAROLINA BAYS PKWY

Grand
Dunes

ATLANTIC
OCEAN

OCEAN BLVD

Broadway
at the Beach

GRISSOM PKWY

Myrtle Beach
Myrtle Beach
Boardwalk

Coastal
Grand

Myrtle Beach
International
Airport

Myrtle Beach
State Park

Miles

© The Countryman Press

Calabash

Conway

Coastal
Carolina
University

Coastal
Grand

Myrtle Beach
International
Airport

Socastee

Intracoastal Waterway

Myrtle Beach
Myrtle Beach
Boardwalk

OCEAN BLVD

Myrtle Beach
State Park

ATLANTIC
OCEAN

Surfside Beach

Garden City Beach

OCEAN BLVD

Murrells Inlet
Marsh Walk

Murrells
Inlet

HUNTINGTON
BEACH
STATE
PARK

BROOKGREEN
GARDENS

Great Pee Dee River

Litchfield
Beach

Pawleys
Island

Georgetown

Miles

Finding Your Base

Fifty years ago, the Grand Strand consisted of a string of vacation villages, separated by miles of sand and thick groves of pine trees. Although the original limits of these communities have blurred with modern development, each retains a distinct personality that can add an extra dimension to your vacation.

Today, all areas of the Strand are easily accessible via automobile, but traffic can be a problem, especially during the busy summer months. Besides, who wants to spend time in the car on vacation? So select your home base with care.

Locations can also be divided into oceanfront and inland. Ocean Boulevard, known as the Boulevard, or sometimes just "the 'Vard," is the road closest to the ocean. However, the Boulevard is not continuous from north to south. One section runs along the coast through North Myrtle Beach then rejoins US 17. Another loops down to the water in Myrtle Beach proper.

The Atlantic Intracoastal Waterway (ICW) comes over the North Carolina line in Little River, splitting the long sandy island of Myrtle Beach off from the mainland. The ICW joins the Waccamaw River before emptying into Winyah Bay, a noted wildlife habitat, just north of Georgetown. The peninsula between the river and the ocean goes by the name of the Winyah Neck.

US 17, also known as the King's Highway, runs north–south through the interior, between the ocean and the ICW. Visitors soon discover that there are several US 17s running through the region, but all parallel the beach. Business 17 splits from Bypass 17 at the northern end of Myrtle Beach, then rejoins it at the southern end of the Strand in Murrells Inlet. A branch of Business 17 follows the waterfront in Murrells Inlet, before looping around to rejoin the main highway north of Litchfield Beach. South of Surfside, the Kings Highway becomes the Ocean Highway, running on through Georgetown to Charleston, about 100 miles away.

SC 31, a new expressway, runs along the western side of the ICW, speeding traffic around the oceanfront congestion and spurring development in Carolina Forest and other mainland communities. New bridges make access to the beaches easier and give drivers a number of alternatives to the congestion often present at the US 501 bridge, once the main entrance to the Grand Strand.

Approaching from the west, US 501 from Conway provides access directly to

Quick tips:

• If you're coming to the Grand Strand down US 17 from North Carolina, make your first stop the **South Carolina Welcome Center** (843-249-1111; www.discoversouth carolina.com) close to the state line in Little River. A few miles farther south on US 17, the **North Myrtle Beach Chamber of Commerce Welcome Center** (843-281-2662; www.northmyrtlebeachchamber .com) is a great source of visitor info about the Strand. Be sure to arm yourself with a local map to help you navigate the many branches of US 17 and find the best traffic work-arounds.

• North Myrtle Beach is often abbreviated in addresses as NMB. Myrtle Beach "proper," also divided into north, central, and southern sections, is sometimes referred to as MB. We'll be using these abbreviations to help you keep your bearings.

the center of Myrtle Beach; SC 9 goes direct to the North Strand; SC 544 from Conway is a shortcut to Surfside Beach and the South Strand.

The Main Street Connector bridge delivers you straight into the heart of shag territory on Ocean Drive's Main Street. The SC 22 bridge leads to the outlet shopping and restaurants in the Restaurant Row/Lake Arrowhead section between North Myrtle and MB proper. If you're headed for Murrells Inlet or Pawleys Island, take SC 707 off SC 544 for a backdoor way around the traffic.

Quick tip: The multiple versions of US 17 and the similarity of street names in North Myrtle and MB proper confuses the dickens out of most GPS systems, not to mention the various online mapping systems. We've arranged our listings by region, so you'll have some idea of which way you're headed. Most attraction websites offer detailed directions. If in doubt, call ahead.

SC 90, a scenic byway, is a backroad alternative to the traffic on the major highways. It runs from Cherry Grove to Conway through fields and forests.

Profiles of each of the Strand's communities follow, moving from Little River at the North Carolina line south to Georgetown, 60 miles north of Charleston. For suggestions on where to party by the water, see our section on Bars, Nightlife, and Happy Hours later in this chapter.

LITTLE RIVER

Little River, a laid-back fishing village on the North Carolina border, has long been a favorite getaway for locals, who headed for the riverfront restaurants and bars for a respite from the frantic tourist season farther south on the Strand. The tourists discovered Little River long since, but the village retains its small-town charm with docks along the river, live oak trees draped with moss overlooking shady streets, and a party reputation that's still going strong.

While many tourists still come to Little River to board headboats or charter vessels for days of fishing at sea, many more voyagers are after different fish—a big payoff aboard the casino boats that take on passengers here, then head out into international waters for a day of legal gambling and Vegas-style buffets. The Sun-Cruz Aquasino (843-280-2933 or 1-800-474-DICE; www.suncruzaquasino.com) and Big "M" Casino (843-249-9811 or 877-250-LUCK; www.bigmcasino.com) both offer slots as well as blackjack, poker, roulette, and other table games aboard day and evening cruises.

Little River is a noted dining destination as well. Favorite restaurants along the waterfront include ✒ Crab Catcher's (843-280-2025; www.crabcatchers.net) and the venerable ✒ Capt. Juel's Hurricane Restaurant (843-249-2211; www.captjuelshurricane.com), serving seafood since 1945.

Quick tip: The Little River casino boats offer many coupons and special deals, so check their websites before you set sail.

Little River's best known annual event is the Blue Crab Festival (www .bluecrabfestival.org), held every May on the historic waterfront. The

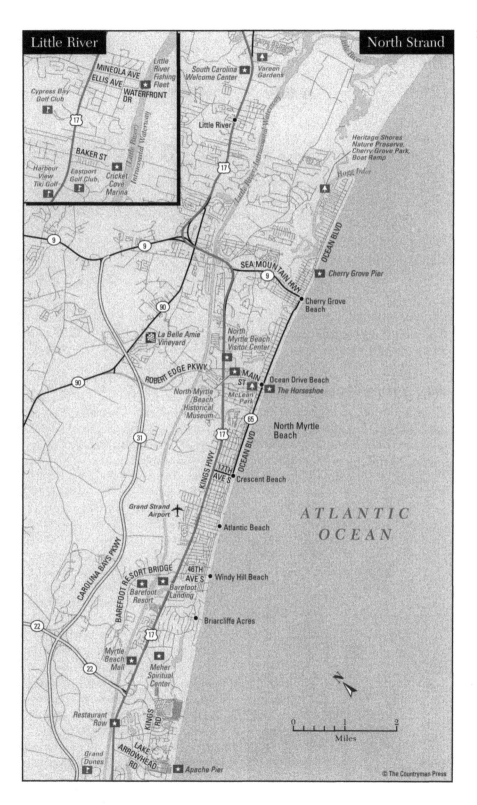

Little River

North Strand

MINEOLA AVE
ELLIS AVE
WATERFRONT DR
Little River Fishing Fleet
Cypress Bay Golf Club
BAKER ST
Harbour View Tiki Golf
Eastport Golf Club
Cricket Cove Marina

South Carolina Welcome Center
Vareen Gardens
Little River
Heritage Shores Nature Preserve, Cherry Grove Park, Boat Ramp
Hogg Inlet
OCEAN BLVD
SEA MOUNTAIN HWY
Cherry Grove Pier
Cherry Grove Beach
La Belle Amie Vineyard
North Myrtle Beach Visitor Center
ROBERT EDGE PKWY
MAIN ST
Ocean Drive Beach
The Horseshoe
North Myrtle Beach Historical Museum
McLean Park
North Myrtle Beach
KINGS HWY
OCEAN BLVD
17TH AVE S
Crescent Beach
Grand Strand Airport
Atlantic Beach

ATLANTIC OCEAN

CAROLINA BAYS PKWY
BAREFOOT RESORT BRIDGE
46TH AVE S
Windy Hill Beach
Barefoot Resort
Barefoot Landing
Briarcliffe Acres
Myrtle Beach Mall
Meher Spiritual Center
Restaurant Row
KINGS RD
LAKE ARROWHEAD RD
Grand Dunes
Apache Pier

0   1   2
Miles

© The Countryman Press

Top 10 Don't Miss: The North Strand

- Play a round of late-night minigolf next to the erupting volcano at Hawaiian Rumble.
- Watch the shaggers (or join in) at Harold's or Duck's on Ocean Drive's Main Street.
- Sun on the locals' "secret beach" along the ICW.
- Eat a mess of crab on the Little River waterfront.
- Sample local wines at La Belle Amie Vineyard.
- Ride a bike along the beach from Ocean Drive to Cherry Grove.
- Tune in to the philosophy of Meher Baba at the Meher Spiritual Center.
- Get a bird's-eye view of the Strand on the second-story deck at the Cherry Grove Pier.
- Chill out in the meditation garden at McLean Park.
- Kayak Hogg Inlet.

October Shrimp & Jazz Festival, sponsored by the Little River Chamber of Commerce (843-249-6604; www.littleriverchamber.org), has the same charm without the huge crowds.

NORTH MYRTLE BEACH

The favorite vacation destination for the baby boomer crowd, North Myrtle Beach (NMB) is actually a collection of four separate beach communities, Cherry Grove, Ocean Drive, Crescent Beach, and Windy Hill, which banded together in 1968 to form the City of North Myrtle Beach (843-280-5555; www.nmb.us).

Cherry Grove is farthest north, set amid marsh near the mouth of the Little River. SC 9, here the Sea Mountain Highway, runs from US 17 straight down to the ocean. Head north on Ocean Boulevard to the Cherry Grove Pier (843-249-1625; www.cherrygrove pier.com), the only ocean fishing pier in NMB. The second-story observation deck here provides a great view of the coast.

Strolling the Strand remains a favorite activity for visitors and locals.

Marshy Hogg Inlet, running behind the northern half of Cherry Grove, is a tremendous resource for crabbing, shrimping, fishing, and bird-watching. A couple of nearby parks offer access: Russell Burgess Coastal Preserve at the end of Duffy Street and the Heritage Shores Nature Pre-serve, with a fishing pier, boardwalks, restrooms, and a floating boat dock,

Main Street in Ocean Drive hosts frequent street festivals.

adjacent to the Cherry Grove Park and Boat Ramp (843-280-5570; http://parks.nmb.us) at the end of 53rd Avenue North. The inlet is a popular spot for kayakers, of both the fishing and birdwatching persuasions.

A short trip south down Ocean Boulevard brings you to Ocean Drive, known as O.D., home base of the shag. The O.D. Pavilion (843-238-3787; www.odpavilion.com), last of the open-air dance halls, sits at the Horseshoe where Main Street meets Ocean Boulevard.

While high-rise time-shares and condominiums have grown up around it, Main Street, O.D., has retained its casual, laid-back beach community character. Sidewalks are lined with local shops, cafés, raw bars, and hot dog stands, mixed in with dance clubs where beach music seeps out the doors all day and well into the night.

> **Quick tip:** The Main Street Connector from SC 31 takes you straight down Ocean Drive's Main Street via a bridge over the ICW.

Main Street provides the setting for many NMB street parties, including the free Music on Main concert series on the first and third Thursdays of each month, May to September. Dancing in the street is highly encouraged.

In addition to the summer concert series, Ocean Drive's Main Street hosts the St. Patrick's Day Parade and Festival, Mayfest on Main, and, in September, the Irish Italian International Festival, complete with a spaghetti eating contest. Check with the North Myrtle Beach Chamber of Commerce (843-281-2662; www.northmyrtlebeachchamber.com) for details.

Other community events, including the Sounds of Summer Concert Series and a free family outdoor movie series, are held a couple of blocks south of Main Street at McLean Park, on Oak Drive. Considered NMB's loveliest outdoor space, McLean Park (843-280-5570; http://parks.nmb.us) has a 2-acre lake, a paved walking and fitness trail, an EVOS "exercise in disguise" playground, lighted tennis courts, and a meditation garden.

As you travel south on either Ocean Boulevard or US 17, Ocean Drive blends seamlessly with Crescent Beach. SC 63/17th Avenue South, leading down to a major beach access, takes you through the center of Crescent Beach.

> **Quick tip:** 🏨 ♿ **Grand Strand Resorts** (1-800-367-6515; www .northmyrtlebeach.com) represents over 60 properties in every section of NMB, including many dog-friendly destinations.

A great place to find out more about the history of the North Stand, from Native American oyster roasts to the birth of the shag, is the North Myrtle Beach Historical Museum (843-427-7668; www.northmyrtlebeachmuseum.com), at 799 Second Avenue North, scheduled to open in 2012.

At 28th Avenue South, Ocean Boulevard is interrupted. There's no through traffic along the ocean in the town of Atlantic Beach, a traditionally African American community that isn't part of NMB. Ocean Boulevard resumes at 33rd Avenue South in the community of Windy Hill, still made up primarily of traditional beach cottages.

At the southern end of Windy Hill, off 48th Avenue South, the Towers at North Beach Plantation (1-800-615-3598; www.northbeachrentals.com), one of NMB's most posh resorts, occupies a secluded oceanfront location next to White Point Swash. Amenities at the resort include a 2.5-acre private water park, the Cinzia Spa (843-361-2772; www.thecinziaspa.com), and the highly acclaimed 21 Main Prime Steak House (www.21main.com), the first location of this family of high-end eateries outside of New York.

The Town of Atlantic Beach (843-663-2284; www.townofatlanticbeachsc .com), known as "the Black Pearl," provided a popular beach resort for African Americans during the era of segregation. Founded in the 1930s, Atlantic Beach was home to numerous hotels, nightclubs, and restaurants owned and operated by African American families. During the 1940s, it became known for its nightlife scene, featuring members of big bands passing through town, and dancing until dawn in the oceanfront pavilions. In 1954 Hurricane Hazel destroyed many of these oceanfront businesses, but Atlantic Beach today remains the only African American owned beach in the nation. Atlantic Beach can be found between 29th and 32nd Avenues South off US 17. There are no connecting streets with the NMB towns on either side. Atlantic Watersports (843-272-2420; www.atlantic watersports.net), offering parasailing, banana boat rides, fun cycle rentals, and refreshments, is located on the beach at the foot of 32nd Avenue.

BAREFOOT LANDING

At the intersection of 48th Avenue South and US 17 sits the North Strand's best-known landmark, Barefoot Landing (843-272-8349; www.bflanding.com). Built on boardwalks over marshlands bordering the ICW, and around a 27-acre freshwater lake, the complex is home to herons, turtles, and alligators, as well as 150 shops, more than a dozen waterfront restaurants, the House of Blues, and the Alabama Theatre.

The *Barefoot Princess* (843-272-2140; www.mbriverboat.com), a riverboat departing from the docks near Greg Norman's restaurant, cruises the ICW on

Top 10 Don't Miss: Barefoot Landing

- Check out the rock and roll music, Outsider art and bottle cap decor at the House of Blues.
- Watch a feeding at Alligator Adventure.
- Take a cruise aboard the *Barefoot Princess*.
- Order up happy hour bargains on Greg Norman's deck.
- Discover the spooky side of the beach at Ghosts and Legends.
- Get your picture taken with endangered tigers at Preservation Station.
- Jet Ski out to visit the dolphins.
- Rev up with a multimedia show at the Alabama Theatre.
- Toss a flounder at the Flying Fish Grill.
- Sample the elderberry wine at Carolina Vineyards.

TOP: Dine aboard a riverboat at Barefoot Landing. BELOW: Bottlecap art at the House of Blues

sightseeing and dinner excursions. The excellent Alligator Adventure, a ghost tour, and an exhibit of endangered tigers add to the appeal for families. A frequent winner of Most Popular Tourist Attraction and Best Place to Take Out-of-Towner Awards, Barefoot's blend of laid-back waterfront shopping and attractions is much imitated. But this is the original.

Just across the ICW from Barefoot Landing, the enormous Barefoot Resort (843-692-2299 or 1-800-548-9904; www.myrtlebeachbarefoot resort.com) offers a wide range of accommodations and amenities, including four championship golf courses. Reached via its own bridge across the waterway at 49th Avenue South, the resort provides an escape from the sometimes frantic pace of life found on the oceanfront. Amenities include more than a dozen pools, walking and biking paths, a free summer shuttle to the beach, and a top-notch spa, Jasmine (843-390-7015; www.jasminespabarefoot.com). Barefoot Water Sports (843-455-4888; www.barefootresortwatersports .com) rents Jet Skis, yachts, and pontoon boats, and conducts Jet Ski dolphin tours.

Shagging in Ocean Drive

While there's not much agreement on where or when the sweet-steppin' dance called the shag developed (see our History & Nature section for an overview), in the 21st century the heart of shag culture definitely can be located on Main Street in NMB's Ocean Drive neighborhood.

Since the first Society of Stranders (SOS) reunion in 1980, dancers and "beach diggers" have made pilgrimages to the clubs along Main Street, looking for the sounds that made the summers of their youth so memorable. That first gathering proved so successful that **SOS** (www .shagdance.com) has expanded to a year-round schedule of events, including annual ten-day Spring Safaris and Fall Migrations, attracting up to 10,000 shaggers at a time, plus weekend gatherings in winter and summer.

Shops dedicated to shaggers line Ocean Drive's Main Street.

At the same time, other beach music and shag events held in NMB have flourished. The annual **Carolina Beach Music Awards** (1-888-323-2822; www.cammy.org), held in November, sets off a week of shagging at the Ocean Drive clubs, capped off with a gala awards ceremony at the Alabama Theatre.

The **National Shag Dance Championships** (www.shagnationals.com) are held on weekends in January and March. The locally based Ocean Drive Shag Club (www.od shagclub.com) and O.D. Pavilion Social & Shag Club (www.odpavilionsocialshagclub .com) sponsor regular events, as do shag clubs from around the South on annual outings.

Plenty of shaggers have retired to NMB—or never left—and today you can listen to beach music, watch shaggers practice their moves, and even learn a step or two your-self, every day of the year on Ocean Drive.

Two clubs that face each other across O.D.'s Main Street a block from the ocean keep the shag fires flaming, hosting live beach music bands and convivial shag gather-ings all year. Y **Duck's Beach Club** (843-663-3858; www.ducksatoceandrive.com) and Y **Fat Harold's Beach Club** (843-249-5779; www.fatharolds.com) have a lot in com-mon—huge wooden dance floors, top DJs spinning beach music, grills where you can stoke your energy with a juicy burger, and great happy hour prices. Wander into the back room at Fat Harold's to see pictures of the many famous shaggers and musicians who have graced these floors, as well as the Keepers of the Dance (www.keepersof thedance.com) wall of fame. The club also offers free introductory shag lessons on Tuesday evenings.

If you like this . . . Fat Harold's has a second location in Cherry Grove, Y **Harold's on the Ocean** (843-249-5601; www.haroldsontheocean.com), otherwise known as HOTO's, hosting outdoor concerts on the beach during the summer.

The OD Beach Club is a popular hangout.

The most iconic of the shag clubs, the **O.D. Pavilion** (843-280-0715; www.od pavilion.net), sits right on the sand at the end of Main Street, an area called the Horseshoe. The last of the open-air dance pavilions that once defined summer on the Carolina coast, this open-sided dance hall drops its shutters in winter, but the beat goes on daily from Memorial Day to Labor Day, plus on weekends in spring and fall.

Across the Horseshoe, the **Ocean Drive Beach and Golf Resort** (1-800-438-9590; www.oceandriveresort.com) provides shaggers with lodging, plenty of additional floors for dancing, and bars for partying, including the ocean-level O.D. Beach Club, opening directly onto the sand; and the ⅄ **Spanish Galleon** (1-800-438-9590; www.thespanishgalleon.net), blessed with an enormous dance floor. The Shaggers Hall of Fame occupies the mezzanine level.

Other Ocean Drive clubs with a special place in the hearts of shaggers include the ⅄ **O.D. Arcade and Lounge** (843-249-6460; www.odarcade.com) in the first block of S. Ocean Boulevard; the **Boulevard Grill** (843-249-1061), across the street; ⅄ (ᵖ) **Deckerz** (843-280-1200; www.deckerznmb.com), a block down Main at Hillside; and ⅄ **Pirates Cove Lounge** (843-249-8942; www.piratescovelounge.com), with its crow's nest deck overlooking the corner of Main Street and Ocean Boulevard and live music every night.

Restaurants along Main Street cater to dancers' appetites. Favorites that have stood the test of time include **Hoskins** (843-249-2014) for breakfast, meat-and-three plates, and fresh seafood; **Duffy's Seafood Shack** (843-281-9840; www.duffyst.com) for its raw bar; **Flynn's Irish Tavern** (843-249-6533; www.flynnstavern.com); and the ⅃ ⅄ **International Café** (843-281-2325; www.theinternationalcafenmb.com), with a late-night menu served till 2 AM and 40 beers from around the world.

Not all the shagging action is on Main Street. ⅃ **Boom Boom's Raw Bar** (843-427-7304; www.boomboomsrawbar.com), at 13th Avenue North in the marina, hosts top beach music bands, no cover required. (ᵖ) **Swillie's Hideaway** (843-280-5301; www.thehideawaynmb.com), across US 17 on Second Avenue North, books blues and jazz bands. At ⅄ **Little John's Bar & Grill** (843-427-4024; www.littlejohnsbarand grill.com), just west of US 17 on Sixth Avenue South, you can party all night with the locals amid walls covered with shag memorabilia.

Shagging even inspires its own retail. Along Main Street, stop by **Beach Memories Art** (843-249-7215; www.beachmemoriesart.com) to see the work of owner Becky Stowe, official artist of the Society of Stranders. That's her artwork up on the O.D. water tower. A block down Main, **Judy's House of Oldies** (843-249-8649; www.judyshouseofoldies.com) stocks the music that will get your feet moving. On US 17 next to Big Lots, the **Shoe Center** (843-272-6515; www.shagshoes.com) has all the right footwear to keep you dancing in style.

Just past Barefoot Landing, the Kings Highway (US 17) enters an area that until recently was largely forested, the home of deer and raccoons rather than high-rise resorts. Today, some of Myrtle Beach's largest shopping destinations are found here, including the enormous Myrtle Beach Mall, a Walmart Supercenter, and the Tanger Outlet Center.

Just south of the malls, the eateries of Restaurant Row sometimes attract a gridlock of crowds during the evening dinner rush.

Twenty years ago, most of the accommodations in this area were campgrounds set amid the pine trees. Now large resorts dominate the oceanfront, although two campgrounds on the beach survive: the Myrtle Beach Travel Park (843-449-3714; www.myrtlebeachtravelpark.com) and the Apache Family Campground (843-449-7323; www.apachefamily campground.com), home of one of the region's longest fishing piers. The Apache Pier (843-497-6486) and its restaurant, Croakers on the Pier (843-497-5331), are open to the public.

Several other stretches of this coast remain largely undeveloped. The Town of Briarcliffe Acres (www.townof briarcliffe.us), developed in the 1940s and one of the region's earliest planned communities, maintains its low-key res-idential profile.

Next door, the 🐾 ♿ Meher Spiritual Center (843-272-5777; www .mehercenter.org) sits on land virtually untouched since the 1940s. Founded by Elizabeth Chapin Patterson, a devotee of the Indian spiritual teacher Meher Baba, on property donated by her family, the center continues to provide a place for spiritual retreats and meditation. The 500-acre property is a designated state wildlife sanctuary with nature trails, two lakes, and a long stretch of unspoiled oceanfront.

The Meher Spiritual Center welcomes visitors to participate in many activities, including music concerts, films, and informal talks on Meher Baba's mes-sage of love and truth. First-time guests are required to take a free tour of the center, usually offered on weekends. Cabins are also available for individuals, families, and groups seeking a place for spiritual renewal.

At the southern end of Restaurant Row, drivers are presented with a choice. The Kings Highway/US 17 Business bears off to the east, leading down toward the oceanfront. The

> **Quick tip:** SC 22, the Conway Connector, crosses the ICW and joins US 17 at the Tanger Outlets.
>
> **Fast fact:** Indian spiritual teacher Meher Baba maintained silence from 1925 until his death in 1969, communicating via hand gestures and the written word. He coined the phrase, "Don't Worry, Be Happy," which inspired Bobby McFerrin's 1989 Grammy Award–winning Song of the Year.

Nature trails provide good birding close to the beach.

US 17 Bypass bears off to the west, taking an inland route that passes Grand Dunes, Broadway at the Beach, and Coastal Grand Mall en route to Murrells Inlet. You can hardly miss the junction: the glittering edifice of the Carolina Opry sits in the V.

DOWNTOWN MYRTLE BEACH

The history of Myrtle Beach is inextricably interwoven with that of the Burroughs family and their business associates, the Collins and Chapin families. Without the vision of these founding families, there might be no Myrtle Beach today.

Before the Civil War, Franklin Burroughs settled in Conway, founding a flourishing turpentine and naval stores enterprise with riverboats running up and down the Waccamaw River. After the war, Burroughs, with partner Benjamin Collins, expanded into tobacco and timber and built a railroad across the swamps that would eventually turn the coast into a major tourist destination. The Burroughs and Collins families built the first seaside hotel, the first bathhouse, the first pavilion, and the first general store.

The Hard Rock theme park, with rock 'n roll coasters and live entertainment, lasted just one season. Will it reopen?

The Conway and Seaside Railroad connected Conway with New Town, now Myrtle Beach, in 1900. The beach got its permanent name the same year in a contest won by Miss Addie, the widow of Franklin Burroughs, who named it for the Southern Wax Myrtle (*Myrica cerifera*), a native shrub that grows abundantly in the area. "Edgewater" was runner-up.

In 1912 the Burroughs family joined forces with Simeon Chapin to form Myrtle Beach Farms, which once owned some 80,000 acres, including the entire coastline between Little River and Murrells Inlet.

Today the company, now called Burroughs & Chapin (www.burroughschapin .com), and still owned and operated by the members of the original families, remains a major landowner and developer in the area. It owns the wildly successful Broadway at the Beach, the Coastal Grand Mall, the Grande Dunes resort, plus hotels, residential communities, golf and miniature golf courses, amusement parks, and water parks up and down the Grand Strand.

The Burroughs & Chapin Company helped shaped the face of Myrtle Beach through many civic bequests. It donated the land for Myrtle Beach State Park to South Carolina, and gave the city of Myrtle Beach property at the foot of most streets leading to the beach, specifying that it remain open for public access to the ocean. Other grants established an art museum, gave land for a convention center,

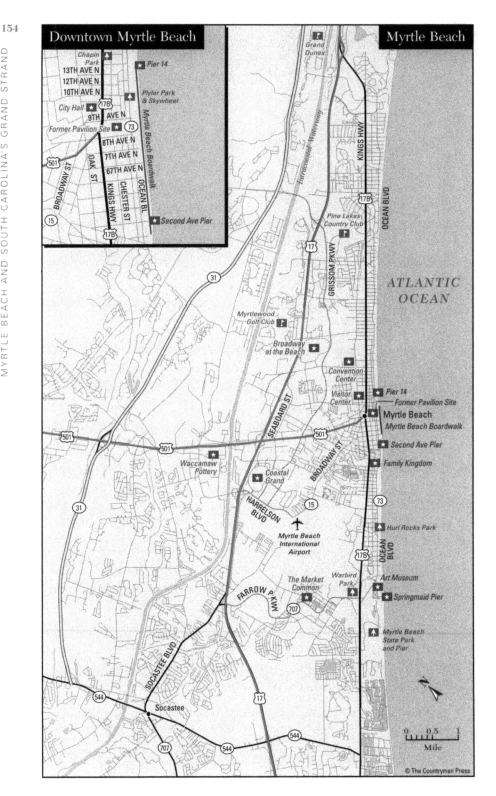

Downtown Myrtle Beach

Myrtle Beach

Chapin Park
13TH AVE N
12TH AVE N
10TH AVE N
City Hall
9TH AVE N
Former Pavilion Site
8TH AVE N
7TH AVE N
67TH AVE N

Pier 14

Plyler Park & Skywheel

Myrtle Beach Boardwalk

BROADWAY ST
OAK ST
KINGS HWY
CHESTER ST
OCEAN BL

Second Ave Pier

Grand Dunes

KINGS HWY

OCEAN BLVD

Pine Lakes Country Club

ATLANTIC OCEAN

GRISSOM PKWY

Myrtlewood Golf Club

Broadway at the Beach

Convention Center

Visitor Center

Pier 14

Former Pavilion Site

Myrtle Beach
Myrtle Beach Boardwalk

Second Ave Pier

Family Kingdom

SEABOARD ST

BROADWAY ST

Waccamaw Pottery

Coastal Grand

HARRELSON BLVD

Hurl Rocks Park

OCEAN BLVD

Myrtle Beach International Airport

The Market Common

Warbird Park

Art Museum

Springmaid Pier

FARROW PKWY

Myrtle Beach State Park and Pier

SOCASTEE BLVD

Socastee

0   0.5   1
Mile

© The Countryman Press

Top 10 Don't Miss: Myrtle Beach

- Enjoy hot dogs and beer after a stroll on the boardwalk.
- Explore the heights of Mount Atlanticus, an indoor minigolf course built in a parking deck.
- Get a bird's-eye view from the top of the SkyWheel.
- Order cocktails on a pier.
- Take in the exhibits at a traditional seaside cottage turned art museum.
- Ride the giant wooden coaster at Family Kingdom.
- Get lost in Ripley's Marvelous Mirror Maze.
- Enjoy happy hour specials at the restaurants in Market Common.
- Shop the day away at Coastal Grand Mall, Myrtle Beach Mall, or the Tanger Outlets.
- Paddle the blackwater Waccamaw River from the dock in downtown Conway.

and provided funding for programs at Coastal Carolina University, Francis Marion University, Horry-Georgetown Technical College, and other institutions of higher learning.

The Seaside Inn, built in 1901 by the Burroughs Company, was the first hotel to open on Myrtle Beach. It had no plumbing or electricity, but you could get three meals and a bed for the night for just $2. The old inn was demolished in the 1920s, but its beachfront pavilion at Ninth Avenue and Ocean Boulevard remained in use as The Attic dance club until 2006.

Although several so-called welcome centers line US 501 on the way into Myrtle Beach, these are privately operated and not affiliated with the official Myrtle Beach Convention and Vistors Bureau. For the real deal, visit the official Myrtle Beach Welcome Center (843-626-7444 or 1-800-356-3016; www.visitmyrtlebeach .com) in the Myrtle Beach Convention Center located at 1200 N. Oak Street in downtown MB. (While you're there, have a look at the South Carolina Hall of Fame and the Wyland Whaling Wall.) A second official welcome center is located in the Myrtle Beach International Airport arrivals area.

Jimmy Buffett's Margaritaville on Lake Broadway

On the Oceanfront

Myrtle Beach's first hotel, opened by the Burroughs family in 1901, sat on the oceanfront near today's Ninth Avenue North, and this remains the focus of the city's entertainment district even today. The new Myrtle Beach Boardwalk (myrtlebeachdowntown.com) provides a centerpiece and gathering spot for visitors of all ages both day and night.

Landmarks here include the Ripley's Believe It or Not! family of attractions, the new SkyWheel, and a real blast from the past, the Gay Dolphin Gift Cove (843-448-6550; www.gaydolphin .com), the Strand's largest and oldest gift shop. Founded in 1946, it has something for everyone among its seven levels of beach souvenirs.

Follow 9th or 10th Avenue North a couple of blocks inland from the boardwalk to find Broadway Street, the heart of old downtown Myrtle Beach and a hidden gem. City hall shares the street with art galleries, cafés, markets, and bars. Landmarks include the recently restored historic ♂ Myrtle Beach Train Depot (843-918-1050; www.cityofmyrtlebeach.com) and Mrs. Fish (843-946-6869; 919 Broadway Street), an unassuming spot popular with locals for inexpensive seafood. The annual Myrtle Beach FAME Festival (www.myrtle beachfamefestival.com) is held on Broadway every April.

North of the boardwalk along Ocean Boulevard, a neighborhood of luxurious beach cottages has been dubbed the Golden Mile. While most accommodations along this stretch are private rentals, the family owned ((y)) Island Vista Oceanfront Resort (1-888-733-7581; www.islandvista.com), a 12-story, all-suite hotel that opened in 2006, occupies a prime spot on the Golden Mile. Its ♂ Cypress Room and Lounge wows diners with a magnificent oceanfront view, plus French-inspired New American cuisine created by Chef Michael McKinnon.

The general location of most Myrtle Beach hotels, restaurants, and other attractions is easily determined by the number of the street address (most often Kings Highway or Ocean Boulevard). The first one or two numbers represent the cross street (1105 S. Ocean Boulevard will be near 11th Avenue South). The numbering system switches from

> **Did you know?** Myrtle Beach is the only incorporated municipality of that name in the United States. It's part of Horry (pronounced OH-ree, sometimes OW-ree) County, named for Brig. Gen. Peter Horry, a Revolutionary War hero who served under Brig. Gen. Francis Marion, the famous Swamp Fox. **Horry County** (843-915-5000; www.horry county.org) includes all the communities from the North Carolina state line, south to Surfside Beach along the oceanfront, and inland as far as the communities of Loris and Aynor. Conway is the county seat.

Most Myrtle Beach hotels have a lazy river to entertain guests.

> **Quick tip:** Despite the exclusive nature of the Golden Mile, public beach accesses, many with parking, are found all along this stretch of coast, and the beach here is likely to be less crowded than in more developed areas. Look for the public access points at the end of cross streets.

The Golden Mile is one of the less developed stretches of the Strand.

north to south at the rather obscure First Avenue, which splits as it reaches the ocean near the southern end of the boardwalk.

Heading south from the boardwalk, Ocean Boulevard is a steady stream of beachfront hotels, broken only by the Family Kingdom amusement park, all the way to the Springmaid Resort at the far southern end. Along this stretch of strand, the ⚓ ⚕ ⚲ ☊ Coral Beach Resort (1-800-556-1754; www.coralbeachmyrtlebeach resort.com) is an excellent choice, especially for families. Selected as the best family accommodations in Myrtle Beach by the Travel Channel, this hotel, located at 1105 S. Ocean Boulevard, has something for kids and their parents to do all day and well into the night. Ten water attractions include a water park with lazy river, two kiddie pools, four jacuzzis, and a heated indoor pool with a cool mermaid theme. The recreation center, with bowling alley, video arcade, pool tables, and a snack bar, hosts glow bowling nightly in season. Live music, karaoke, comedy, and magic shows entertain at the outdoor Beach Bar and MacDivot's Sports Pub. Rooms have private balconies, microwaves, and free WiFi. Suites and efficiencies with full kitchens are available.

If you like this . . . the Coral Beach's sister hotels in the family of ☊ Myrtle Beach Resorts (1-888-889-8113; www.myrtlebeach-resorts.com), the Sea Crest Oceanfront on South Beach, and the Holiday Inn Oceanfront at the Pavilion, devote similar attention to family activities.

If you follow Ocean Boulevard to its southern end and go straight across Kings Highway onto Farrow Parkway, you'll find yourself at the Strand's newest, hottest mixed-use destination, the Market Common (www.market commonmb.com). Numerous dining and shopping options are grouped together here, along with a movie theater and frequent free events.

The Coral Beach Resort rates among the best for families.

On the Bypass
Just south of the US 17 Business/Bypass split, Grande Dunes Boulevard leads down to the banks of the ICW and one of the Strand's finest new resort complexes. Developed by the Burroughs &

Chapin Company, Grande Dunes includes several hotel and restaurant options, including a Ruth's Chris Steakhouse, plus a golf course and marina. The star of the show, however, is the luxurious ♂ (ᵗᵖ) Marina Inn at Grande Dunes (1-866-437-4113; www.marinainnatgrandedunes.com). Rooms and suites equipped with high-end bedding, indoor and outdoor pools, access to a private beach cabana, plus golf, tennis, and fitness facilities, pontoon and Jet Ski rentals, and a selection of spa services, are a few of the amenities. The on-site ✍ Waterscapes Restaurant (843-913-2845), helmed by Chef James Clark, presents farm-to-table dishes that rank among the best on the Strand; and the seasonal Anchor Café (843-315-7855) at the marina is one of the region's best places to watch the sun set.

The Mediterranean-style Marina Inn at Grande Dunes overlooks the ICW.

A few blocks farther down the bypass brings you to Burroughs & Chapin's signature development, Broadway at the Beach (www.broadwayatthebeach.com). With more than 100 stores, 22 restaurants, an IMAX theater, Ripley's Aquarium,

The world's only pyramid-shaped Hard Rock Café at Broadway at the Beach

Top 10 Don't Miss: Broadway on the Beach

- Ride the historic carousel.
- Watch the fireworks from beside the Hard Rock Pyramid.
- Swirl your wand in MagicQuest.
- Discover the topsy-turvy world of Wonder-Works.
- Do the seventh-inning stretch at a Myrtle Beach Pelicans game.
- Slip-slide all day at Myrtle Waves.
- Gun your engine at the NASCAR Speed Park.
- Dance the night away at the clubs in Celebrity Square.
- Take a musical trip down memory lane at Legends in Concert.
- Walk below the sharks at Ripley's Aquarium.

the Palace entertainment hall, and a nightlife zone, this all-in-one festival experience combines shopping, entertainment, dining, and accommodations into a single award-winning destination, frequently winning the title of South Carolina's Top Tourist Attraction. The entertainment complex surrounding a 23-acre lake includes the Hard Rock Café pyramid, Planet Hollywood's globe, Legends in Concert, the world's first NASCAR Speed Park, plus a minor-league baseball stadium, and many hotels. You can take a boat ride, play miniature golf, watch a film, ride an antique merry-go-round, or just shop, shop, shop the day away at the many specialty stores. There's plenty of parking, and every space is free.

SURFSIDE BEACH & GARDEN CITY BEACH

A quiet beach town popular with retirees and families, Surfside Beach (843-913-6111; www.surfsidebeach.org) is mainly residential with a few hotels and restaurants at the foot of Surfside Drive, next to the Surfside Pier. Several time-share resorts occupy the west side of US 17, along with numerous shopping options.

From Surfside, Ocean Boulevard continues south along the oceanfront, becoming Waccamaw Drive as it enters Garden City Beach. The Pier at Garden City (843-651-9700; www.pieratgarden city.com), the community's main landmark, is located at the intersection with Atlantic Avenue, where a variety of seasonal rides and amusements can also be found. Several restaurants, including the 24-hour Sam's Corner, are located here as well.

Beyond Atlantic Avenue, Waccamaw Drive stretches far south on a peninsula between the ocean and a salt marsh. Two watering holes here, the Gulfstream Café (843-651-8808; centraarchy.com) and the Marlin Quay Marina Restaurant & Bar (843-651-6544; www.marlinquaymarina.com), offer fine views west across the marsh toward the Murrells Inlet Marsh Walk and the setting sun.

The Garden City Pier is considered the Strand's best.

Annual events in Surfside include free Sunday Serenade Concerts during the summer in the gazebo at the corner of Surfside Drive and Willow Drive; and the community Christmas tree lighting and Christmas Parade, in December.

The area is a popular one for camping. Myrtle Beach State Park (843-238-5325; www.southcarolinaparks.com), with RV sites and rental cabins, is just to the north of Surfside. If you prefer more amenities, three of the area's surviving oceanfront campgrounds lie next door. Pirateland Oceanfront Campground (1-800-443-2267; www.pirateland.com); Lakewood Camping Resort (843-238-5161 or 877-525-3966; www.lakewoodcampground.com); and Ocean Lakes Family Campground (877-510-1413; www.oceanlakes.com) all offer fun on both beach and freshwater lakes, with family activities during the summer months.

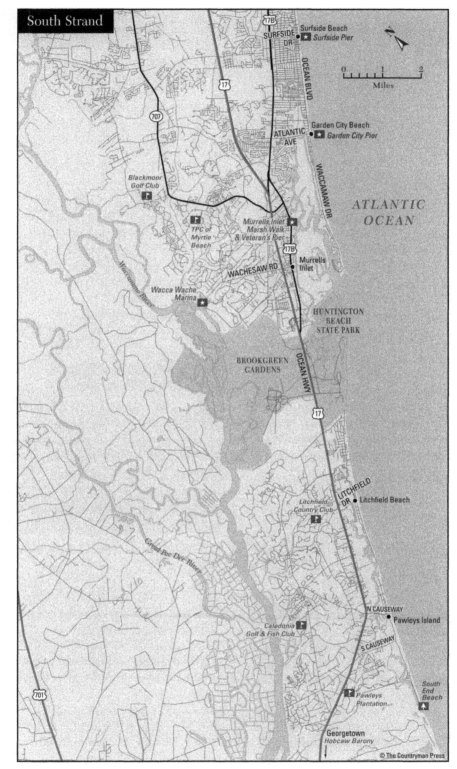

South Strand

Surfside Beach
SURFSIDE DR
Surfside Pier

OCEAN BLVD

Garden City Beach
ATLANTIC AVE
Garden City Pier

WACCAMAW DR

ATLANTIC OCEAN

Blackmoor Golf Club

TPC of Myrtle Beach

Murrells Inlet Marsh Walk & Veteran's Pier

WACHESAW RD
Murrells Inlet

Wacca Wache Marina

Waccamaw River

HUNTINGTON BEACH STATE PARK

BROOKGREEN GARDENS

OCEAN HWY

Great Pee Dee River

Litchfield Country Club
LITCHFIELD DR
Litchfield Beach

N CAUSEWAY
Pawleys Island

S CAUSEWAY

Caledonia Golf & Fish Club

Pawleys Plantation

South End Beach

Georgetown
Hobcaw Barony

© The Countryman Press

Top 10 Don't Miss: The South Strand

- Stroll the Murrells Inlet Marsh Walk in the moonlight, enjoying live music and seafood along the way.
- Bring your camera to Brookgreen Gardens, the perfect combination of natural beauty and sculpture.
- Tour the spooky ruins of Atalaya in Huntington Beach State Park.
- Paddle a kayak through the Murrells Inlet saltmarsh and around Goat Island.
- Explore the history and ecology of the Hobcaw Barony.
- Discover the life of dolphins aboard an offshore cruise.
- Hike the Sculpted Oak Trail at Myrtle Beach State Park.
- Bike the Neck.
- Cast a line (or just enjoy the party) at the Garden City Pier.
- Visit the red wolves at the Sewee Visitor & Environmental Education Center in Arendaw.

If you'd like to enjoy the camping lifestyle, but don't have an RV, most campgrounds have trailers or villas available for rent, often at a price below what you'd pay for a hotel room.

MURRELLS INLET

Make your first stop in Murrells Inlet the South Strand Welcome Center (843-651-1010; www.visitmyrtlebeach.com) at the junction of US 17 Business and the Ocean Highway.

Murrells Inlet sits on the border between Horry County and Georgetown County, which also includes Garden City Beach, Litchfield Beach, Pawleys Island, and the historic port of Georgetown, an area now nicknamed the Hammock Coast. For information on visiting these South Strand communities, contact Georgetown County Tourism (843-546-8436; www.hammockcoastsc.com) or the Georgetown County Chamber (1-800-777-7705; www.visitgeorge.com).

While the traffic rushes by on US 17/Ocean Highway, US 17 Business bends off to the east, taking a shady route along the shore of Murrells Inlet, once a sleepy fishing village, today renowned as the Seafood Capital of South Carolina. No visit to the Grand Strand is complete without a stroll

The marsh walk in Murrells Inlet makes a great destination day or night.

along the marsh walk (www.murrells inletmarshwalk.com), with its many dining, entertainment, and watersports options. At the Crazy Sister Marina and Veteran's Pier, adjacent to the marsh walk, you can cast a line, board a headboat for a day of fishing, or rent a Jet Ski for a tour of the historic waterfront. Many of the older buildings along the water are part of the Murrells Inlet Historic District (www.nationalregister.sc.gov).

Fast fact: The Hot and Hot Fish Club, established in the early 1800s, was originally built on Drunken Jack Island. This gentlemen's club, dedicated to the "epicurean pursuits" of dining and the drinking of spirits, as well as fishing and hunting, included several South Carolina governors among its members.

While you're cruising Business 17, stop at ✒ Lee's Inlet Apothecary and Gifts (843-651-7979; www.inletrx.com) for an old-fashioned egg cream, phosphate, or cherry limeade at its classic soda fountain.

Morse Park Landing, farther south on US 17 Business at the end of Swale Avenue, is the site of annual dedications at the Lost at Sea Memorial (www.lostat seamemorial.com) every April. The park also has a boat ramp for launching kayaks, a crabbing dock, picnic tables, and wonderful views across the marsh. Other annual events at the Inlet include the Blessing of the Inlet (www.blessingoftheinlet .com) in May, Fourth of July boat parade and fireworks, a November oyster roast, and the Christmas parade.

The Inlet Sports Lodge (877-585-9360; www.inletsportslodge.com), a new luxury hotel close to the marsh walk, returns to Murrells Inlet's sporting past, offering packages that include fishing and hunting adventures, as well as golf, biking, kayaking, and more. The excellent Bliss Restaurant, one of the best in the region, is just across the patio.

For more information about ecotourism adventures in Murrells Inlet, visit Murrells Inlet 2020 (www.murrellsinletsc.com) or the website of the Low Country Companion (www.lowcountrycompanion.com).

LITCHFIELD BEACH & PAWLEYS ISLAND

After US 17 Business rejoins the Ocean Highway at the southern edge of Murrells Inlet, drivers pass through a stretch of woodlands, with Brookgreen Gardens on the west side of the road, Huntington Beach State Park and the ruins of Atalaya Castle on the east. Where the forest ends, the highway enters Litchfield Beach and Pawleys Island.

Originally the summer retreat of colonial rice plantation owners, who brought their families here to avoid the malaria and fevers so prevalent in the interior, Pawleys Island (843-237-1698; www.townofpawleysisland.com) is one of the country's oldest beach resorts. The Pawleys Island Historic District (www.national register.sc.gov) includes cottages dating back to the late 1700s through the mid-1800s, strung along 3 miles of oceanfront. Built of cypress, with deep porches to catch the breeze, these homes, survivors of both wind and time, lend the island its signature moniker: "arrogantly shabby." A 🐾 public beach access is located at the island's southern end.

You can stay in one of Pawley's historic beach cottages. The P. C. J. Weston

House now houses the Pelican Inn (843-325-7522; www.pawleyspelican.com), with eight air-conditioned guest rooms. Breakfast and lunch are included in the room price. Or for an old-fashioned beach vacation, with sea breeze replacing air-conditioning, books, and games instead of television, and no clocks, telephones, or locks, plan a stay at the 1937 Sea View Inn (843-237-4253; www.seaviewinn.net), where rates include three meals every day. The Inn also welcomes guests who just want to try its famous Lowcountry cuisine, with advance reservations only.

On the mainland, even locals have trouble locating the border between Litch-field and Pawleys Island along US 17, here thickly lined with shops and restau-rants. The Hammock Shops (www.thehammockshops.com), a shady village built around the home of the world-famous Pawleys Island rope hammocks, is a land-mark to look for on the east side of the highway. Dating back to 1938, this is one of the most relaxed shopping experiences on the planet, with more than 20 shops and restaurants clustered under the moss-draped oaks amid a garden of azaleas and camellias surrounding the Original Hammock Shop (843-237-9122; www .hammockshop.com). You can watch hammocks being made in the Hammock Weavers Pavilion.

Before the Civil War, much of the interior land between the beach and the Waccamaw River contained rice and indigo plantations. Today the fields have returned to marsh, but huge live oak and cypress trees remain to maximize Lowcountry charm. Nearly a dozen golf courses, includ-ing some of the top rated on the Strand, now occupy these former plantations. Two stay-and-play resorts, the Pawleys Plantation Golf & Country Club (1-800-367-9959; www.pawleysplantation.com) and its sister resort, Litchfield Beach & Golf Resort (843-237-3000; www .litchfieldbeach.com), are favorites with golfers. Both properties offer a variety of accommodations, mostly condominium units, as well as numerous amenities.

Pawleys Island is noted for its atmospheric shopping options.

Local Flavors

Taste of the town—local cafés, restaurants, bars, bistros, etc.

Throughout most of our listings, we'll divide spots to visit by their location, north to south. North Strand listings include attractions from Little River to Barefoot Landing. Myrtle Beach listings run from Restaurant Row to the Market Common. The South Strand includes destinations from Surfside through Murrells Inlet to Pawleys Island, and beyond.

With nearly 3,000 (and counting) restaurants strung along the Strand, finding nourishment is not that challenging a task. We've picked out a few to highlight, places that you might overlook without a heads-up, along with places that are iconic Grand Strand experiences that you shouldn't miss.

RESTAURANTS

North Strand

Many, many dining options are available in North Myrtle, but most of them are more casual spots. For a special sit-down meal, head north up US 17 to

Quick tip: You can save considerably on your vacation expenses by doing as the locals do: graze your way through the region's numerous happy hours, where you'll typically find lowered prices on both drinks and appetizers. Even fine-dining spots often offer happy hour in their lounges, where you can taste many house specials at discount rates. Visit www.myrtlebeachhappyhour.com for a good rundown on local deals.

the ☏ ⅄ (((•))) Brentwood Restaurant (843-249-2601; www.thebrentwoodrestaurant.com) in Little River. The elegant 1901 Queen Anne Victorian farmhouse, situated on a hill, is one of the region's top-rated eateries, noted for its authentic and beautifully prepared menu created by owner Eric Masson, a classically trained French chef. Offerings hit all the high notes of French cuisine, from escargot to an award-winning seafood bouillabaisse, as well as a vegetarian menu, a healthy—and French—children's menu, a four-course prix fixe, and a seven-course tasting menu. If you're not quite white-tablecloth ready, by all means stop by the Brentwood for a look around. The Wine Bistro offers a more casual dining experience, with numerous reasonably priced wines by the glass, free WiFi, half-price appetizers—including those escargot—during happy hour, and a ghost.

If you like this . . . the ☏ Parson's Table (843-249-3703 or 910-579-8298; www.ParsonsTable.com), also on US 17 in Little River, occupies a former Methodist church, built in 1885, now embellished with a collection of antique stained glass from around the South. Make reservations to sample the famous prime rib, or drop by the lounge for the daily happy hour.

As you drive by on US 17 through North Myrtle, you might think ↩ SeaBlue (843-249-8800; www.seablueonline.com) is just another seafood joint located in a strip mall. But step inside the doors, and you'll realize you couldn't be more wrong. Effective lighting, local art, and modernistic design create a dim, blue-tinged interior with an underwater feel, one of the most romantic on the Strand. The menu is equally forward thinking, using organic produce and locally sourced seafood. Much of the award-winning wine selection is available by the glass at the bar, where you'll also find weekday happy hours. Dinner is served Tuesday–Saturday.

For a casual lunch at great prices, join the locals at 🍴 Goodfella's Seafood Hut (843-272-3079; www.the seafoodhut.com), a locally owned and operated spot along US 17 in the Windy Hill section, serving fried and broiled seafood at prices below what you'll find elsewhere, without skimping on quality. For a real deal, arrive before 6 PM for the seafood lunch special.

Barefoot Landing has a number of excellent restaurants, but none has the buzz of 🍴 Greg Norman's Australian Grille & Pub (843-361-0000; www.greg normansaustraliangrille.com). Occupying a superb location along the ICW, this multitiered restaurant is handcrafted from imported Australian wood and decorated with aboriginal art and a huge mural of Ayers Rock, in addition to its owner's golf memorabilia. The menu features wood-grilled seafood, steaks, and chops, accompanied by a large selection of Australian wines, including Norman's signature vinos. Add a daily happy hour in the Shark

Bar and live music on the Waterway Deck, and you have an unforgettable spot to watch the boats go by or the sun go down.

Restaurant Row
Set between North Myrtle and Myrtle Beach proper, just north of the US 17 "split," Restaurant Row is famous for its many restaurants, as well as its sometimes frustrating traffic backups around the dinner hour. You'll find restaurants specializing in nearly every style of food here, from steaks to sushi to steamed seafood. A couple of Japanese steakhouses and a Mexican cantina fill out the offerings. The ICW runs close to US 17 here, so many spots on the west side to the road have decks overlooking the water.

The star of the show on Restaurant Row is 🍴 🍸 Cagney's Old Place (843-449-3824; www.cagneysoldplace .com), one of the original restaurants. Owned by two local boys, both named Dino, Cagney's is known for its slow-roasted prime rib, lobster, and steak specials, and original seafood dishes, such as Flounder Cagney, a butter-wine sauced baked fillet on a bed of parmesan-dusted tomato slices. But the thing that really sets this restaurant apart is the history on display. Over the years the Dinos salvaged woodwork and antiques from many local landmarks, including the beach's original showplace, the Ocean Forest Hotel. The Dinos are shaggers, and folks gather in the restaurant's dancin' room to cut the rug on weekend nights.

If you like this . . . visit the 🍴 *Flamingo Grill (843-449-5388; www .flamingogrill.com), also owned by the two Dinos, at Kings Highway and 71st Avenue North in MB. You'll find more Myrtle Beach memorabilia here, plus the popular fried lobster chunks, a Flamingo Grill favorite.*

A happy hour spread at Greg Norman's Australian Grille

Special Events for Foodies

While the Grand Strand has never been a noted foodie destination, that's changing thanks to an active chapter of the American Culinary Federation, programs in culinary arts at local colleges, and a growing number of chef-owned restaurants opening their doors. Locally sourced seafood and produce are gaining ground, highlighted in annual festivals. Check local food writer Becky Billingsley's *Food Restaurant News* blog (www.myrtlebeachrestaurantnews.com) for the latest on events, openings, and closings along the Strand.

JANUARY

Mr. Fish Myrtle Beach Oyster Festival (843-568-3778; www.myrtlebeachoyster festival.com).

Restaurant Week Myrtle Beach (www.restaurantweekmyrtlebeach.com), a nine-day festival of special discount meals at area restaurants.

FEBRUARY

Little River Taste of the South (www.littleriverchamber.org).

APRIL

Coastal Uncorked Food, Wine and Spirits Festival (843-839-8818; www.coastal uncorked.com), a weeklong event with wine dinners, a culinary competition, and a trolley tour to participating restaurants that benefits culinary arts and hospitality students at Horry-Georgetown Technical College and Coastal Carolina University.

FAME (Food, Arts, Music and Entertainment) Festival (myrtlebeachfamefestival .com), held on historic Broadway Street in Downtown Myrtle Beach.

Omar Shriners' Smoke on the Beach (843-971-0131; www.smokeonthebeach.com), annual barbecue cook-off at Family Kingdom.

Spring Sensation: Salads and Sweets (www.myrtlebeachacf.com), American Culinary Federation competition held at Market Common's Valor Park.

When Cagney's opened on Restaurant Row back in 1976 only one other restaurant, the Chesapeake House (843-449-3231; www.thechesapeake house.com), opened by the Cribb family in 1971, could be found along this stretch of US 17, at the time mostly farmland. Both restaurants are still going strong today, but they've been joined by some two dozen other eateries along this short stretch of highway.

Restaurant Row also is home to an impressive number of the Strand's iconic eateries—seafood buffets. Original Benjamin's Calabash Seafood (843-449-0821; www.originalbenjamins .com) is a kid's favorite, with an indoor pirate-themed playground. Grown-ups enjoy the nautical and fishing memorabilia, as well as the many ship models created in-house by carver Jimmy Frost, including a 30-foot-long model of the *Queen Elizabeth* ocean liner.

Visit the Original Benjamin's during December to see entries in its annual Gingerbread House competition. Admission is free.

Locals consider the 30-item Sunday brunch buffet served at Chestnut Hill (843-449-3984; www.chestnuthill

Trio Dinner Coastal Culinary Experience (www.triodinner.org), Myrtle Beach Hospitality Association event showcases dishes created by professional chefs teamed with college and high school culinary students.

MAY

Blue Crab Festival (www.bluecrabfestival.org), Little River's signature annual event.
Coastal Food & Music Festival (www.coastalfoodandmusicfest.squarespace.com), a new festival showcasing local chefs and music groups.

SEPTEMBER

Beach, Boogie & Barbeque Festival (www.grandstrandevents.com), a barbecue cook-off drawing entries from nationally ranked pit masters, plus great beach music bands.

OCTOBER

Loris Bog-Off (www.lorischambersc.com), features tastes of the local specialty, a rice-based chicken stew, plus a parade, entertainment, arts festival, and family fun in downtown Loris.
Taste of the Town (843-448-6062; www.totmb.com), an annual one-day event, brings 50 restaurants to the Myrtle Beach Convention Center competing to win awards from judges and the crowd.
Little River Shrimp and Jazz Festival (www.littleriverchamber.org).

NOVEMBER

Murrells Inlet Oyster Roast (843-357-2007; www.murrellsinletsc.com), an all-you-can-eat affair. Bring your favorite oyster knife.
Souper Supper (www.myrtlebeachacf.com), an American Culinary Federation soup competition held at Market Common's Valor Park.
Taste of Georgetown (www.tasteofgeorgetownsc.com), a restaurant crawl along historic Front Street.
Taste of the Inlet (843-357-2007; www.murrellsinletsc.com), part of Murrells Inlet's annual autumn gala.

dining.com), a fine-dining spot on Restaurant Row, the best in town, naming it best Sunday brunch for 20 consecutive years. Open only for dinner (and happy hour) other days of the week, this long-time favorite is known for its hand-cut Certified Angus steaks and fresh seafood.

Runners up for best brunch in the polls? The House of Blues and the Sea Captain's House.

Downtown Myrtle Beach
Free-standing restaurants right on the oceanfront are the exception rather than the rule in Myrtle Beach, where every foot of beachfront is worth its weight in gold. The ⚓ Sea Captain's House (843-448-8082; www.sea captains.com) is that exception. Operated by the same folks for more than 40 years, the restaurant specializes in fresh local seafood served in dining rooms with unobstructed views of surf, sand dunes, and pelicans, or you can step outside to enjoy the salty breeze on the patio. Housed in a gray-shingled beach cottage built in the 1930s (one of the very few to survive both hurricanes and the invasion of high-rise

Did you know? When the Ocean Forest Hotel opened in 1930, it was one of the finest resorts on the Southeast coast, with a wedding-cake central tower standing ten stories high. It was demolished in 1974, replaced by the Ocean Forest Villas, one of the Sands family of resorts. Today all that remains is a traffic circle, the memorabilia at Cagney's, and the Ocean Forest Country Club, renamed—and famous as—Pine Lakes.

hotels), this local favorite serves many traditional dishes, including an awesome she-crab soup, award-winning hush puppies, shrimp salad, crabcakes, and desserts. A perennial winner of *Southern Living*'s Reader's Choice Award for Best Seafood Restaurant in the South, this landmark at Ocean Boulevard and 30th Avenue North serves breakfast, lunch, and dinner, seven days a week.

The Sea Captain's House especially welcomes families and offers

The Sea Captain's House is the last oceanfront restaurant in an old beach cottage.

children a unique and educational menu that includes kid-size portions of crabcakes, shrimp, and oysters, served fried or broiled, as well as facts about ocean ecology.

Waits can be long at the Sea Captain, thanks to its popularity with both locals and visitors, as well as its no reservations policy. To best enjoy your meal, go at a less busy time.

If you like this . . . join the locals for a bargain breakfast or lunch buffet at ✍ *Magnolia's at 26th* (843-839-3993; *www.magnoliasat26th.com), on Ocean Boulevard at 26th Avenue North, where you'll find home cooking, including an array of fresh vegetables, just like grandma used to make, and at prices she might have paid decades ago.*

Myrtle Beach's top-rated chef-owned restaurant, the ✍ Y ↝ Aspen Grille (843-449-9191; www.aspen-grille .com) pleases diners with contemporary Southern fare, served in a sleek, black-awning spot in the Colony Square Shopping Center near 52nd Avenue North on the Kings Highway. Owner and chef Curry Martin, a true foodie with international chef chops, haunts local farmer's markets and day boats looking for the freshest local fish, heirloom tomatoes, and other produce for his seasonal menus. Dinner only is served with live jazz on tap several nights a week, plus a popular happy hour in the bar.

A bit off the beaten track on Grissom Parkway at 38th Avenue North in the Bank of North Carolina building, Y Croissants Bistro and Bakery (843-448-2253; www.croissants.net) is what diners often call "a find." Serving three meals a day, Croissants is casual during the mornings and afternoons, then steps up its game for dinner with chef-prepared specialties crafted from local

Pimento cheese is a regional favorite found on many Grand Strand menus.

fish and produce, plus a variety of gourmet flatbreads and European-style steak *frites*. In between it's a great spot for coffee and pastries, with one of the town's top bakeries on-site. Live jazz plays some nights, and, during the off-season, Croissants sponsors wine tastings, beer dinners, and other special events.

Located on the west side of Ocean Boulevard at 19th Avenue North, ⚓ 𝗬 Lulu's Cafe (843-712-1890) features bright decor, a view of the ocean from its patio, and a menu that appeals to all ages. This is a place you can actually order green eggs and ham or peanut butter and jelly pancakes. And that's on the adult menu! You can also order a beach picnic to go. Open from early morning to late night and 24 hours a day during the busiest season.

Quick tip: Watch for dishes featuring Palmetto Cheese (www .palmettocheese.com), a spicy local version of the Southern classic invented in Pawleys Island.

*If you like this . . . in downtown MB, join the locals at **Sun City Café** (843-445-2992), at 801 Main Street, for fresh Mexican-inspired cuisine and great margaritas.*

One of the nicest dining experiences along the Myrtle Beach Boardwalk can be found at the ⚓ Pier House Restaurant and Pier View Bar (843-445-7437; www.secondavenue pier.com) on the Second Avenue Pier. Located near the south end of the boardwalk, at Second Avenue North, this family-owned restaurant was recently completely refurbished, and an open-air bar was added on top. Kids of all ages will rock out with the Tabor City Toast, stuffed with peanut butter and bananas, or you can start the day with shrimp and grits topped with country ham and red-eye gravy. The Pier View Bar has its own menu served all day, plus lots of shady seating with a view, and welcomes guests in their beach attire.

If you like this . . . ⚓ 📶 Pier 14 Restaurant & Lounge (843-448-4314; www.pier14.com), a locally owned spot on the 14th Avenue Pier at the north end of the Boardwalk, serves a variety of surf and turf items, plus pitchers of frosty cocktails, in its scenic dining room and on the open-air deck.

⚓ ♿ Damon's Oceanfront Grill (843-626-8000; www.ribsribsribs.com) is known for its succulent baby back ribs and great onion rings, but the menu has many more options, including salads, sliders, pulled-pork barbecue, prime rib, and chargrilled steaks. It's a great spot to take a break from the relentlessly seafood-oriented menus found at most Strand restaurants, but the real reason to visit Damon's is its excellent location. Situated at the far south end of Ocean Boulevard in MB, this restaurant occupies a wonderful beachfront building with a huge bar, wide decks, and great views.

At Downwind Watersports (843-448-7245; www.downwindsailsmyrtle beach.com), located on the deck at Damon's, you can arrange parasail trips or banana boat rides; rent a Hobie cat, ocean kayak, or Jet Ski; or sign up for kiteboard lessons. If you'd like something a bit more relaxing, take a sunset sail to Surfside Beach aboard a catamaran.

The Market Common (www .marketcommonmb.com), located just south of Myrtle Beach International Airport, is the hottest dining destination on the Grand Strand right now, with numerous high-quality eateries. A standout among them, ♿ ⛾ Travinia Italian Kitchen (843-233-8500; www .traviniaitaliankitchen.com), a curvaceous and contemporary restaurant and lounge, serves to-die-for pastas, risottos, and Italian specialties. The award-winning wine list includes over 40 wines by the glass priced under $10. Live jazz is on the menu, too, several nights a week. Gluten-free menu available.

♿ ⛾ Tommy Bahama's Tropical Café (843-839-1868; www.tommy bahama.com) is another must-stop in Market Common, a palace of a restaurant with a huge bar, cushion-strewn booths, and frequent live Island-style music. The specialty cocktails are huge and creative; ditto the fabulous desserts. Menu highlights spotlight the island connection, with sesame-and-caper-laced ahi tuna poke, worthy of any Hawaiian gourmet spread; coconut shrimp; and macadamia-crusted snapper. Island Time, its daily happy hour, offers great discounts on appetizers and cocktails.

Market Common makes a great location for a bar crawl, with popular happy hours at ✈ P. F. Chang's China Bistro (843-839-9470; www.pfchangs .com); sports bar King Street Grille (843-238-3900; www.thekingstreet grille.com); and Gordon Biersch Brewery Restaurant (843-839-0249; www.gordonbiersch.com), with specials after 10 PM and all day Sunday as well. ⛾ Nacho Hippo (843-839-9770; www .nachohippo.com) serves up live music several nights a week and $3 margaritas all the time.

You can score a gourmet quality meal at miniscule prices by making reservations at Beach Bistro 354 (843-477-2040; www.hgtc.edu), where culinary arts students from Horry-Georgetown Technical College polish their chops. Lunch and dinner are served Monday–Thursday and feature a revolving menu of international specialties for just $10. Located at 950 Crabtree Lane in the HGTC Conference Center near Market Common, the Bistro occupies the former officer's club of the U.S. Air Force 354 Squadron and is decorated with military memorabilia.

Travinia's picatta is Italian cuisine at its best.

Quick tip: Looking for a quality kosher meal on the Strand? Check out the **Diner at the Beach** (843-839-2032; www.dineratthebeach.com) at 105 S. Kings Highway, serving glatt kosher and Mediterranean specialties, as well as Shabbat meals to go or delivered. Closed Saturdays.

Five-course lunches prepared by senior culinary students in the Fowler Dining Room (843-349-5334) on the Conway HGTC campus are also available by reservation.

Surfside Beach & Garden City Beach
On the US 17 Bypass just south of the SC 544 overpass in Surfside Beach, ✆ California Dreaming (843-215-5255; www.centraarchy.com), one of the CentraArchy family of restaurants, occupies a light and airy building with soaring atrium. The menu offers American classics carefully prepared, including crisp salads with house-made dressings, huge plates of nachos, and fat sandwiches stuffed with goodies. House specialties are Danish baby back ribs, prime rib, and steaks prepared Pittsburgh-style with a charred exterior crust.

If you like this . . . a second California Dreaming is located on US 17 in North Myrtle Beach (843-663-2050). The CentraArchy group also operates the ✆ Carolina Roadhouse (843-497-9911) in Myrtle Beach, where the menu features many items found at California Dreaming.

✆ 🍴 🍸 Dagwood's Deli & Sport Bar (843-828-4600; www.dagwoods deli.com) serves award-winning, over-stuffed sandwiches in an atmosphere sure to enchant any sports fan. Over 50 flat-screen TVs crowd the walls, including one at every booth. Darts, billiards tables, video games, and a big beer selection add to the fun. A second location (843-448-0100), on 11th Avenue North in MB, serves the same huge sandwiches.

Surfside Drive, running from US 17/Kings Highway down to the oceanfront, harbors a charming little business district with several eateries and bars. The standout among them is the Charleston Café (843-238-2200; www.charleston-cafe.com), housed in a distinctive pink building. Inside you'll find a tastefully done, white-tablecloth restaurant, one of the top-rated romantic spots on the Strand, serving a menu of well-executed Lowcountry specialties, including she-crab soup, grits topped with shrimp or fish, and a seafood soufflé that would do credit to any Charleston society matron's table. The award-winning desserts are made in-house. Lunch and daily sunset specials reveal the same gourmet touches, but at bargain prices. Upstairs, a comfortable lounge with sofas, its own

The romantic Charleston Café in Surfside Beach has a cozy upstairs lounge.

menu of appetizers, and daily happy hours, is a popular local gathering spot. Closed Sundays.

Near the southern end of Garden City Beach, the ⊕ Gulfstream Café (843-651-8808; www.centraarchy.com) sits between the ocean and Murrells Inlet and has one of the best views on the Strand. The upstairs bar and rooftop deck are perfect spots to watch the sun go down and the lights come on at the Murrells Inlet Marsh Walk, directly across the water. The menu draws inspiration from New Orleans, including spicy BBQ shrimp in butter sauce and a seafood loaf styled after the famous po'boy on thick-cut toast found at Casamento's in New Orleans. The rooftop deck is the scene of oyster roasts during off-season months. Reservations are suggested for the popular Sunday brunch and build-your-own Bloody Mary bar.

Murrells Inlet

There's not much doubt that 𝖸 ⊕ Bliss (843-282-6737; www.true-bliss .com) is the best restaurant in Murrells Inlet. The only real question is whether it's the best restaurant on the Grand Strand. Operated as a labor of love by Ernest Bledsoe, the Grand Strand's most celebrated chef, and his wife, Kimberly, Bliss abounds in delicious flavors. The former executive chef at Pawleys Island Plantation, Bledsoe has won just about every cooking competition in the region, and is noted for his creative dishes using the best locally sourced products. Since launching his own restaurant in fall 2010, the chef has developed a creative and ambitious menu that suits the white-tablecloth, elegantly appointed dining room in this totally refurbished old fish house. Items change with the season, but among the memorable standards are flounder, pan-seared in basil *beurre*

> **Fast fact: Benjamin's Bakery** (843-477-1100; www.benjaminsbakery .com), in Surfside Beach, provides many of the quality fresh-baked rolls, breads, pastries, and buns found at local restaurants and grocery stores. The bakery sells mostly wholesale, but check its Facebook page to see if there are any discounted breads, or maybe some awesome glazed chocolate donuts, for sale in the office. ((ψ)) **Surfside Subs & Deli** (843-238-2425), located in front of the bakery, serves sandwiches, grinders, and fresh-baked bagels.

noire; an award-winning crab-crusted grouper; buffalo meatloaf rolled around smoked gouda; and a grilled romaine salad laced with smoked bacon and Asiago cheese vinaigrette, one of several wonderful dressings available by the bottle to take home. The cozy Reel Bar next to the restaurant spills out onto a covered porch and courtyard centered on an outdoor

Ernest and Kimberly Bledsoe operate Bliss, Murrells Inlet's best bet for dinner.

fireplace, with cocktail service and a light menu available. Bliss serves lunch and dinner daily, with breakfast on weekends. The restaurant is part of the Inlet Sports Lodge (877-585-9360; www.inletsportslodge.com), an upscale new spot aimed at fishers and hunters, located along US 17 Business south of the marsh walk.

If you like this . . . make reservations at Austin's Ocean One (843-235-8700; www.austinsoceanone.com) at the ↭ Litchfield Inn (www.litchfield inn.com). Executive chef Bill Austin is an honors CIA grad and another of the Strand's top chefs. Go before dark to best enjoy the expansive ocean views.

Given the huge volume of business they handle during the summer season, the restaurants along the marsh walk do a pretty good job keeping diners happy. For a meal in a refined setting with views of the inlet, Capt. Dave's Dockside Restaurant (843-651-5850; www.davesdockside.com) is your best bet. The building, designed to resemble an old farmhouse, has an elegant, open feel created by a wall of windows facing the marsh. Piano music from the grand piano in the lounge provides a serene background for a menu featuring live Maine lobster, fresh seafood, charcoal grilled steaks, and the best key lime pie ever. Complimentary docking is available if you arrive by boat.

Capt. Dave's serves dinner only, so if you're looking for something light, or a more party-like atmosphere, head out back to ✎ ♈ Bubba's Love Shak (843-651-5850; www.bubbasloveshak.com). This colorful spot on the marsh walk, named for local fisherman and kitchen regular Jerome Smalls, aka Brother Love, serves up fish tacos, po'boys, burgers, and fresh seafood, as well as live entertainment many evenings.

Fast fact: Drunken Jack's is named for a legendary pirate, reputedly stranded on a nearby island by the notorious Blackbeard with nothing for sustenance but kegs of rum. The story inspired several scenes in Disney's *Pirates of the Caribbean* movies.

✎ ♈ ↭ Drunken Jack's Restaurant (843-651-2044; www.drunken jacks.com) is one of the marsh walk's most popular dining destinations, and waits at dinner time can be daunting. Better option: grab a stool on the covered deck out back, where you'll have an unobstructed view of Goat Island, and laze the afternoon away with a jumbo softshell crab or a Drunken Jack's sampler of scallops, shrimp, crabcakes, and beef tips, washed down with an award-winning margarita or a refreshing glass of Goat Island Tea, worthy of any pirate.

A resident of Goat Island in Murrells Inlet

If you like this . . . you may need to work up a thirst with a little activity. Head across Business 17 from Drunken Jack's to **Express Watersports** *(843-357-7777; www.expresswatersports .com) and rent a kayak or paddleboard for a quick cruise around Goat Island. You can also sign up for banana boat rides, kayak tours of the inlet, parasailing, and dolphin cruises.*

Arrange a private dinner cruise aboard the colorful *Bahama Mama* (843-602-1637; www.bahamamama chartercruises.com), an authentic wood-hulled shrimp boat now adapted for use as a passenger vessel. Your meal will be grilled right on board, and you can chose from a whole Maine lobster, fish of the day, shrimp, or filet mignon. Cruises depart from Capt. Dave's docks.

With so many great restaurants along the waterfront in Murrells Inlet, you might overlook a spot along busy US 17/Ocean Highway, but the ✍ Salt Water Creek Cafe (843-357-2433; www.saltwatercreekcafe.com), a friendly spot with star-quality food, is worth seeking out. A bright blue neon sign leads you to a cedar-shingled building with outside dining under a huge live oak. Locally owned and operated by Keith and Wendy Wolff,

Did you know? You can take your dog to dinner at Shell Crackers Outback Grill on the grounds of **A Dog's Way Inn** (843-357-4545; www.adogswayinn.com) on the Murrells Inlet bypass. The 8-acre canine resort also offers overnight boarding, doggie day care, grooming, and a fenced dog park complete with swimming pond.

another chef-and-wife combo, this spot offers lunch and dinner menus available all day and well into the evening. Locals love the café for its blue light specials, happy hour and early bird menus, and the Thanksgiving dinner, complete with stuffing and cranberry sauce, served daily. The popular weekend brunch includes marquee dishes such as surf and turf Benedict and lobster omelets.

Litchfield Beach & Pawleys Island

The exterior of the historic old grocery located at the foot of the causeway to Pawleys Island belies the restaurant that lies within. ❦ ((ᵖ)) Frank's Restaurant and Frank's Outback (843-237-3030; www.franksandoutback.com) provide one of the region's most upscale dining experiences, with white tablecloths, candlelight, a lengthy list of wines by the glass, and menu prices to match. The grouper, either pan-seared or crusted with cornmeal and black pepper, is a favorite with many repeat customers. Franks' Outback, in a little house next door, offers a romantic spot for dining, with a separate menu exhibiting a down-home emphasis, entrée salads, and wood-fired pizzas. But wait! There's more! Out back of the Outback, a tented area set beneath old live oaks hosts a casual scene much favored by locals for live jazz and community gatherings around the outdoor fireplace and bar. Frank's is named for Frank Marlow, who operated a landmark supermarket and gas station on US 17 near the causeway to Pawleys Island beginning in the 1930s.

For something completely different, seek out the PIT, short for ✍ ❦ Pawleys Island Tavern (843-237-8465; www.pawleysislandtavern.com), a blue-jean casual place at the end of a dirt road. Eat on the patio under the trees or inside, where patrons past have

At the PIT in Pawleys Island, dine outside under shady live oaks.

hung up dollar bills with witty sayings on the walls and ceiling. The menu features local favorites from great crab-cakes and house-made pimento cheese to a garlicky white pizza, complemented by local microbrews and wines by the glass. Locals drop by regularly for the lunchtime blue plate specials. Stay long enough and the music will start to play. Closed Mondays.

BARBECUE

No trip to the South is complete without a good feed of 'cue. The Grand Strand has its share of great places for pig, served smoked and chopped Carolina-style, but you can also find beef brisket and other styles of barbecue if you know where to look. Besides Damon's Grill, discussed in our restaurants section, here are some other spots to get your smoked meat on.

The Bar-B-Que House (www.best bbqonthebeach.com), with locations on US 17 in North Myrtle Beach (843-249-6901) and Surfside Beach (843-477-1801), serves hickory-smoked Boston butt and pork ribs, chicken fried or smoked, and a full array of sides from collards to banana pudding.

Big KT's Barbecue Shack (843-427-4117; www.bigktsbbq.com), on US 17 near Barefoot Landing, adds beef brisket and mesquite smoked turkey to the usual chopped pork, BBQ chicken, and pork ribs menu. If you can't decide, the sampler platter with beef, pork, chicken, and ribs is a great solution. A full-service bar and some unusual sides, such as fried green beans, two types of potato salad, and that Southern classic, tomato pie, round out the menu.

Palmetto Pig at the Beach (843-390-9600; www.palmettopig.com), on SC 9 west of NMB, serves a popular barbecue buffet with chopped pork, fried chicken, and homemade sides such as a tasty hash made of Boston butt, onions, and tomatoes. Drive-through is available if you don't have time to sit down for a meal.

Myrtle Beach

It's nothin' fancy, but Little Pigs BBQ (843-692-9774) is the hands-down favorite for chopped pig, winning first place in local polls year after year. Look for it on the frontage road where 62nd Avenue North meets the US 17 Bypass. Hams are slow smoked over hickory coals, then chopped and served unsauced so you can add your choice of four different homemade dips.

Sticky Fingers (843-839-7427; www.stickyfingers.com), located next to the Coastal Grand Mall, wins the Best Ribs Award in every local poll. Order them Carolina sweet, Habanero

The Grand Strand offers plenty of places serving great barbecue.

hot, or Memphis-style, wet or dry—it's hard to go wrong. Other great choices include hickory-smoked jumbo wings, smoked beef brisket, and stacked apple pie. Sticky Fingers' five original sauces, including our favorite, Tennessee Whiskey, are award-winning and available for sale. This regional chain, founded in 1992 in nearby Mount Pleasant, South Carolina, has another location in North Myrtle Beach (843-663-7675).

Quick tip: Sticky Fingers is conveniently located near the Myrtle Beach International Airport, so stop in for a slab of ribs to take home.

South Strand

Located in a rustic building across from the Hobcaw Barony on US 17, ✔ Ý Hog Heaven (843-237-7444; www.hogheaveninc.com) serves fried and steamed seafood, as well as a very low-priced, all-you-can-eat buffet crowded with barbecued pork, fried chicken, and a wealth of Southern side dishes, from stewed tomatoes and field peas to chicken bog and fruit cobbler.

Make your way to the back deck to join the locals under the live oak trees where a bar and occasional entertainment add to the fun.

Several regions of the Carolinas have their own distinctive barbecue sauces. Eastern North Carolina sauce is thin and vinegary with flecks of red pepper. Lexington-style sauce is also thin and based on vinegar, but has a bit of tomato and sweetness added. Western Carolina barbecue sauce is thicker and tomato based with a ketchup consistency. South Carolina–style barbecue sauce is based on mustard. Try them all to find your favorite. Another Carolina tradition is putting coleslaw on the bun with the chopped barbecue. You may be offered a choice between red and white slaw. White is the usual kind of coleslaw found across the country. Red slaw is made with spicy red vinegar sauce and adds extra kick to your sandwich.

BREAKFAST SPOTS

No trip to the Grand Strand is complete without a visit to one of the area's legendary pancake houses. Once upon a time, the Kings Highway was lined with these mom-and-pop eateries. Most of them opened at 10 PM and closed for a few hours at 2 PM just to get the floors swept. People stayed up late and ate breakfast before they went to bed in those hard-partying days.

Quite a few of those classic pancake houses survive, although most don't keep those long hours now, usually opening at sunrise for breakfast, then closing in early afternoon after the lunch crowd thins out. In fact, it can be difficult to find an all-night spot to satisfy those 2 AM breakfast munchies. All of the restaurants listed here are open only for breakfast and early lunch, unless otherwise noted.

North Strand

The ✿ Golden Griddle Pancake House (843-249-2227; www.golden griddlepancakehouse.com), on Main Street in North Myrtle Beach, has a lot more going for it than just those famous buttermilk pancakes. Daily specials and low-priced kids' and senior menus help keep many a vacation on budget.

Myrtle Beach

Since 1953 ✿ Mammy's Kitchen (843-448-7242; www.mammyskitchen.com) has been a landmark of Southern homestyle cooking on Kings Highway at 10th Avenue North. Generations of visitors and locals make regular pilgrimages to fill up at the all-you-can-eat breakfast and dinner buffets. Country classics such as ribs and chicken, plus fresh seafood, crowd the dinner buffet. Midday, Mammy's serves traditional "meat-and-three" plate lunches.

Quick tip: Mammy's breakfast and fruit buffet, served until 1 PM daily, is one of the Strand's great bargains. Also, the kitchen here willingly handles special dietary requests.

Wildly popular for 20 years on the Surfside Pier, Nibils (843-448-6789; www.nibilsrestaurant.com) lost its lease and moved north to a new location on Kings Highway at 33rd Avenue North. Open only for breakfast and lunch, Nibils has stood the test of time thanks to its reasonable prices, three-egg omelets, and fresh seafood, including a great broiled flounder plate and popular shrimp salad.

If you like this . . . 📶 *Wood-haven Pancake House (843-448-2277;*

www.wafflecam.com), at 26th Avenue South, is notable for its huge servings and free WiFi access.

There's a special welcome waiting for current and former servicemen and women at the Veterans Café & Grille (843-232-8387; www.veteranscafeand grille.com), located on Shine Avenue near Market Common, on the former U.S. Air Force Base. Breakfast and lunch, starring Philly cheesesteak sandwiches, come in at very reasonable prices.

South Strand

Like many of the mom-and-pop restaurants across the South, the Omega Pancake House (843-238-5292; www .omegasurfside.com) is operated by a Greek family. Unlike most of those places, however, Omega serves Greek specialties, including gyros, souvlaki, spanakopita, and Greek salads, in addition to well-executed breakfast dishes and Southern plate lunches. Open 6 AM to 2 PM on the Kings Highway at 16th Avenue North in Surfside Beach.

The Village Café (843-477-8029; www.villagecafesurfside.com), a long-time favorite on Surfside Drive, serves breakfast all day plus a nice selection of sandwiches, pizza, and plate lunches.

If you like this . . . another good breakfast/lunch option in Surfside is the ✿ Golden Egg Pancake House (843-238-4923; www.goldeneggonline .com), serving a huge menu of favorites on US 17 Business, the Kings Highway.

Farther down US 17 in Pawleys, the ✿ Litchfield Restaurant (843-237-4414; www.litchfieldrestaurant.com) is a red-and-white landmark familiar to locals for its good and inexpensive diner-style food. The menu includes local specialties such as fish and grits with stewed tomatoes, and chicken pilau, as well as all the breakfast standards and popular meat-and-three plates for lunch.

For a reliable breakfast at reasonable prices, check out local favorite Eggs Up Grill (843-650-5515; www.eggsupgrill.com), a local chain with locations in Surfside Beach, Pawleys Island, Conway, and the MB, all open from 6 AM to 2 PM daily.

BREWPUBS & BREWERIES

New South Brewing (843-916-2337; www.newsouthbrewing.com), located at 851 Campbell Street in Myrtle Beach, creates small-batch craft beers, including several award winners. Beer buffs over 21 can take a free tour of the brewery and sample the varieties on tap on Tuesday and Thursday afternoons. Many local restaurants and bars carry New South beers on draft, and its popular white ale, a Belgian-style wheat, is available in cans at retail outlets throughout the region.

Liberty Steakhouse & Brewery (843-626-4677; www.libertysteakhouse andbrewery.com) was Myrtle Beach's original brewpub, introducing its first beers in 1995. The enormous facility at Broadway at the Beach includes a dining room, plus a huge bar area and outside beer garden, where you can enjoy a very popular daily happy hour and samplers of the current beers on tap, including Liberty Ale, Rockets Red Glare, and a tasty raspberry wheat. Tours of the brewery are available.

If you like this . . . Liberty's fresh, award-winning beers, along with other microbrews from near and far, are also available on tap at other restaurants of the TBonz group (www.tbonz.com), including the Liberty Tap Room & Grill (843-839-4677; www.libertytaproom.com) on the Kings Highway at 76th Avenue North; Flying

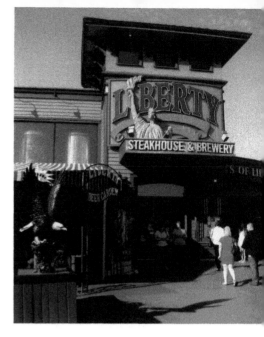

The Liberty was Myrtle Beach's first brewpub.

Fish Market and Grill (843-663-3474; www.flyingfishmarket.com) in Barefoot Landing; and TBonz Gill & Grill (www.tbonzgillandgrill.com), with locations at Barefoot Landing (843-272-7111) and Seaboard Commons (843-946-7111) near Broadway at the Beach.

Down in Pawleys Island, fans of fresh beer should seek out   Quigley's Pint & Plate (843-237-7010; www.pintandplate.com), a brewpub founded by a veteran of both Liberty and New South Brewing. Tucked into a retail area set next to a pleasant pond on the west side of US 17, Quigley's offers an interesting menu of reasonably priced favorites, such as black-eyed pea hummus, fish tacos, and meatloaf with mushroom ale gravy, as well as a great happy hour, occasional live music, an outside deck overlooking the pond, and at least eight hand-crafted brews on tap. If you're curious about the brewing process, request a tour.

If you like this . . . the ☙ Gordon Biersch Brewery Restaurant (843-839-0249; www.gordonbiersch.com) in Market Common produces a variety of German-style brews, including an award-winning black beer.

On an entirely different note, try Pig Swig, the house brand at Piggly Wiggly (www.thepig.net), a Southern born-and-bred chain and the first self-service grocery in the nation, with several locations along the Strand.

The website of Myrtle Beach Craft Beer (www.myrtlebeachcraftbeer.com) is a handy resource to help hops-lovers locate beer and beer-related events on the Strand. ☙ ♈ For What It's Worth (843-497-5000; www.fwiwbar.com), a gastropub in Myrtle Beach, carries one of the area's largest selections of craft brews and let's you build your own beer dinner.

BURGERS & DOGS

Most meals on vacation need to be casual—and fast. The Grand Strand has its fair share of the usual national fast-food eateries, including the hot Five Guys (www.fiveguys.com) chain, but there are plenty of spots serving great burgers and hot dogs in more interesting surroundings.

Prime spots for a burger fix are the several locations of the ☙ ♿ River City Café (www.rivercitycafe.com), a consistent award winner among both locals and visitors. Seven stores along the Strand mean that a juicy burger paired with hand-cut fries or hand-battered onion rings is just seconds away. The oceanfront location in Surfside Beach (843-232-9797) is especially scenic, with tables on a deck set high above the sand. Burgers come with a wide choice of toppings, and you can switch out the beef for a chicken, veggie, or turkey burger, or even meatloaf. Kids love this place—especially eating the free

peanuts and throwing the shells on the floor. In fact, *USA Today* declared the River City Café "one of the best places in the nation to feed the kids."

North Strand
In Little River, 2 Dogs a Walk'n (843-4277178; www.2dogsawalkn.com), on US 17, serves hand-patted, charcoal-grilled burgers, old-fashioned chili dogs, fried bologna sandwiches, inexpensive breakfast specials, and at dinner time, the area's least-expensive version of shrimp and grits.

Heading down the Sea Mountain Highway into Cherry Grove, look for Beaches Burgers (843-663-5777), where you can sit outside at a picnic table and wrap your mouth around a Carolina-style burger topped with mustard, chili, and onions, or a bun filled with house-smoked pork barbecue.

Tucked away on 48th Avenue in North Myrtle Beach, Hamburger Joe's (843-272-6834) is a longtime local favorite for the big three—burgers, barbecue, and beer.

Myrtle Beach
☙ Burky's Grill (843-626-2888; www.burkysgrill.com), at 39th Avenue North on the Kings Highway in Myrtle Beach, combines a 1950s vibe with tasty burgers, Cincinnati-style chili mac, stuffed baked potatoes, veggie burgers, and kids' meals. The Myrtle Beach Car Club (www.myrtlebeach carclub.com) holds weekly cruise-ins here, attracting some 50 classic cars, year-round.

South Strand
At Joey Dogg's Dogs, Burgers and Fries (843-238-5639; www.joeydoggs.net), on US 17 Business in Surfside Beach across from the Ocean Lakes Campground, most menu items are made fresh; meat is ground daily on-site; and chili comes from a 75-year-old

Grand Strand Wine Tour

If your favorite vacation activity is visiting wineries to sample new vintages (and add to your wineglass collection), you needn't miss out during your stay on the Strand. Several wineries in the area offer tastings and tours. Most feature wines made with the super healthy muscadine grape, as well as vinifera vintages.

Star of the show is **La Belle Amie Vineyard** (843-399-9463; www.labelleamie.com) on SC 90 in Little River. In addition to tastings and tours, this family-operated winery offers a busy schedule of concerts and special events. Wines here include muscadines made from local grapes, plus wines from small family vineyards in southern France not available elsewhere.

⊤ **Carolina Vineyards** (843-361-9181; www.carolinavineyards.com) at Barefoot Landing, and its sister store, ' **Boardwalk Winery** (843-712-1944; www.boardwalkwinery.com) at Broadway at the Beach, offer tastings daily. Both are working wineries, making wines from vinifera grapes (grown elsewhere) and a variety of fruits, including that famous Southern classic—elderberry wine—a refreshing treat after a day on the sand.

In Conway, **Hyman Vineyards** (843-397-2100; www.hymanvineyards.com) crafts wines, ranging from dry to spicy sweet, from several varieties of muscadine grapes growing on this family farm. In addition to tastings and tours, Hyman offers muscadine juice, neutraceuticals, and health care products featuring grape seed extract, plus a wide variety of unusual jams and jellies. (Try the purple sweet potato butter.)

Travel over the border into North Carolina to visit two other wineries. ♂ **Silver Coast Winery** (910-287-2800 www.silvercoastwinery.com), near Ocean Isle Beach, offers tastings of award-winning wines, tours of the vineyard and winemaking facility, plus an art gallery and two gift shops. The 🍴 ♂ ⅄ **Grapefull Sisters Vineyard** (910-653-2944; www.grapefullsistersvineyard.com), located on a former tobacco farm now converted to vines, offers wine tastings, picnic baskets, and evenings of bluegrass music. There's also a campground and a country inn on the property.

You can sample a wide variety of vintages at the **Wine Shoppe** (843-272-6941; www.thewineshoppenmb.com) in North Myrtle Beach, which sponsors free tasting events each week.

Several area restaurants make good destinations for wine lovers. **Travinia Italian Kitchen** (843-233-8500; www.traviniaitaliankitchen.com) in Market Common has a self-serve Enomatic wine dispenser, plus 60 carefully selected wines by the glass. In Little River, at the other end of the Strand, the ⅄ (📶) **Brentwood Restaurant** (843-249-2601; www.thebrentwoodrestaurant.com) offers great happy hour deals on wine and other libations in its Wine Bistro. Don't miss the interesting collection of corkscrews in the restaurant hallway.

Celebrate Beach Tradition at Peaches

Since 1937, ☞ **Peaches Corner** (843-448-7424; www.peaches-corner.com) has been pleasing the crowds along the oceanfront with foot-long dogs, double burgers, catfish sandwiches, and ice-cold draft beer. Located just a block from the surf at Ocean Boulevard and Ninth Avenue North, this landmark in Old Myrtle Beach has been discovered by a new generation of beachgoers who find this is the perfect stop for refreshment after a stroll on the new boardwalk. Stop by to gobble down a foot-long corndog, or to take the Peaches Challenge—finish 5 pounds of food in 20 minutes for a prize. You'll receive a great welcome and a taste of Grand Strand past.

family recipe. Try the gourmet quality Super Duper burgers stuffed with cheddar or blue cheese.

☞ ☜ ▾ Sam's Corner (843-651-3233; www.samscornerhotdogs.com), long a landmark across from the Garden City Pier, serves hot dogs that have won top honors for 20 years, plus breakfast platters, burgers topped with pimento cheese, and 5¢ cups of coffee. Open 24 hours a day, a rarity now on the Strand, it also has a full bar, with screwdrivers on special all the time.

Sam's Corner, famous for its hot dogs, stays open 24/7.

COFFEEHOUSES

Downtown on Broadway at 10th Avenue North, the alcohol-free ☞ ((•)) Fresh Brewed Coffee and Music House (843 251-8282; www.freshbrewedcoffee house.com) provides an island of cool near the boardwalk. Live music in a wide variety of styles is the draw here, paired with a comfortable lounge and patio, billiards, and darts.

Over at Broadway at the Beach, KISS Coffeehouse (843-626-KISS; www.kisscoffeehouse.com) is a java joint with attitude. Filled with KISS memorabilia, souvenirs, and sounds, this is not the place for a laid-back cup of joe. Look for the 20-foot-tall boots out front.

The Chocolate and Coffee House (843-237-7874), in the Litchfield Exchange, features a full espresso bar, handmade chocolates, Wholly Cow ice cream, and a selection of teas. It's also the home of CLASS (843-235-9600; www.classatpawleys.com), offering yoga and art classes, plus literary events, and Art Works (843-235-9600; www.artwrks.net/), a gallery of local art.

Just down US 17, ((•)) Latte Litchfield Espresso Bar & Creamery (843-235-7575; www.lattelitchfield.com) serves hot and cold coffee and tea drinks. Local art, used books, and occasional live music complete the experience.

SEAFOOD STEAMERS & RAW BARS

Many visitors arrive at the beach wanting to eat seafood for every meal. It's a vacation tradition, and nearly every menu on the Strand features seafood front and center. How do you choose from so many options? Here's some help: a listing of spots that are favorites among locals, with reasonable prices and fresh local seafood. Nothing fancy, these are places where you can roll up your sleeves and dive into a bucket of steamed oysters, peel some shrimp, or savor a steam pot stuffed with crab, oysters, shrimp, mussels, sausage, and corn on the cob.

North Strand

Duffy Street Seafood Shack (www .duffyst.com), with three locations in Cherry Grove (843-249-7902), Main Street in Ocean Drive (843-281-9840), and Restaurant Row (843-449-2233), is the North Strand's go-to spot for oyster po'boys; award-winning crabcakes; buckets of steamed oysters, clams, and shrimp; and authentic key lime pie. Kids love the free peanuts while their parents enjoy the daily raw bar happy hour.

The fish literally fly at the Flying Fish Public Market and Grill (843-663-3474; www.flyingfishmarket .com), located on the ICW next to the Alabama Theatre in Barefoot Landing. Fishmongers in the market area toss fish à la Seattle's Pike's Place, and young diners may get a chance to try their hands after a brief—and free— lesson. You can dive into a steamed feast, select your fresh catch from the market, or belly up to the bar for the popular daily happy hour featuring raw oysters, sushi, and other discounted apps and cocktails.

Join the locals and relax with a cocktail at Rockefellers Raw Bar (843-

Outdoor oyster roast on the deck at Gulf-stream Café

361-9677; www.rockefellersrawbar .com), a ramshackle place along the Kings Highway, as the bartender prepares your kettle of steamed seafood. The selection here is unusually wide, including scallops, lobster chunks, and crawfish, as well as the more usual shrimp, mussels, and clams.

Restaurant Row

Craving oysters on Restaurant Row? Hunt out Bimini's Oyster Bar and Seafood Café (843-449-5549; www .biminisoysterbar.com) on Lake Arrowhead Road, where you'll find a boisterous group of locals wolfing down 99¢ oyster shooters, steam pots, crab legs, and other treats from the sea. This tends to be an adult spot—often smoky and noisy, especially when there's live music—but food is served until late most nights of the week.

Myrtle Beach

The Original Mr. Fish Restaurant, Market & Steam Room (843-839-3474; www.mrfish.com), a no-frills spot on Kings Highway at 34 Avenue North, is owned and operated by father-daughter team Ted and Sheina Hammerton. Ted, Mr. Fish himself, is an internationally known consultant in seafood processing and markets, his daughter is a noted seafood chef, and together they operate one of local folks' favorite spots for seafood, prepared a million different ways. Their seafood market is located just two doors down from the modest storefront restaurant; stop for a mess of hot steamed blue crabs to go.

In the heart of the action at the corner of Kings Highway and First Avenue South, the Noizy Oyster (843-444-6100; www.thenoizyoyster.com) is a great find when you're in the mood for a bucket of steamed oysters or middle neck clams, or some blue crabs steamed in beer. Preparations here are Maryland-style, with Old Bay Seasoning featured.

If you like this . . . on the boardwalk you can get your oyster fix, steamed, fried, or blackened, at Dirty Don's Oyster Bar & Grill (843-213-1632; www.dirtydonsmyrtlebeach .com), where Ninth Avenue North meets the ocean.

Surfside Beach & Garden City Beach

Backfinz (843-357-3069; www.backfinz .com), on US 17 Business in Garden City Beach, is a great place to crack some crab while watching a Baltimore Ravens or Orioles game, hosted by a family that transplanted here from Maryland. The local blues are steamed Maryland-style with rock salt added, and the crabcakes are authentically created from super lump-grade meat with just the right spices and no filler at all.

Murrells Inlet

A drive along US 17 Business through Murrells Inlet takes you past one seafood spot after another. Beyond the marsh walk, look for the ☙ Inlet Crab House & Raw Bar (843-651-8452; www.inletcrabhouseandrawbar.com), a laid-back spot operated by a fishing boat captain, serving oyster and clam roasts, an outstanding she-crab soup, and a wide selection of other seafood specials.

Nearby, Lee's Inlet Kitchen (843-651-2881; www.leesinletkitchen.com) continues its tradition of well-prepared local seafood and Angus steak dinners, which began in 1948, making this the oldest family-owned restaurant on the Grand Strand. The she-crab soup is award winning, and entrées feature your choice of large fantail or sweet creek shrimp from the local marshes. Closed during the winter.

Located near the northern end of Business 17, ☙ Flo's Place (843-651-7222; www.flosplace.com) is another spot that has stood the test of time, welcoming guests for more than 30 years. Mardi Gras is the theme here, complete with Dixieland jazz, beads, and *bon temps*. Oyster or crawfish boils are on the menu, along with gumbo and alligator stew.

Steamed mussels appear on many menus around the region.

If you like this . . . Nance's Creekfront Restaurant (843-651-2696; www.nancescreekfrontrestaurant.com), near the southern end of Business 17, is an old-style oyster house, complete with holes in the tables where you discard the shells. Local oyster clusters are the specialty, when available.

Litchfield Beach & Pawleys Island
Among the many restaurants up and down the Grand Strand, you'd be hard pressed to find a more family-friendly spot than the ♂ Litchfield Beach Fish House (843-237-3949; www.litchfield beachfishhouse.com), where a pirate ship playground and complimentary pirate hats are just the beginning of the fun activities. Fried local fish is the specialty, with flounder receiving high marks. The fish house is located on US 17—here the Ocean Highway—near the corner of Litchfield Drive. Look for the shark breaking through the roof.

A bit farther south on US 17 in the Indigo Exchange Plaza, ♂ Captain John's Seafood Grill (843-235-9300; www.captainjohnsseafoodgrill.com) offers patrons a quick trip to the shores

Did you know? Roadside stands located on the routes leading to the Grand Strand sell the freshest local produce. Depending on the season, you'll find strawberries, vine-ripened tomatoes, watermelons, collard, beet and turnip greens, Vidalia onions, peaches, and many other local crops. Look for pit-cured Red Jewel sweet potatoes—they'll keep all winter. Another local delicacy worth trying: boiled green peanuts, a salty snack found at many stands along US 501. Watch out! They're addictive.

of New England with classic dishes such as Ipswich whole-belly clams, New Bedford scallops, Maine-style lobster rolls, and fresh haddock dishes, as well as authentic creamy clam chowder.

If you like this . . . follow US 17 a few more blocks to the ♂ Blue Crab (843-979-2722; www.bluecrabrawbar .com) for oysters on the half shell, steamed blue crabs, snow crabs, little neck clams, mussels, or shrimp, along with a variety of seafood entrées, served in a fun, casual atmosphere.

SPECIALTY MARKETS & TAKEOUT

A trip to the beach calls for lots of seafood, and the best place to find the freshest local catch is at markets in the region's fishing villages. Here fish and seafood are just off the boat, directly from offshore local waters.

The Grand Strand has major fishing ports at either end: Little River, South Carolina, and Calabash, North Carolina, at the northern extreme; and Murrells Inlet and Georgetown on the South Strand. Look for seafood stands along Mineola Avenue and Waterfront Drive in Little River. In Murrells Inlet, two spots to look for along US 17 Business are Seven Seas Seafood Market (843-651-1666; www.sevenseasseafood.com) and Harrelson's Seafood Market (843-651-5707).

If you like this . . . Fish Monger Seafood (843-903-2722; www.fish mongerseafood.org), on US 17 in Surf-side Beach, sells fresh seafood, most of it local, although they do carry products from other parts of the country, including haddock and soft clams.

In MB, on the Kings Highway at 13th Avenue North, the Fresh Seafood Company Restaurant & Market (843-

Meet the Crab Cake Lady

A little shack along the US 17 Bypass in Murrells Inlet is a landmark for seafood lovers. This is the shop of An Mathis Springs, the **Crab Cake Lady** (843-651-0708; www.thecrabcakelady.com), a Vietnamese woman who arrived in Murrells Inlet in 1973. Seeing the rich salt marshes all around, she began to set crab traps and harvest the local blue crabs, turning them into crabcakes and deviled crabs that soon became the talk of the town. Today the matriarch of a family of fishermen, Mrs. Springs, now in her 70s, and her grandsons head an expanding empire of retail and wholesale seafood sales. Since the Travel Channel featured the Crab Cake Lady as the area's top attraction, business has soared. The crabcakes, made according to her original recipe, continue to be her best sellers, now joined by shrimp-filled egg rolls, blue crab dip, and she-crab soup. All are available at the Crab Cake Lady store, as well as at the family-owned Harrelson's Seafood Market (843-651-5707), at Piggly Wiggly groceries, and online. *The Crab Cake Lady of Murrells Inlet, The Story of An Mathis Springs: From Rice Paddies to Crab Cakes,* a book by Sara L. Powell, tells Mrs. Springs's inspiring story.

448-9043) offers fresh seafood, raw or cooked, including the house specialty, Alaskan snow cod.

Some local fish to try include hogfish (sometimes known as lobster fish, thanks to its firm texture and sweet meat), trigger fish, red snapper, and grouper, as well as sweet creek shrimp, blue crabs, and cluster oysters. All are caught in local waters and are available seasonally.

Several farmer's markets operate from spring to fall along the Grand Strand. In downtown Myrtle Beach, Myrtle's Market (843-918-1014; www.myrtlesmarket.com), on Mr. Joe White Avenue at Oak Street, sells a wide variety of local fruits, vegetables, seafood, and crafts, all day on Wednesday, Friday, and Saturday. An organic farmer's market operates nearby on Wednesday afternoons at the ✪ Gallery on 8th (843-429-0018; www.cccmg.com /farmers_mkt.htm). Offerings here include organically grown produce, free-range meats, hormone-free dairy products, herbs, and organic wines.

*If you like this . . . visit the seasonal farmer's markets in North Myrtle Beach, Conway, and Loris, all part of the **Waccamaw Market Cooperative** (843-365-6715; www.waccamawmarkets.org). **Georgetown County** (843-545-3275; www.georgetowncountysc.org) sponsors seasonal markets at Parkersville Park in Pawleys Island on Wednesday mornings and East Bay Park in the city of Georgetown on Saturday mornings.*

✪ Lee's Farmers Market (843-651-7398; www.leesfarmersmarket.com), on the Ocean Highway/US 17 in Murrells Inlet, offers local and organic fruits and vegetables, plus deli sandwiches made with Carnegie corned beef and pastrami, 200 varieties of cheese from around the world, an extensive Italian food section, imported sausages, hand-cut steaks and chops, and live Maine lobsters. Open year-round.

Pawleys Island has two excellent gourmet markets, both on the Ocean Highway/US 17, offering prepared foods to make feasting in your vacation cottage or condo easy. ⅄ (ᵖ) Perrone's Fine Food and Wine Market (843-235-9193; www.perronesmarket.com) fills its cases with chef-prepared gourmet treats, and offers panini, tapas, sushi, and an eclectic selection of wines and microbrews for takeout or to enjoy at the new wine bar equipped with a cuvenee system. Get Carried Away Southern Takeout (843-314-3493; www.getcarriedawaypi.com) features the Lowcountry delicacies served at the Sea View Inn on Pawleys, such as tomato pie, Palmetto Cheese, chicken pilau, and their specialty, Lowcountry boil in a bucket. Delivery is available in Litchfield and Pawleys Island.

VEGETARIAN FARE & NATURAL FOODS

Although the Grand Strand doesn't harbor any strictly vegetarian restaurants, several spots have extensive vegetarian offerings in a wide variety of cuisines.

(ᵖ) ⏻ Bay Naturals (843-448-0011; www.bay-naturals.com), at Kings Highway and 76th Avenue North, is the area's foremost purveyor of healthful and organic products of all kinds. The café on-site serves a menu of healthful foods, from hormone-free chicken salad to fully vegan and vegetarian soups, sandwiches, and quiches, plus fresh-squeezed juices.

Habibi's Café & Market (843-236-0150), located in a modest storefront

on Waccamaw Boulevard off US 501, on the west side of the ICW, serves excellent Middle Eastern dishes, including hummus, baba ghanoush, and a tasty falafel, plus great desserts and many hard-to-find grocery items. Order a Greek salad from the pizzeria next door to complete your meal.

If Asian is more your style, head for one of the E Noodles & Co. Asian Bistro (www.enoodlesco.com) locations on the Strand, at 20th Avenue South (843-916-8808) in MB and on US 17 in North Myrtle (843-663-1628). Chef Eddie Kwong and his staff can prepare many of the dishes, inspired by Japanese, Chinese, Thai, and Vietnamese cuisines, in vegetarian versions.

Several Mexican restaurants on the Strand offer good selections of vegetarian dishes, including La Hacienda Mexican Restaurants, a Charleston-based chain with a couple of Myrtle Beach locations, including a waterfront spot along the ICW in Socastee (843-650-3588) and in Carolina Forest (843-903-3399), and the easier to find Mexico Lindo (www.ilovemexicolindo.com) restaurants with locations along US 17/Kings Highway in MB (843-626-4566) and North Myrtle (843-361-4667).

🐟 Redi-et Ethiopian Cuisine (843-238-2879; www.redi-et.com), conveniently located at the intersection of US 501 and US 17 Business in the heart of Myrtle Beach, offers a menu of ten 100 percent vegan dishes served on large platters with Ethiopian *injera* bread, used to scoop up the stew-like entrees. If you like spicy food, or something different, this is the spot for you.

For a vegetarian fix in Pawleys Island, head over to Quigley's Pint and Plate (843-237-7010; www.pintandplate.com), where the vegan burger, constructed from black-eyed peas, mushrooms, and wild rice, earns rave reviews.

GETTING YOUR BEARINGS

While the 60 miles of the Grand Strand are hard to cover in a single short visit, this itinerary lets you hit the high spots without getting stuck in traffic.

Once you're settled into your hotel, condo, or beach cottage, set out to get your bearings. If you're in North Myrtle, head down to Main Street in Ocean Drive and check out the shag clubs. If your digs are at the south end of the Strand, take a walk along the Murrells Inlet Marsh Walk. At both destinations you'll find plenty of nightlife going on until late.

If the family is along, consider a game of minigolf if the weather cooperates. Many courses stay open very late, and it's a great way to work off the extra energy built up from being cooped up in a car.

DAY 1

Early Breakfast
Fill up with pancakes at one of our recommended breakfast spots, then head for the beach.

Take a Spin
Stroll or bike ride along Myrtle Beach's new mile-long boardwalk. If you skipped breakfast, catch up with some caffeine at the Boardwalk Coffee House (843-839-1230; www.boardwalk coffeehouse.com). Next, take a spin on the Strand's newest attraction, the SkyWheel (www.skywheelusa.com).

Stop for Lunch
Grab a dog at Peaches Corner (843-448-7424; www.peaches-corner.com),

or a bucket of steamed oysters and a beer at Dirty Don's Oyster Bar & Grill (843-213-1632; www.dirtydons myrtlebeach.com) on the boardwalk.

Afternoon Sightseeing
Head out to the bypass for an afternoon of strolling Broadway at the Beach (www.broadwayatthebeach .com), the region's largest and most popular shopping and entertainment destination. Poke your head into all the shops, take a ride on the historic carousel, or marvel at the fire-breathing dragon guarding the minigolf course. Stop along the way for a craft beer at Liberty Brewery or a wine tasting at Boardwalk Wines. Or go on a hunt for the best margarita. Ripley's Aquarium, MagiQuest, and WonderWorks provide plenty of options for family fun.

If shopping and bar hopping just aren't your thing, head south down US 17 to the amazing Brookgreen Gardens (843-235-6000; www.brook green.org), where you'll find a world-class collection of sculpture set amid beautifully landscaped grounds. Then cross US 17 to Huntington Beach State Park for shell hunting along an unspoiled strip of beach.

Street legal electric golf cars are a popular way to get around.

The Hard Rock pyramid at Broadway at the Beach is a popular stop for all ages.

Apparently, the folks who make these kinds of decisions in the Hard Rock home office felt Myrtle Beach needed a pyramid. So they built one, the only pyramid-shaped Hard Rock Café (843-946-0007; www.hardrock .com) in the world. It's become both a landmark and an icon, putting the remarkable Broadway at the Beach complex on the map, while establishing a tradition of mega-architecture that sets the Myrtle Beach mood. Prowl the Egyptian-themed interior of the pyramid and check out the cool music memorabilia, enjoy a Legendary Burger, and ask about a behind-the-scenes tour. The outdoor patio has a great view of Celebrity Square and Lake Broadway, plus live music several nights a week. Hard Rock is also a favorite hangout for celebrity look-alikes from the Legends in Concert show next door, so keep an eye out for Elvis.

Dinner & a Show

With the broad range of entertainment available on the Strand, you can take your pick from tribute shows featuring music of past decades, live-action dinner theater, country western and patriotic reviews, music concerts, comedy by national headliners, and even minor league baseball. Check our listings of live shows to see all your options.

For dinner, select a restaurant close to your chosen theater, or fill up at happy hour and put off your meal until after the show if you don't want to be rushed.

Late Night

Pay an after-dark visit to the Myrtle Beach Boardwalk to enjoy the carnival atmosphere and lights. Or go for a stroll along the Murrells Inlet Marsh Walk—perfect on a moonlit evening.

DAY 2

Brunch

If today is Sunday, don't miss the gospel brunch at the House of Blues (843-272–3000; www.houseofblues .com). Talented gospel groups raise a joyful noise as you pile your plate with breakfast favorites, plus jambalaya, catfish, and prime rib. Take a stroll around the music venue to admire the unique Outsider artworks and bottle-cap decor, and to make room for the wickedly addictive white chocolate bread pudding with Jack Daniel's sauce. It's all-you-can-eat, so come hungry. You won't leave that way.

If your second day doesn't fall on a Sunday, consider breakfast or brunch at the Sea Captain's House (843-448-8082; www.seacaptains.com), the last of the seaside cottages serving meals on the Strand. Iconic Southern breakfast dishes here include pecan waffles and blueberry pancakes, along with a wonderful seafood omelet, crabcakes Benedict, and a sinfully rich Brie and bacon omelet.

Shopping and Strolling

After lunch, explore the shops and attractions at Barefoot Landing (www

.bflanding.com), one of the earliest examples of nature-based tourism. There's plenty of entertainment for all ages, including the excellent Alligator Adventure, sightseeing cruises on the ICW, and a Ghosts and Legends show that runs all day.

Lunch before You Go

For a relaxing meal before you head home, try the waterside deck at Greg Norman's Australian Grille & Pub (843-361-0000; www.gregnormans australiangrille.com) in Barefoot Landing. Here you'll have an unequalled view of the "back" side of the Strand along the ICW, far from the sun and surf, and often preferred by locals.

Greg Norman's Australian Grille occupies a prime spot along the ICW.

Extend Your Stay

ART MUSEUMS & GALLERIES

At the south end of Ocean Boulevard in Myrtle Beach, the Franklin G. Burroughs–Simeon B. Chapin Art Museum (843-238-2510; www.myrtle beachartmuseum.org) hosts changing exhibits of regional and national art in a charming 1924 beach cottage near Springmaid Pier. This free museum is open Tuesday–Sunday.

The Burroughs-Chapin Art Museum occupies a traditional seaside cottage.

Did you know? The **Myrtle Beach Convention Center** (843-918-1225; www.myrtlebeachconvention center.com) at 21st Avenue North is home to one of the famous Wyland Whaling Walls. The enormous, 250-foot-long mural, *Right Whales off the South Carolina Coast*, covers the center's exterior west wall. Also at the convention center: the **South Carolina Hall of Fame** (843-626-7444; www.the officialschalloffame.com), with portraits and touch-screen bios of famous South Carolina natives, past and present, including President Andrew Jackson, jazz legend Dizzy Gillespie, and many more. The hall of fame is open Monday–Friday 8–5, and admission is free.

A right whale painted by Wyland swims along the outside of the Myrtle Beach Convention Center.

If you like this . . . plan a visit to the ☂ Collector's Cafe & Gallery (843-449-9370; www.collectorscafeandgallery.com) on North Kings Highway, where you can browse six rooms filled with art while enjoying an espresso or a cocktail. Locals love to drop by for dessert or after-work libation.

On the 17 Bypass in Murrells Inlet, ((•)) Ebb & Flow Art Co-op (843-651-2386; www.ebbandflowartco-op.com) features works by local artists, plus live music and great coffee.

Pawleys Island at the south end of the Strand is something of an artist's haven, with numerous galleries strung along US 17, including Art Works at the Litchfield Exchange (843-235-9600; www.artwrks.net) and the Cheryl Newby Gallery (843-979-0149 or 1-800-435-2733; www.cherylnewbygallery.com). The Island Art Gallery (843-455-9007; www.pawleysislandart.com) in the Village Shops offers works by Betsy McDonald and other local artists, plus classes and workshops in art techniques.

Many local artists are members of the Seacoast Artist Guild (843-655-1800; www.seacoastartistguild.com). Their work is available at the new Seacoast Mall Gallery at Inlet Square Mall (www.inletsquaremall.com) on the US 17 Bypass in Murrells Inlet. Or you can enjoy artworks by members along with breakfast or lunch and free WiFi at the ((•)) Applewood House of Pancakes (843-979-1022; www.applewoodhouseofpancakes.com), located in the Exchange Shops of Litchfield Beach. Additional exhibits by Seacoast Artist Guild members hang at the Socastee Library (843-215-4700; www.horry.lib.sc.us) and at the Horry-Georgetown Technical College Grand Strand Campus (843-477-0808; www.hgtc.edu).

If you like this . . . Coastal Carolina University (843-349-6454; www .coastal.edu/bryanartgallery) sponsors changing exhibits in a wide variety of art forms and traditions in its free Bryan Gallery on campus.

Maximize your local art exposure by planning your visit during the annual Pawleys Island Festival of Music and Art (843-626-8911; www.pawleysmusic .com), held for two weeks in late September. Along with numerous concerts, films, and wine tastings, the festival includes a Sunday Gallery Crawl featuring a dozen galleries and studios from Murrells Inlet to Georgetown.

GARDENS & NATURE CENTERS

Bring your camera for a visit to ✈ 🍴 ♿ ⚥ Brookgreen Gardens (843-235-6000; www.brookgreen.org), the loveliest spot on the Grand Strand. This 300-acre garden, which recently celebrated its 80th anniversary, houses over 1,400 works of figurative American sculpture set amid formal gardens in the European mold. Highlights include an alley of 250-year-old moss-draped live oaks; Carl Milles's Fountain of the Muses, formerly in NYC's Metropolitan Museum of Art; a butterfly house; and a medieval labyrinth.

Children enjoy the Discovery Center, with interactive exhibits, as well as the Lowcountry Zoo, exhibiting native animals, including otters, foxes, alligators, and wild turkeys, in their natural habitats. The Cypress Aviary features boardwalks through a swamp inhabited by local birds. Another section of the zoo exhibits animals used on area plantations, including the Carolina Marsh Tacky, a unique breed of horse dating to Colonial days, and other heritage species.

Tickets to Brookgreen are good for a week, so come back another day for a pontoon boat tour of the abandoned ricefields that surround the gardens, or a minibus tour to the old plantations along the Waccamaw River, including Oaks Plantation, said to be haunted by Theodosia Alston, the daughter of Aaron Burr. The lovely young woman was lost at sea in 1813, but her son and husband are buried here.

The equestrian statue at the entrance to Brookgreen Gardens is by founder Anna Hyatt Huntington.

Check the table outside the Welcome Center as you arrive to find out what's blooming during your visit. A short film tells the history of Brookgreen. Lunch and refreshments are available at several cafés within the gardens, including the ((ɣ)) Pavilion Restaurant. Shuttles take visitors to various parts of the grounds.

The graveyard at Vereen Gardens dates to colonial days.

The ruins of Atalaya retain Moorish ironwork and a courtyard of palms.

Across from the Brookgreen entrance, Huntington Beach State Park preserves the eerie remains of ♿ Atalaya (843-237-4440; www.huntingtonbeachstatepark .com), home of the Garden's founders, Anna and Archer Huntington. Now a crumbling ruin, the huge house is designed in the Moorish style, with more than 30 rooms, including kennels and bear pens where Anna kept subjects for her sculptures. The palm court, centered on a ruined minaret, evokes a lost age— guaranteed to give you a shiver. Admission to Atalaya is $1, which includes either a self-guided or docent-led tour, or you can rent an audio tour.

At the north end of the Strand, the Vereen Memorial Historical Gardens (843-249-4157; www.cclittleriver.org), located just a mile south of the North Car-

Did you know? Archer Huntington inherited the fortune of his father, railroad industrialist Collis Huntington, who founded the city of Newport News, Virginia, as well as the shipbuilding company that became today's Northrop Grumman. In 1930, after his marriage to sculptress Anna Hyatt, Archer purchased four former rice plantations as a setting for her sculptures, as well as the couple's growing art collection. The couple built a winter home on an adjacent stretch of beachfront, naming it Atalaya. Archer, a noted expert on Spanish culture, designed the Moorish mansion himself and had it built with local labor. Today, Atalaya is the centerpiece of Huntington Beach State Park, while the plantations across US 17 are open to the public as Brookgreen Gardens. The golden equestrian statue at the Gardens' entrance is the work of Anna Hyatt Huntington.

olina border in Little River, preserves part of the Vareen Plantation, owned by the same family since the early 1800s. Trails and boardwalks lead through native woodland down to a salt marsh on the ICW. Historic features include the Vareen Family Cemetery, with graves dating to the Revolutionary War era, and section of the Old Kings Highway, one of the few stretches to retain its original sandy surface. The gardens are located off US 17 on SC 179/Calabash Road. Trail maps and information are available at the C. B. Berry Community and Historical Center at the Gardens' entrance. Admission is free.

*If you like this . . . in Surfside Beach, **Martin Park** (843-650-4131; www .surfsidebeach.org) on Floral Lake, with a scenic footbridge, fountain, dogwood trees, and serene swans cruising the waters, makes a pleasant spot for a picnic or stroll.*

Festivals at Huntington Beach State Park include the Atalaya Arts and Crafts Festival (www.atalayafestival.com), held in late September; and Three-in-One Day, held on March 10, honoring the Huntington's birthdays and anniversary. Across the street, Brookgreen sponsors many festivals and special events, including the most spectacular, Nights of a Thousand Candles, when the gardens are lit with thousands of candles and other lights during the holiday season.

HISTORY & HERITAGE

Once rice was king in this region, with many plantations located on the Waccamaw Neck, the peninsula of land between the Waccamaw River and the ocean, where one of the largest holdings was the Hobcaw Barony, a 1718 royal land grant of over 17,000 acres. Eventually subdivided into more than a dozen plantations, the Barony was reassembled by native South Carolinian and Wall Street financier Bernard Barush in 1905 for use as a winter hunting retreat. His 1930 mansion, containing mementos of the visits of Winston Churchill, FDR, and other luminaries, is included on van tours of the Hobcaw Barony (843-546-4623; www.hobcaw barony.org), available by reservation only. The tour visits several other historic properties, as well as Fairfield Village, the last intact slave village on the Waccamaw Neck. Barush's daughter, Belle, established a foundation on the barony dedicated to ecological research. The free ♂ & Discovery Center, with exhibits on local history and ecosystems, and a large aquarium of local species, is open weekdays. Numerous special programs, including bike, kayak, fishing, and birding expeditions, plus summer day camps, take place on the property, now part of the North Inlet-Winyah Bay National Estuarine Research Reserve (www.northinlet.sc.edu).

The manor house at Hobcaw Barony hosted presidents and foreign dignitaries.

If you like this . . . journey south along US 17 to the 🐾 ♿ Sewee Visitor & Environmental Education Center (843-928-3368; www.fws.gov/seweecenter/) in the Francis Marion Forest for more information on the local ecology and a visit with a family of red wolves.

Fast facts:
• *Hobcaw* is a Native American word meaning "between the waters."
• The **Horry County** website (www.horrycounty.org) offers historical brochures for download with driving tours to a number of local historic sites, including Gallivants Ferry, Little River, and Socastee.

After the Civil War, before tourism came to the region, much of the population of Horry County made their living on hardscrabble farms growing tobacco, peanuts, and vegetables; raising milk cows and hogs; and plowing their fields with mules. Two living-history farms in the area preserve and demonstrate this way of life.

Located off US 701, the 🐾 L. W. Paul Living History Farm (843-365-3596; www.horrycountymuseum.org), a project of the Horry County Museum, re-creates life on a one-horse farm in the early 1900s. 🐾 Freewoods Farm (843-650-9139; www.freewoodsfarm.com), off SC 707 in Burgess, brings an African American agricultural village of the late 1800s to life, with a working, animal-powered farm, a rural Main Street of shops, and a wetlands walk. Activities at the farms change with the seasons and include grinding grits, making lye soap and cane syrup, milking cows, and other everyday activities.

If you like this . . . visit the 🐾 🌳 Historic Myrtle Beach Colored School Museum and Education Center (843-918-1050; www.cityofmyrtlebeach.com /coloredschool.html) to discover more about the region's African American heritage. This re-created 1932 schoolhouse contains exhibits and a library. Admission is free.

At the free 🐾 🌳 Horry County Museum (843-915-5320; www.horrycounty museum.org) on Main Street in Conway, exhibits explore local flora and fauna, including the American alligator and black bear; the region's days as a logging and turpentine center; local crafts; tobacco farming; and artifacts from the CSS *Pee Dee*, a Confederate gunboat scuttled near the Mars Bluff Naval Yard.

If you like this . . . tour the 1912 Historic Bryan House (843-488-1966; www.hchsonline.org), headquarters of the Horry County Historical Society, also located on Conway's Main Street.

Galivants Ferry (www.palmettohistorysc.org), on the eastern bank of the Little Pee Dee River on US 501, west of Conway, has more than a dozen buildings listed in the National Register of Historic Places, including tobacco barns, a century-old general store, and a vintage 1922 gas station, now a museum with tin signs and antique pumps. Since 1876 locals have gathered here in even-numbered years to meet politicians and eat chicken bog at stump speakings, a tradition that continues today. The Galivants Ferry Stump (www.galivantsferrystump.com) is the longest-running Democratic gathering of this type in America.

Civil War buffs will enjoy the 🌳 South Carolina Civil War Museum (843-

Gallivants Ferry is home to the country's longest-running political stump meeting.

293-4344; www.mbisr.com/sccivilwar museum.html) on the US 17 Bypass adjacent to the Myrtle Beach Indoor Shooting Range. Exhibits include artifacts recovered from the Confederate Mars Bluff Naval Yard on the Pee Dee River.

During World War II the Myrtle Beach Air Force Base played an important part in the war effort. Today the airfield forms the basis of Myrtle Beach International Airport, but the air force days are commemorated at Warbird Park (843-918-1014; www.cityofmyrtle beach.com/wall.html) on Farrow Parkway, where three aircraft once stationed at the base are on display. The nearby Veterans Café & Grille (843-232-8387; www.veteranscafeandgrille.com) exhibits military memorabilia.

If you like this . . . visit the Hall of Heroes (1-800-978-9598; www.sands resorts.com/heroes) at the Ocean Dunes Resort on the beach at 75th Avenue North in Myrtle Beach. Exhibits include a replica of the Vietnam Veterans Memorial Wall, a Gold Dog Tag display, flags, and more.

If the history of the automobile is your passion, visit the ☂ Wheels of Yesteryear (843-903-4774; www.wheelsofyesteryearmb.com), located near the Myrtle Beach Speedway off US 501 on the western side of the ICW, where Paul Cummings's collection of over 100 classic American cars and trucks is on display.

LIVE SHOWS

Often compared to Branson, Missouri, and Pigeon Forge, Tennessee, the numerous live shows along the Strand provide a wealth of family-friendly entertainment options mixed with Vegas-style production values.

The first and still the best by many standards is the ♿ Carolina Opry (843-913-4000; www.thecarolinaopry.com), founded in 1986 by Calvin Gilmore, an Ozarks Mountain farm boy fresh from Nashville. Today his ever-changing country music review attracts the best talent from around the country and an army of returning fans who come to the show each year. Opry performances share the stage at the 2,200-seat, state-of-the-art theater with *Vibrations!*, a high-energy show set to hits of the '60s, '70s, and '80s; a laser light show; and a popular Christmas special.

The ☂ ♿ Alabama Theatre (843-272-1111; www.alabama-theatre.com) in Barefoot Landing presents a new variety show each year, plus a Christmas show and a lineup of top country legends, rhythm and blues greats, and big bands. Sometimes you'll even find Alabama—the country supergroup who began this theater in 1993 to honor their Grand Strand roots as house band at the Bowery—on stage here. You'll certainly see much Alabama memorabilia on the walls.

Tribute shows are some of the most popular on the Strand, and ☂ ♿ Legends

The Palace at Broadway at the Beach is the Strand's grandest theater.

in Concert (843-238-7827; www.legendsinconcert.com) is the don't-miss entry in this category. With sister shows in Las Vegas and around the world, Legends features talented impersonators who rotate every four months, ensuring an experience that's always fresh. The Legends show, long a stalwart presence in Surfside Beach, recently moved into a free-standing theater next to Planet Hollywood at Broadway at the Beach.

If you like this . . . the ら Celebration Music Theatre (843-839-5483; www.celebrationmb.com), produced and directed by a team long associated with Legends in Concert, presents SuperStarz! Live at the former Legends theater in Surfside Beach.

More legends of the past can be found at ら ⵎ *Dino's TV Variety Show* (843-234-2229; www.dinostvvarietyshow.com), based on the Dean Martin shows of the '60s and '70s, featuring Dino and his Gold Diggers and celebrity guests of the era. Shows take place in the Starlight Room, a cabaret room with cocktail and dinner service at the 2001 Entertainment Complex on Lake Arrowhead Road. A second show, *The Marvelous Wonderettes*, features music from the 1950s.

The spectacular ⵌ ら Palace Theatre (843-448-9224; www.palace theatremyrtlebeach.com), a 2,700-seat showplace at Broadway at the Beach, offers a variety of family-friendly shows year-round. Kid favorites include *Le Grand Cirque*, *Christmas on Ice*, and a

Fast fact: Shows at the Palace Theatre are produced by David King (www.spiritshows.com), originator of the hit touring show *Spirit of the Dance*.

troupe of Irish stepdancers and singers, while the *Hooray for Hollywood* tribute show brings back memories from favorite movies of the past.

If you like this . . . two dinner theaters cater principally to the younger crowd. ♪ Ꮣ *Medieval Times Dinner & Tournament (843-236-4635; www .medievaltimes.com) appeals to horse lovers and princess hopefuls.* ♪ Ꮣ *Pirates Voyage (843-497-9700; www.piratesvoyage.com), Dolly Parton's new show, takes aim at swashbucklers of all ages.*

The new Pat Boone Family Theater (843-213-6880; www.pbftheater.com), occupying the former NASCAR Café site across from Broadway at the Beach, books shows by master illusionists, as well as performances by singer Pat Boone, members of his family, and recording artists from his record label.

MUSIC, THEATER & DANCE

Although the Grand Strand is known for its music halls, those with a taste for more traditional forms of entertainment will find plenty of offerings, especially in the off-season.

Atlantic Stage (877-287-8587; www.atlanticstage.com), founded by faculty and staff from the Coastal Carolina University arts departments, teaming with local theater professionals, presents professional-quality productions, as well as new play readings, wine soirees, and more at their theater at 79th Street North off the 17 Bypass in Myrtle Beach.

In downtown Conway, the Theatre of the Republic (843-488-0821; www .theatreoftherepublic.com) presents plays, a popular Holiday Revue, and children's theater productions in the restored Main Street Theatre.

If you like this . . . two other community theater groups produce plays in the region. The Murrells Inlet Community Players (843-651-4152; www.mictheatre .com) presents a broad range of plays during the off-season in a former schoolhouse. In Georgetown, the Swamp Fox Players (843-527-2924; www.swampfox players.com) stage musicals and comedies year-round in the historic Strand Theater, a landmark on Front Street.

The Long Bay Symphony (843-448-8379; www.longbaysymphony.com) offers symphony and chamber music concerts, as well as family and pops events.

During the academic year, Coastal Carolina University (843-349-2502; www.coastal.edu) presents nationally known music and dance companies in Wheelwright Auditorium on the Conway campus. The ensembles that make up the CCU Music Department (www.coastal .edu/music), including guitar, flute, and percussion ensembles, a jazz big band, and a gospel choir, offer concerts during the school year, especially near the end of term. The CCU Theatre Department (www.coastal.edu/theatre) presents an aggressive schedule ranging from comedies to classics, including Broadway hits, musicals, new plays, and physical theater in the Cirque du Soleil–style.

Fast fact: Look for the lights made of tomato cans donated by local restaurants and the resident "mouse" during shows by the Murrells Inlet Community Players.

Did you know? Entertainment is easy to find on the Grand Strand, with numerous street festivals, free concerts, and fireworks displays sponsored by both private and public groups. **Myrtle Beach Downtown** (www.myrtlebeachdowntown .com) sponsors Hot Summer Nights, with entertainment centered on Plyler Park and the boardwalk throughout the summer. **North Myrtle Beach** (www.nmb events.com) sponsors the Sounds of Summer concert series in McLean Park, as well as Music on Main, bringing bands to Ocean Drive. **Barefoot Landing** (843-272-8349; www.bflanding.com) hosts Summerfest, with street entertainers, fireworks, and camel rides. **Broadway at the Beach** (843-444-3200; www.broadway atthebeach.com) schedules fireworks and free shows all year. At the **Market Common** (843-839-3500; www.marketcommonmb.com), Music in the Streets presents blues and jazz bands. Also check out the laid-back weekend concerts at **La Belle Amie Vineyard** (843-399-9463; www.labelleamie.com) and the wicked popular Sunday Funday concerts at the *♂* **Boathouse Waterway Bar & Grill** (843-903-2628; www.boathousemb.com).

For a unique theatrical experience, make reservations for the monthly dinner theater held at the historic *♂* Cooper House (843-236-7077; www.thecooper house.net), located next to the Socastee Swing Bridge over the ICW.

BARS, NIGHTLIFE & HAPPY HOURS

For an update on happy hours up and down the Strand, visit www.myrtlebeach happyhour.com. For the latest in live music, check the listings at www.listenupmb .com.

Beachfront Bars

If your idea of a great day at the beach is sand between your toes and a cold beer in hand, you need to find an oceanfront bar. Alcohol is prohibited on the beach, so seek out spots where you can relax on private property while still enjoying access to the surf. Although high beachfront values have made spots like this less numerous, we've found a few clubs where you can kick back and enjoy. At the majority of these spots, you can walk right in from the beach, bare feet and all. Traveling from north to south along the oceanfront, here are our favorites.

In Cherry Grove, the place to hang is *♂ Ⓨ* Fat Harold's on the Ocean (843-249-5601; www.haroldsontheocean.com) at the corner where Sea Mountain Highway meets Ocean Boulevard. The sister club of Harold's Beach Club in Ocean Drive, this little club, known by fans as HOTO's, serves up beach music concerts on its oceanfront deck, steamed seafood, great burgers, and plenty of floor for shagging.

A bit farther down the beach, two popular clubs sit on either side of the Horseshoe at the end of Main Street in Ocean Drive. The Ⓨ Spanish Galleon/OD Beach Club (843-249-1436; www.thespanishgalleon.net), part of the Ocean Drive Resort (1-800-438-9590; www.oceandriveresort.com), spills out onto the beach, with several bars, and both indoor and outdoor floors for shagging. On the south

The outside dance floor at the O.D. Beach Club is a favorite with shaggers

side of the Horseshoe, step back in time at the ⚓ 🐾 ((•)) O.D. Pavilion (843-280-0715; www.odpavilion.net), the last open-air shag hall on the Strand. DJs spin shag favorites for the grown-up crowd; kids enjoy the arcade; and the Sunset Grill serves beach favorites. During the summer, amusement rides join the fun.

⚓ 🐾 ⟙ 🍸 Molly Darcy's Irish Pub & Restaurant (843-272-5555; www.mollydarcy.com), at the end of 17th Avenue South in the Crescent Beach section of NMB, sits right on the sand, with two levels of patio for great views. There's a game room for kids, frequent live entertainment, Irish and otherwise, and a menu of Irish specialties, including Irish breakfast, complete with bangers and grilled tomatoes, served all day.

Join the pool party at 🍸 Ocean Annie's Beach Bar (1-888-266-4375; www.oceanannies.com) in the Sands Ocean Club Resort (1-800-726-3783; www.sandsoceanclub.com), with live music and dancing on the deck March–November. To find the resort, take Lake Arrowhead Road to Shore Drive, then follow it south to the end.

In MB, St. Clements Beach Bar & Grill (843-449-1112; www.properattire 2000.com), next to the Caravelle Resort at 70th Avenue North, is noted for its friendly, laid-back vibe, ocean views, frozen cocktails, and inexpensive beach fare. Open seasonally.

🍸 Bummz Beach Café (843-915-9111; www.bummz.com), tucked in among the high-rise resorts between 19th and 20th Avenues on N. Ocean Boulevard, makes a great homebase for days at the beach. Come sundown, tiki torches begin to blaze and local acoustic acts entertain the crowd.

Several bars are located along the new Myrtle Beach Boardwalk, but for live local music, and a seat directly on the boardwalk, the 🍸 Ocean Front Bar & Grill (843-448-5142; www.oceanfrontgrill.com) is your best bet. Originally established in 1948, this spot has survived hurricanes and economic downturns thanks to its ice-cold beer and excellent chili.

If you like this . . . on the south end of Myrtle Beach, look for McAdoo's Cafe Oceanfront Beach Bar (843-448-3863) on the north side of the Family Kingdom amusement park at Second Avenue South; and Mako's Oceanfront Bar and Grill (843-808-MAKO; www.facebook.com/makosoceanfront), home of the Jaws Burger, in the Reef Resort at 21st Avenue South.

On Surfside Beach, 🍸 Scotty's Beach Bar (843-238-9363; www.surfsidebeach resort.com), at the Surfside Beach Resort offers live music during the summer season, karaoke, and a Monday night luau with free refreshments.

In Garden City Beach, the Conch Café (843-651-6556; www.conchcafe .net), about a half mile north of the pier, serves seafood and refreshments on its oceanfront deck.

The bright and breezy 🐚 Cabana Café and Beach Bar (843-235-8700; www.litchfieldinn.com) at the Litchfield Inn, has a lot going for it—a location right on the beach, plus the creative dishes of Bill Austin, one of the Strand's top chefs, all in a casual setting. Find it at the eastern end of Litchfield Drive.

Many Grand Strand beach clubs are just steps from the ocean.

At many beach bars you can come in barefoot from the sand. Karen Wright

Locals know the best parties happen on the ICW. Excellent waterfront views and superb sunsets are the draw here, but you'll also find plenty of fun going on, with bands and happy hour specials. You can even arrive by boat. Most of these spots offer complimentary docking for patrons. Starting in Little River, we'll hit the hot spots all the way to Murrells Inlet.

The Patio Tiki Bar (843-727-7228; www.patiostikibar.com) sits on a multilevel deck with live oaks growing through it, just behind the SunCruz Casino boat offices, right on the water in Little River, with unmatched views of the marsh, a menu of specialties from its sister restaurant, the award-winning Little River Deli (843-399-9492; www.littleriverdeli.com), and live music at sundown.

Close by, the Y Key West Crazy Waterfront Grill & Tavern (843-249-6163; www.keywestcrazyrestaurant.com) serves up a long happy hour, steamed and fried seafood, and live music. On Sundays, there's a make-it-yourself Bloody Mary bar and crabcake brunch.

If you like this . . . Fibber's on the Water (843-280-2271; www.fibbers littleriver.com), an Irish-themed spot with extensive outside decks and a kids' playground, has great views of the docks and an all-day happy hour.

If you're up for a bar crawl, head around the corner to Y (( )) Rum RunnerZ (843-427-4459; www.rumrunnerzbar.com), a casual, smoke-free joint with free WiFi, free Wii sports, an Internet juke box set to shag, a popular happy hour, and a weekly blues jam.

A bit farther south on the ICW, Snooky's on the Water (843-249-5252; www.snookysonthewater.com), located on a second-floor deck at the Cricket Cove Marina (843-249-7169; www.cricketcovemarina.com), is a local secret, popular for its sunset gatherings and daily happy hour. If you're coming by boat, look for mile marker 345; approaching by car, turn east at the Little River light on Baker Street and go to the end.

A couple of bars bracket Cherry Grove's double bridges: Y Capt. Poo's Blue Marlin Yacht & Fishing Club (843-249-7881; www.captpoos.com), a real local hangout with a big outside deck, seats along the waterfront, and frequent live music; and Y Filet's on the Water (843-280-5200; www.filetsonthewater.com), in Harbourgate Marina on the south side of the Swing Bridge, with dancing on the tiki deck and freshly rolled sushi as the sun goes down.

Y Boom Boom's Raw Bar (843-427-7304; www.boomboomsrawbar.com) at 13th Avenue North in NMB occupies a prime waterside spot in one of North Myrtle's most popular marinas. Frequent live music, cornhole tournaments, happy hour specials, steamed seafood, and a late-night menu are the draws.

Located on the west side of the ICW, Y Docksider's Grille (843-

Along the ICW you can bar crawl by boat.

390-4745; www.docksidersgrille.com) draws a crowd from the surrounding Barefoot Resort. Overlooking the docks of Barefoot Marina, this is a more casual experience than you'll find across the Waterway at Greg Norman's Australian Grille (843-361-0000; www.gregnormansaustraliangrille.com), although Norman's does have a beautiful waterfront patio, equipped with fireplaces for cool evenings, and some nice happy hour specials.

Situated far out on the docks at the Grande Dunes Marina, Anchor Cafe (843-315-7855; www.marinainnatgrandedunes.com) is a very special place to celebrate the sunset. Featuring a menu from the award-winning kitchens of the Marina Inn and a variety of tropical cocktails, the café is open only seasonally, April–October.

If you'd rather have a rockin' party than a serene waterfront view, then the ✍ ❤ Boathouse Waterway Bar & Grill (843-903-2628; www.boathousemb.com) is for you. Located on the west side of the ICW, on the south side of the US 501 bridge, the boathouse has decks and lawns dotted with hammocks and weeping willow trees leading down to the waterfront; daily promotions; family-friendly movie nights; and a free Sunday summer concert series open to all ages.

Off the beaten track, but well worth finding, ✍ ❤ (📶) Hannah Banana's Sunshine Cabana (843-357-3655; www.hannahbananascabana.com) overlooks the ICW, here also the Waccamaw River, at mile marker 383. The huge deck shaded by an ancient cypress is the location of many a sundown celebration. Hannah Banana's is in the Wacca Wache Marina (843-651-2994 or 1-800-395-6694; www.waccawachemarina.com). To find it, turn west off US 17/Ocean Highway in Murrells Inlet on Wachesaw Road and follow it to the end.

Quick tips:

• On the Saturday following Thanksgiving each year, the **Intracoastal Christmas Regatta** (www.christmasregatta.com) kicks off the holiday season with a lighted boat parade from the Little River waterfront to Dock Holidays Marina at 13th Avenue in North Myrtle Beach.

• If you're planning a big night out, arrange for the folks at Hannah Banana's to send out their complimentary "sober shuttle," which will both pick you up and take you home.

The bridge at Grande Dunes is a landmark along the ICW.

Murrells Inlet after Dark

Just walking along the marsh walk (www.murrellsinletmarshwalk.com) after dark is a pleasure, with the brightly lit restaurants on one side and the tranquil marsh on the other. Take a stroll on a summer evening and listen to the bands competing for your attention. The bars along the marsh walk don't generally charge covers, so you

Look for the statue of Brother Love along the Murrells Inlet Marsh Walk.

can spend the evening wandering from one to the next.

Beside Capt. Dave's Dockside, Bubba's Love Shak (843-651-5850; www.bubbasloveshak.com), with its bright Caribbean colors and good-time vibe, hosts live bands every evening during the summer season, weekend nights all year. Happy hour appetizer specials include fish tacos, bacon-wrapped scallops, and steamed mussels, all from the excellent Dockside kitchen.

Other spots along the marsh walk that host live bands during the summer months include Drunken Jack's (843-651-2044; www.drunkenjacks .com); Wahoo's Raw Bar & Marina (843-651-5800; www.wahoosbar.com), a tropics-themed tiki hut with a menu drawn from the Divine Fish House (843-651-5800; www.divinefishhouse .com) next door; and CreekRatz (843-357-2891; www.creekratz.com), with live bands most nights and shagging on Sunday afternoons. A special kids' corner keeps the youngsters entertained.

The Dead Dog Saloon (843-651-0664; www.deaddogsaloon.com) is another family-friendly stop, with a fun, doggie theme; humorous art; live music during the summer; and the best patio on the marsh walk. Across the parking lot at Crazy Sister's Marina, Spud's (843-651-9987; www.spudsdining.com) sponsors music and other fun goings-on at its waterfront tiki bar.

Fast fact: Bubba's Love Shak is named for Jerome Lorenzo Smalls, aka Bubba Love, a much-beloved local character and self-proclaimed mayor of the marsh walk who has worked in various restaurants along Murrells Inlet since he was a small boy. Bubba is currently employed at Drunken Jack's, where one of his duties is feeding the goats and peacocks on Goat Island. He also receives royalties for the use of his name and likeness in the Love Shak and on souvenir items. Look for a statue of Bubba Love as you stroll the marsh walk. It's a favorite photo op.

Farther south down US 17 Business, the ⏚ Ⅶ Hot Fish Club (843-357-9175; www.facebook.com/hotfishclub) hosts bands in its marshside gazebo. Sit on the back deck or relax in a lawn chair overlooking the water. There's a playground out there for youngsters.

Comedy Clubs

Located on Restaurant Row, the Ⅶ Comedy Cabana (843-449-4242; www.comedy cabana.com) is the Strand's top laugh factory, featuring five-star comedians seen on Comedy Central, HBO, and the late-night talk shows. Dinner and drinks are served, and shows are for adults only. Teens can attend with a parent.

If you like this . . . in Murrells Inlet, Ⅶ Stand Up Carolina Comedy Club (843-651-7819; www.standupcarolina.com) stages very popular shows with top comedians.

Looking for a family-friendly evening of laughs? The Carolina Improv Company (www.carolinaimprov.com) presents audience-participation shows suitable for all ages at Uptown (843-272-4242; www.uptownmb.com), a facility that also offers an art gallery and improv classes for kids and adults. It's located inside the Myrtle Beach Mall along Restaurant Row.

Dance Clubs

Myrtle Beach has a teen-only nightclub for people 13–19. Karma Ultimate Nightlife (843-455 6061; www.karmamb.com) has an ocean-view party deck, state-of-the-art sound and light show, 14-foot video screens, and a cool vibe. Karma is located three blocks north of the late, lamented Attic on the boardwalk. Teens are also welcome at the family-friendly concerts at ⸨ᵧ⸩ Fresh Brewed (843 251-8282; www.freshbrewedcoffeehouse.com), an alcohol-free coffeehouse on Broadway at 10th Avenue North.

The Ⅶ 2001 Entertainment Complex (843-449-9435; www.2001nightclub .com), on Lake Arrowhead Road in the Restaurant Row area, offers nightlife for everyone. The enormous facility houses two nightclubs, plus a theater with two live shows. Club Touch is a multilevel dance club, with DJs spinning video mix-ups for dancing until dawn. Next Level, with a wooden floor ideal for shagging, features local and national bands playing beach, oldies, and soul; two bars; lots of seating; and nonsmoking areas.

At Cagney's Old Place (843-449-0288; www.cagneysoldplace.com), nearby on Restaurant Row, couples dance to the oldies on weekend nights amid mementos of Myrtle Beach's past.

For something a bit different, ▼ ⸨ᵧ⸩ Time Out! (843-448-1160; www .timeoutmbsc.com), the Strand's top gay night club, offers dancing and drag shows every night of the week at 520 Eighth Avenue North, Myrtle Beach.

Celebrity Square is the center of nightlife at Broadway at the Beach.

A one-time $5 membership fee is collected at the door from first-time guests.

As in most things, Broadway at the Beach (www.broadwayatthebeach.com) takes nightlife to an over-the-top experience. Much of the action centers on Celebrity Square, located between the Hard Rock Café pyramid and Lake Broadway. Here you'll find a New Orleans–style street-party atmosphere, with clubs offering everything from dueling pianos to video DJs. Themes change frequently, but most of the clubs belong to two companies with plenty of entertainment experience: Fantastic Clubs (www.fantasticclubs.com) and Celebrations Nightlife (843-444-3500; www.celebrationsnitelife.com). Hot spots include Ƴ Crocodile Rocks (843-444-2096), a dueling piano bar; the family-friendly ◈ ⊤ Ƴ Broadway Louie's, with an arcade and karaoke for the kids and a sports bar with 36 screens for Dad; and Ƴ Blarney Stone's Pub & Cigar Bar (843-626-6644), with live music, dancing, and free admission. Upstairs, Z Bar provides an oasis of calm above the crowds where you can enjoy a martini and cigar.

Celebrations' venues participate in a free Tuesday Night Pub Crawl along with Fat Tuesday (843-444-3255; www.fat-tuesday.com), a Mardi Gras–themed spot with the world's largest selection of frozen cocktails.

Broadway at the Beach is the perfect place for a do-it-yourself pub crawl. Margarita lovers can work their way along Lake Broadway's north shore, with stops at Señor Frog's (843-444-5506; www.senorfrogsmyrtle beach.com) and sister restaurant, Carlos'n Charlie's (843-712-1952; www.carlosandcharlies.com), ending up at ◈ Jimmy Buffett's Margaritaville (843-448-5455; www.margaritavillemyrtlebeach.com), where the music, laid-back vibrations, and booze in the blender (delivered by a special-effect hurricane) never stop.

> **Fast fact:** Tucked away inside the ◈ Ƴ **Surfside Bowling and Family Entertainment Center** (843-238-2695; www.surfside bowlingcenter.com), the Brickhouse Lounge hosts a variety of social dancing and lessons each week, including country two-step, line dancing, shag, ballroom, and Latin/salsa.

Live Music

The iconic ♿ Ƴ House of Blues (843-272–3000; www.houseofblues.com) rises to the top of any live music venue list. National and international bands of every genre take the stage here, and the decor couldn't be better—a giant tin-roofed tobacco barn, decorated with millions of brightly painted bottlecaps and bodacious examples of Outsider art. The adjacent restaurant hosts live music as well as a popular happy hour. You can also hear gospel music on Sundays or attend a murder mystery dinner theater.

The legendary Bowery (843-626-3445; www.thebowery.com), located close to the Myrtle Beach Boardwalk on Ninth Avenue North, has been entertaining locals and visitors since 1944. It's the honky-tonk from which the supergroup Alabama hatched back in the 1970s, and continues to offer down-home, good-time music every night of the week, except during the winter months. Alabama memorabilia covers the walls here, and members of the band have been known to show up and sit in. Those in the know order several mugs of beer at a time.

Fast fact: Alabama served as house band at the Bowery from 1973 to 1980, often playing for tips as they worked on the original songs that would soon vault them to national fame.

Quick tip: Check to see if your visit coincides with the date of a **South by Southeast Music Feast** (www.southbysoutheast.org) for a unique musical experience. The ticket price includes a potluck supper, beverages, socializing with the local music community, and an intimate concert at the old Myrtle Beach Train Depot in downtown MB. Proceeds provide assistance and support to local music education programs.

The PIT, short for Pawleys Island Tavern (843-237-8465; www.pawleys islandtavern.com), is a real find for those who love the blues. And we do mean "find"; look for its bright-green mailbox behind the Island Shops on the west side of US 17/Ocean Highway, and turn down the dirt road behind the Mole Hole. Your persistence will be rewarded with excellent music of the blues and bluegrass variety; a laid-back, friendly atmosphere; and local brews. Closed Mondays.

For additional live music and events along the Grand Strand, consult the *Sun News* Kicks online edition (www.thesunnews.com/kicks-online); the *Weekly Surge* (www.weeklysurge.com), and *Listen Up Myrtle Beach* (www.listenupmb.com).

Piano Bars
In Little River the Wine Bistro at the Brentwood Restaurant (843-249-2601; thebrentwoodrestaurant.com) hosts a piano bar on weekends featuring George Devens performing tunes from the Golden Age of Hollywood and Broadway musicals.

On Restaurant Row, Rossi's (843-449-0481; www.rossismyrtlebeach.com), one of the Strand's top Italian venues, features Rat Pack–style entertainment in the Eighty-Eights piano bar until 2 AM.

If you like this . . . Martini's (843-249-1134; www.martinisfinedining .com), a fine-dining hotspot on US 17 in North Myrtle Beach, offers entertainment in its piano bar nightly, as well as a great happy hour and early-bird specials.

FAMILY-FRIENDLY ACTIVITIES

The North Strand
The O.D. Pavilion (843-238-3787; www.odpavilion.com), located at the Ocean Drive Horseshoe, puts exciting rides and fun games right on the oceanfront. All the popular carnival attractions are here and admission is free; you pay only to ride. Open seasonally, late afternoons and evenings.

At Indigo Farms (843-399-6902 or 910-287-6794; www.indigofarms market.com), owned by the Bellamy family for six generations, kids can pick strawberries, blackberries, blueberries, or pumpkins, then visit the heritage animals in the barnyard and pick out a snack in the bakery.

At the ⚔ T.I.G.E.R.S. Preservation Station (843-361-4552; www.tigerfriends .com), one of the Strand's most unusual attractions, get up close and personal with adult tigers and cubs and baby apes. This living exhibit is free to visit, but consider having a picture taken, or visit the gift store. Proceeds go toward the preservation of the big cats of the world. Call for hours.

*If you like this . . . arrange a **Wild Encounter Tour** of T.I.G.E.R.S.'s 50-acre preserve, where you'll meet "animal actors" who have appeared in numerous films, television shows, and commercials. Species at the preserve include tigers and other big cats, orangutans, gray wolves, and the world's largest cat, a "liger," a rare cross between a lion and a tiger.*

Alligator Adventure at Barefoot Landing

The creatures at ⚔ 🐊 Alligator Adventure (843-361-0789; www .alligatoradventure.com), tucked into the marsh at Barefoot Landing, aren't nearly as cuddly, but quite fascinating all the same. This is the home of a wide variety of animals, from black bears to pythons, plus lots of alligators, including rare albinos, and the largest crocodile in captivity. Live alligator feedings and snake handling shows daily. Tickets are good for two visits within seven days.

If the gators aren't scary enough, stop by ⚔ 👻 Ghosts and Legends Theatre (843-361-2700; www.ghost shows.com), a live-action show where ghosts bring Grand Strand history to life. Blackbeard the pirate, the Gray Man, and other (former) residents all make appearances thanks to Disney-quality special effects. You can also attend a Blackbeard séance, discover the "other side" with a psychic, or take an evening ghost walk that will reveal a side of Barefoot Landing that you'd never imagine in the daylight.

Kids 4–12 can attend the 90-minute Skool 4 Pirates at the Ghosts and Legends Theatre while Mom and Dad shop at Barefoot Landing.

Other family-friendly entertainment at Barefoot Landing includes the Barefoot Carousel, the Coca Cola Cool Zone, and the MirrorMaze (843-663-2700; www.mirrormazeusa.com), with infinite ways to get lost, plus fun house mirrors and the Vault Laser Beam Challenge.

Myrtle Beach

The boardwalk (www.myrtlebeachdowntown.com), running from the 14th Avenue Pier to the Second Avenue Pier, is Myrtle Beach's new destination for family fun. The action centers around the blocks north of the old location of the Pavilion, beginning at Ninth Avenue North where it meets the ocean.

New attractions are beginning to replace the old Pavilion rides, most magnificently the SkyWheel (843-839-9200; www.themyrtlebeachskywheel.com). Located at the end of 11th Avenue North, the 200-foot wheel, with glass-enclosed, climate-controlled gondolas, provides unmatched views of the beach and far out to sea. A million LED lights put on a lightshow nightly. If you need a bit of liquid courage before or after your ride, the new Jimmy Buffett's LandShark Bar and Grill (843-788-0001; www.facebook.com/LandSharkMyrtleBeach), with a deck overlooking the ocean and Parrothead music on tap, is next door.

Nearby, at 12th Avenue North, ⚡ Myrtle Beach Thrill Rides (843-444-8255; www.myrtlebeachthrillrides.com) operate the Sling Shot, propelling riders up to 300 feet in the air, the Screamin' Swing, the Sky Tower, and the more mild-mannered Balloon Tower and Jump Around for younger thrill seekers.

If you like this . . . adrenaline junkies will like the Skyscraper, billed as the fastest, most extreme ride in the world, at Third Avenue South and Ocean Boulevard.

Just off the boardwalk, ⚜ Ripley's (843-448-2331; www.ripleys.com) provides a full block of fun on Ocean Boulevard between 9th and 10th Avenues North. Ripley's Believe It Or Not! Odditorium; the truly scary Ripley's Haunted Adventure; the Marvelous Mirror Maze; and the 3D Moving Theater are perfect for a rainy day, or for late-night fun. All are open until midnight during the summer season.

If you like this . . . venture into the Nightmare Haunted House (843-626-0022; www.beachscream.com) to meet the Monsters of the Midway, including a very evil clown, or paranormalist Nobody Jones, master of clairvoyance.

For a tamer day of fun, the nearby ⚡ ⚜ Children's Museum of South Carolina (843-946-9469; www.cmsckids.org) specializes in interactive activities for younger children.

⚡ Family Kingdom (843-626-3447; www.family-kingdom.com), on the ocean-front at Third Avenue South, offers 30 classic rides, including the Swamp Fox wooden roller coaster built by the famous Philadelphia Toboggan Company, a log flume, miniature railroad, Ferris wheel, go-carts, bumper cars, and a historical carousel. From Memorial Day to Labor Day, a water park keeps families cool with flumes, slides, and lazy rivers. The amusement park is open April–October. You can pay per ride, get all-day wristbands, or just watch for free.

> **Did you know?** You can reserve the SkyWheel's VIP gondola with glass floor and leather seats for special events.

An excellent rainy-day choice is the new Family Fun Center (843-748-0302; www.funwarehousemb.com) for its combination of roller skating and laser tag, plus an inflatable area, unique laser maze, snack bar, video arcade, and even Zumba classes for Mom, all under one roof.

Combine pizza with your fun at ⚜ ⚡ Ultimate California Pizza Game Zone (843-449-1160; www.ultimatecaliforniapizza.com) on Lake Arrowhead Road near Restaurant Row. The 30,000-square-foot facility houses a vast selection of video games, plus a sports bar serving delicious pizza pies from the Ultimate California chain, consistently voted best on the beach.

If you like this . . . also on Lake Arrowhead Road, 🏊 ⛵ *Lazer FX-Lazer Tag*   209
(843-467-2229; www.lazerfxlazertag.com) offers themed competition with the latest
equipment in an arena filled with fog and mazes, plus an arcade with more than
40 games.

For night of family entertainment, visit 🏊 Angelo's Steak & Pasta (843-626-2800; www.angelosteakandpasta.com) on the Kings Highway at 20th Avenue South. Kids love the all-you-can-eat Italian buffet and the illusions performed tableside by Magic Idol winner Michael Bairefoot, while their parents are mesmerized by the reasonable dinner tab.

Located on the west side of the ICW off SC 707, 🏊 🐾 Waccatee Zoological Farm (843-650-8500; www.waccateezoo.com) provides a home for over 100 species of animals, presented in their natural environments.

The Myrtle Beach Pavilion Amusement Park provided the beating heart of the Grand Strand for nearly 60 years. Beginning in 1948, when a traveling carnival set up on a lot behind the oceanfront Pavilion dance hall, the park grew into a prime day-and-night destination for families, dates, parties, and teens, with 11 compact acres of roller coasters, water rides, go-carts, and all the traditional thrill rides. For generations, locals and visitors alike gave directions as either "north of the pavilion" or "south of the pavilion." In 2006, Burroughs & Chapin, owner of the amusement park, announced the entire complex would be demolished and the land used for a new development. Several of the most beloved rides were moved to Broadway at the Beach, also a Burroughs & Chapin property. Since the park's demolition, the large tract of land bounded by N. Ocean Boulevard, the Kings Highway, and Eighth and Ninth Avenues North, has remained vacant, its future yet to be determined. Gone, but not forgotten.

Broadway at the Beach

For sheer concentration of amusement options, Broadway at the Beach (843-444-3200; www.broadwayatthebeach.com) is hard to beat, not only by any destination on the Strand, but by any mixed-use tourist destination anywhere. Imagine a Downtown Disney/Pleasure Island concept that includes IMAX movies, minigolf, water parks, go-cart racing, and a wealth of family activities, shops, nightclubs, and restaurants, all surrounded by acres and acres of free parking.

The Pavilion Nostalgia Park and the Carousel Park (843-913-9400; www.pavilionnostalgiapark.com) preserve many of the beloved rides from the old oceanfront pavilion, including the tea cups, the pirate ship ride, Red Baron airplanes, the caterpillar, and

Quick tip: Carousel Park is in the southwest corner of the complex across from the Palace Theatre; the Nostalgia Park is behind the Carmike Cinema in the southeast corner.

Fast fact: The Herschell-Spillman Carousel at Broadway at the Beach is a real treasure, one of only 27 that survive from this top maker of wooden merry-go-rounds in the early years of the 20th century. On this rare menagerie model, in addition to the usual horses, you can mount camels, elephants, ostriches, lions, pigs, dragons, roosters, or the world's only carousel elk.

MagiQuest, great for a rainy day

more. A spin on the 1912 Herschell-Spillman Carousel is a must. The 400-pipe, hand-carved German Baden bandwagon, now located on the midway, was built for the Paris World Exposition of 1900 and is decorated with twirling ladies and cherubs. Open seasonally, the Nostalgia Park and Carousel Park are free to enter; you pay per ride. Combo tickets and all-day wristbands are also available.

MagiQuest (843-916-1800; www.magiquest.com), on Celebrity Circle, combines the best features of a computer game and a treasure hunt. State-of-the-art technology gets your little magicians off the couch and into the world of magic, where 150 different waves of a magic wand activate interactive features. On the first visit, each magician receives an individualized magic wand to take home; return visits are much less expensive. Accompanying adults without a wand receive an "Ancient Book of Wisdom" and admission for $5; but this game is fun for all ages. Give it a try.

Ripley's Aquarium of Myrtle Beach (843-916-0888 or 1-800-734-8888; http://myrtlebeach.ripleyaquariums.com) is one of South Carolina's top tourist attractions, housing thousands of fish in huge aquariums that literally surround visitors. Children six and over can swim with the stingrays for an unforgettable experience.

WonderWorks (843-626-9962; www.wonderworksonline.com), the latest addition to Broadway at the Beach's family attractions, occupies a building turned upside down that contains over 100 interactive exhibits, including an inversion tunnel, hurricane shack, antigravity chamber, indoor ropes course, and bed of nails. Outside, Soar + Explore (843-448-7627; www.soarandexplore.com), the area's only zip line and a pirate-themed ropes course, combines a thrilling ride above the lagoon with problem-solving skills. Reduced rate combo tickets are available.

The Works Eatery, a full-service restaurant and bar at WonderWorks, doesn't require admission and hosts music on the outside deck some summer evenings.

On the west side of the US 17 Bypass across from Broadway at the Beach,

Special pool areas for young guests are a feature at many resorts.

Myrtle Waves is one of several water parks on the Strand.

Myrtle Waves Water Park (843-913-9260; www.myrtlewaves.com) is South Carolina's largest water park with a huge wave pool, numerous slides, and raft rides for all ages. Open summers only; twilight prices are available.

At the ✐ ⍟ NASCAR SpeedPark (843-918-8725; www.nascarspeedpark .com), seven tracks offer racing in NASCAR-themed cars. The park also includes a Skycoaster, kiddie rides, huge arcade, batting cages, climbing wall, and minigolf, all with NASCAR's patented style. Visits by drivers and other racing celebs are frequent. Most attractions are priced individually, or you can buy an all-day wristband.

The South Strand

✐ Wild Water & Wheels (843-238-3787; www.wild-water.com), on US 17 Business in Surfside Beach, offers 16 acres of minigolf, bumper boats, go-carts, and kiddie rides, plus 24 water slides for all ages.

The two and one-half acre wooden maze at ✐ ⍟ Maze Mania (843-651-1641; www.mazemaniasc.com) on US 17 in Garden City is changed every day to keep you confused. Gilligan's Island Funland Miniature Golf (843-651-4220) is next door; combo tickets to both attractions provide a full day of fun.

For rainy day family fun on the South Strand, plan a visit to the ✐ ⍟ ⍭ Surfside Bowling and Family Entertainment Center (843-238-2695; www.surf sidebowlingcenter.com), where 32 glow-in-the-dark lanes host bowling until midnight. Young bowlers just learning the game can get an introduction at the Hwy 66 Mini Bowling lanes. The complex also includes a full-service grill and sports lounge, dancing several nights a week, an arcade, and the Balladium, a black-light arena where kids four and up can battle it out with cannons firing Nerf balls.

For some free fun for kids, visit the ✐ ⍟ All Children's Park (843-650-4131; www.surfsidebeach.org), at 10th Avenue South and Hollywood Drive in Surfside

Beach. The complex includes two playgrounds with accessible equipment, picnic tables, and restrooms.

If you like this . . . the new ♂ ͳ Ỷ Frank Entertainment Center (843-651-9400; www.franktheatres.com) at the Inlet Square Mall (www.inletsquaremall .com), on the bypass in Murrells Inlet, includes an 11-screen movie theater, a bowling alley with disco evening sessions, an arcade and game room, and a full-service restaurant and bar.

Near Georgetown, ♂ ⇸ Millgrove Farms (843-546-5075; www.millgrove farms.com), a family farm following heritage agricultural traditions, schedules many kid-friendly activities. The ♂ SC-CARES Animal Sanctuary (843-546-7893; www.sc-cares.org), off US 701 outside of Georgetown, is home to more than 150 rescued animals. Families can tour by appointment.

OUTDOOR ADVENTURES

Beach Parks

North Myrtle Beach (843-280-5684; http://parks.nmb.us) has numerous public beach accesses, including the ♿ Cherry Grove Oceanfront Park at 22nd Avenue North and ♿ City Park on the Atlantic Ocean at First Avenue South in Ocean Drive. Both offer restrooms, picnic areas, and beach showers. In Ocean Drive, many streets end in parking and beach access. In addition, large accessible accesses can be found at the end of 17th Avenue South in the Crescent Grove section and at the end of 46th Avenue South in Windy Hill.

In Myrtle Beach itself, nearly every street end offers public access to the beach, many with parking, thanks to bequests from the Burroughs family. One special place to check out is ♿ Hurl Rock Park (843-918-1014; www.cityofmyrtlebeach.com), near the end of 20th Avenue South on Ocean Boulevard, with a boardwalk, restrooms, beach access, and parking. On his tour of the South in the mid-1700s, naturalist William Bartram named the area for its unusual outcrop of black rock on the otherwise sandy shore.

To enjoy undeveloped beachfront, visit one of the area's state parks, which charge a small fee ($5) for admission. Located at the south end of Myrtle Beach along US 17, Myrtle Beach State Park (843-238-5325; www.southcarolinaparks .com), preserving a pristine stretch of beach and a patch of rare maritime forest, has restrooms, changing facilities, and outdoor showers, as well as a fishing pier with snack bar and boardwalks crossing the dunes. The Nature Center (843-238-0874; call for hours) offers saltwater aquariums, live reptiles, and information on

Quick tip: Always check websites and coupon books for money-saving deals before you head out for minigolf, seafood buffets, watersports, or any activity.

Fast fact: Many public beach accesses on the Grand Strand are fully accessible. Beach wheelchairs are available from the North Myrtle Beach Parks & Recreation (843-280-5570). Myrtle Beach also has complimentary wheelchairs. From April 15 to September 15, just ask the closest lifeguard. The rest of the year, call 943-918-1382. In Surfside Beach, contact the Public Safety Department (843-913-6368) to reserve a beach wheelchair.

Public beach accesses line the Strand.

the area's ecology. You can stay in the park at rental cabins and apartments or at a campground with hookups.

Huntington Beach State Park (843-237-4440; www.southcarolina parks.com), across the street from Brookgreen Gardens just south of Murrells Inlet, includes 3 miles of undeveloped beach and acres of pristine salt marsh, RV camping, a boat ramp for power boats or kayaks, nature trails, tours of historic Atalaya, and an education center (843-235-8755; call for hours) with a saltwater touch tank and interpretive exhibits.

On the South Strand, Surfside Beach (843-650-4131; www.surfsidebeach.org) has numerous public accesses with parking. Restrooms and showers are available at Third Avenue North, 13th Avenue South, and the Surfside Pier.

Swimming and pets are allowed at the public South End Beach Access (843-545-3275; www.georgetowncountysc.org) on Pawleys Island.

Biking
North Myrtle Beach is a bike-friendly community where you can ride on the beach or along bike lanes on Ocean Boulevard. Other great spots to bike are McLean Park and the Barefoot Resort. At Wheel Fun Rentals (843-280-7900; www.wheel funrentals.com), close to the Horseshoe on Ocean Boulevard, you can rent a beach

The Sunset Beach Pier provides a focus for fun in this South Strand community.

The World Capital of Miniature Golf

No one knows exactly how many miniature golf courses are on the Strand. Resorts and campgrounds keep building more, and every amusement park has its own. Reliable estimates hover around 50, and a drive down US 17 will reveal numerous waterfalls, several pirate ships, downed airplanes, dinosaurs, fire-breathing dragons, trains, acres of fiberglass creatures, at least three volcanoes, and various temples of questionable derivation.

Playing minigolf on the Strand is not your average putt-putt experience. Great time, energy, and money have gone into many of these courses, to tell a story and set the stage. For families, in the summer season especially, minigolf makes the perfect evening activity after a day in the sun.

In addition to the sheer number of courses, the Grand Strand is the national center of professional minigolf. The **U.S. ProMiniGolf Association** (843-458-2585; www.prominigolf.com) is based in North Myrtle Beach, and USPMGA tournaments, including the Masters National ProMiniGolf Championship, played annually in September, and the America's Championship every May, are held on the Hawaiian Rumble and Hawaiian Village courses.

Minigolf at Runaway Bay

Then there is that Myrtle Beach innovation, indoor minigolf. Going far beyond a room full of black light murals, the indoor courses on the Strand lead you deep into a Mayan pyramid, inside an active volcano, and on a visit to a 50,000-year-old minigolf resort that broke away from a sunken continent and came to shore high above Myrtle Beach. The beauty of indoor minigolf is that it's good for those very hot days when you don't want to be in the sun, as well as for rainy days.

Mount Atlanticus Minotaur Goff (843-444-1008; www.mountatlanticus.com), the original indoor course, sits atop the old Chapin Company department store at Kings Highway and Eighth Avenue North. Although showing its age a bit, the multilevel Atlanticus is a must-play for its elaborate exploration of the Atlantis myth and torch-lit huts with outstanding views of the ocean. Ace the tricky 19th hole and you win a lifetime pass.

The Grand Strand has two other (partially) indoor miniature golf courses. At **Molten Mountain** (843-280-5095; www.moltenmountaingolf.com), on US 17 in NMB, you brave Pele's wrath in air-conditioned caverns inside a volcano. **Cancun Lagoon** (843-444-1098) at 21st Avenue South in MB features play inside a 50-foot Mayan pyramid. Both are part of Paradise Entertainment, which also operates the Caribbean-themed **Mutiny Bay** (843-249-7844; www.mutinybaygolf.com) in North Myrtle, an outdoor course with live pirate shows and a 45-foot animated pirate ship.

Hawaiian Rumble (843-272-7812; www.prominigolf.com/rumble.html), in North Myrtle Beach at 33rd Avenue South, can hardly be missed thanks to the towering volcano that erupts at regular intervals. Voted the best minigolf course in the country, Rumble enhances its Hawaiian theme with leis, talking parrots in the gift shop, and a soundtrack of "feel-good" tunes by James Taylor, Jimmy Buffet, and the Beach Boys. Its sister course, the ♿ **Hawaiian Village Golf Course** (843-361-9629; www.pro minigolf.com), just down the road at 43rd Avenue South, has a pineapple plantation theme, with a steam locomotive and caboose that were air-lifted in. Check out the limited edition Indian motorcycle, one of only five like it in the world, in the gift shop.

Between Little River and Ocean Drive, the North Strand's third volcano can be found at ♿ **Tribal Island Tiki Adventure Golf** (843-249-9117; www.harbourviewgolf .com), with eruptions every hour. Part of the Harbour View Golf Complex, along with a par 3 course and a driving range, the entire facility is lighted for evening play.

Also on the North Strand, **Dinosaur Adventure Golf** (843-272-8041; www.lost treasuregolf.com) at Seventh Avenue North contains a full roster of popular dinosaurs. Its sister course, **Professor Hacker's Lost Treasure Golf** (843-272-5467; www.lost treasuregolf.com), at 17th Avenue South, NMB, features a train that takes golfers up a mountain to the first tee.

Another landmark North Strand course, **Mayday** (843-280-3535; www.mayday golf.com) at Seventh Avenue North showcases a 1945 U.S. Navy Lockheed PV-2 Harpoon airplane and a Bell UH-1 "Huey" helicopter, both authentic decommissioned vehicles.

In Myrtle Beach, ♂ **Jungle Lagoon** (843-626-7894; www.junglelagoon.com), at Fifth Avenue South, is a well-kept family-owned course with waterfall caverns (popular for weddings), a saltwater inlet, and a variety of jungle animal statues.

Located next to the lake at Broadway at the Beach, **Dragon's Lair Fantasy Golf** (843-913-9301; www.myrtlebeachfamilygolf.com) makes a lasting impression with its animatronic, 30-foot tall, fire-breathing dragon—even if you aren't playing golf. This course belongs to the Burroughs & Chapin family of minigolf courses, which includes **Shipwreck Island Adventure Golf** (843-913-5330), a whale-infested course at 33rd Avenue South and Ocean Boulevard in MB; **Jurassic Golf** (843-913-5333) on 29th Avenue South, with animatronic dinosaurs; ♿ **Captain Hook's Adventure Golf** (843-913-7851) at 22nd Avenue North, with animated crocodiles; and **Jungle Safari Golf** (843-315-0311) on 71st Avenue North, with life-size elephants and giraffes. Check the website (www.myrtlebeachfamilygolf.com) for coupons and tickets to play a round at all five at a discounted rate.

On the bypass in Murrells Inlet, the Jamaican-themed ♿ **Runaway Bay** (843-215-1038; www.tupelobay.com), centered on a full-size seaplane, is part of the Tupelo Bay complex with a par 58 executive course, par 3 course, award-winning driving range, and disc golf course, all lighted for evening play.

A tricky hole at Runaway Bay

cruiser or surrey for a run up the beach to the Cherry Grove Pier, or a romantic tandem bike for a trip along Main Street. Bike Doctor of the Carolinas (843-249-8152 ; bikedoctorofthecarolinas.com) in Cherry Grove also rents two- and three-wheeled bikes, plus surfboards, bodyboards, kayaks, and beach equipment, and will repair a broken bike within 24 hours.

Myrtle Beach has several dedicated multiuse paved bike paths, including a path paralleling the Grissom Parkway from the ICW to Harrelson Boulevard, where it joins a bikeway running from Coastal Grand Mall to the airport. Paved paths also line both sides of the Farrow Parkway. Rent beach cruisers, mountain bikes, and road bikes at the Beach Bike Shop (843-448-5335; www.beachbikeshop .com) on Broadway Street, three blocks from the ocean.

If you like this . . . Bodacious Bob's Beach Bicycle Tours and Rentals (843-241-2731; www.beachbicycletours.com) offers daily and weekly bike rentals; plus guided or self-guided tours to the planetarium in Ocean Isle Beach and to local wineries.

On the South Strand, cyclists, skaters, or hikers can "bike (or hike) the neck" on the new Waccamaw Neck Bikeway (843-237-4486; www.biketheneck.com), a shady, 17-mile paved path running from Murrells Inlet to Litchfield Beach.

Cyclopedia (843-235-6500; www.cyclopediaonline.com), in Litchfield Market Village, is a convenient spot to rent bikes close to one end of the bikeway. Grand Strand Bicycles (843-652-3700 ; grandstrandbicycles.com) in Murrells Inlet also offers rentals, sponsors group rides, and offers indoor training during inclement weather.

Another scenic South Strand ride is the 3.5-mile Pawleys Island Loop (www .scgreatoutdoors.com), beginning at the Pawleys Island Nature Park on the north causeway (Waverly Road), or at the Food Lion on US 17 at the south causeway.

Mountain biking trails can be found in Myrtle Beach at Mallard Lake Park (843-918-1188; www.cityofmyrtlebeach.com), just off the Farrow Parkway, next to the South Bark Park. Near Conway, the Cox Ferry Lake Recreation Area (843-527-8069; www.fws.gov/waccamaw) contains miles of newly constructed trails.

Birding

The Waccamaw Audubon Society (843-347-6222; www.waccamawaudubon.org) meets six times a year on first Thursdays in the spring and fall. Visitors welcome. The society hosts the annual Litchfield Beach–Pawleys Island Christmas Bird Count, which usually documents over 250 species.

If you like this . . . join professional naturalist Jerry Walls for Guided Birding Trips (843-933-1556; www.georgetowncountysc.org) through the Hobcaw Barony on the third Saturday of every month.

Free birding programs are offered at Huntington Beach State Park (843-237-4440; www.southcarolinaparks

Kayaking is a great way to explore the salt marsh.

.com), considered one of the top birding destinations on the East Coast during the winter migration.

The best time to see migrating songbirds is during the spring and fall. Migrating shorebirds, including sandhill cranes, rosette spoonbills, and swallow-tailed kites, come through in fall, winter, and spring.

Canoeing & Kayaking

The Lowcountry of South Carolina contains a variety of excellent paddle options, on blackwater and red water rivers, freshwater swamps and saltwater marsh, down canals and through abandoned rice fields, and into the ocean to meet the dolphins.

The knowledgeable folks at the Conway Kayak Company (843-488-0999; www.conwaykayak.com), located along the river walk in downtown Conway, will guide you along the blackwater Waccamaw River and deep into the cypress swamp. Or you can rent a kayak and explore on your own. Signs have been posted throughout the swamp with snippets of local history. Conway Kayak offers tours and rentals all year.

If you like this . . . at Little Pee Dee State Park (843-774-8872; www.south carolinaparks.com), off SC 57 near Dillon, you can rent a jon boat, canoe, or kayak for a paddle on 54-acre Lake Norton, a water-filled Carolina bay.

Several state and local agencies conduct kayak and canoe tours. Check with Horry County Parks and Recreation (843-915-5330; http://parksandrec.horry county.org) for paddles on the Waccamaw River. Huntington Beach State Park (843-237-4440; www.southcarolinaparks.com) offers two-hour paddles through the salt marsh. Register in advance to ensure a spot.

You can rent a canoe with or without a trailer for the weekend from Georgetown County Parks and Recreation (843-545-3275; www.georgetowncountysc.org /parks). Horry County Parks and Recreation (843-915-5330; http://parksandrec .horrycounty.org) loans out freshwater fishing equipment for kids and adults for free.

Ecotours

Cricket Marina in Little River is home port for several eco-adventures, including Enchanted Charters (843-283-4873; www.enchantedcharters.com) and Getaway Adventures (843-663-1100; www.myrtlebeachboatcruises

Quick tip: Download a map of the Conway Blueways Paddle Trail at the Conway Parks and Recreation website (www.conwayparks andrecreation.com).

.com), offering shelling trips to off-shore islands, dolphin watches, and sightseeing cruises.

In North Myrtle Beach, Thomas Outdoors Watersports (843-663-7433; www.mbjetski.com) conducts guided kayak tours of the Cherry Grove salt marsh, jet boat ecotours, Jet Ski dolphin watches, and sunset cruises from the Anchor Marina.

In Murrells Inlet, Blue Wave Adventures (843-651-3676, 843-340-7713; www.bluewaveadventures.com) offers dolphin watch cruises and kayak trips to an island used by pirates from the marsh walk.

From the Wacca Wache Marina, on the ICW side of Murrells Inlet, Plantation Tours (843-651-2994; www.plantationrivertours.com) will take you into the backwaters aboard

Banana boat rides are a fun and inexpensive family activity.

the *Waccamaw Cooter* airboat for up-close views of alligators, ospreys, and abandoned rice fields.

Myrtle Beach Segway (843-477-0800; www.mbsegway.com) offers guided tours through the wildlife refuge at Huntington Beach State Park. Rentals and self-guided tours of Market Common are also available.

In Pawleys Island, Surf the Earth (843-235-3500; www.surf-the-earth.com) conducts guided paddleboard and kayak tours of the Pawleys Island marsh, yoga paddleboard tours for women, full moon tours, and an exclusive North Inlet kayak trip from the Hobcaw Barony (reservations: 843-546-3623).

Fishing Charters

The fishing villages of Calabash, North Carolina, and Little River on the North Strand, and Murrells Inlet and Georgetown on the South Strand, are home to most of the fishing charter boats in the regions. The experienced captains of these boats will take you on an inshore adventure or offshore after the big game species in the Gulf Stream.

The ♦ Little River Fishing Fleet (843-361-3323 or 1-800-249-9388; www.littleriverfleet.com) has several larger boats available for charter or for per-person fishing trips. The 90-foot *Pride of the Carolinas* headboat, carrying up to 80 people, makes half-day and night fishing trips.

At the Crazy Sister Marina in Murrells Inlet, the *New Inlet Princess* (843-651-3676 or 1-866-557-3474; www.captdicks.com), the state's largest party boat, makes trips to the continental shelf for sea bass and other deepwater species, as well as overnight trips to the Gulf Stream.

Back country fishing is especially popular in the southern part of the Strand, where the waters of the Pee Dee, Black, Waccamaw, and Sampit Rivers flow into Winyah Bay. A number of outfitters in the region specialize in light tackle and fly fishing the shallow estuary waters, where a favorite activity is sight-fishing schools of red fish. Speckled trout, flounder, and, in summer, giant tarpon are also caught here.

Outfitters specializing in fly and light tackle fishing in the Pawleys Island and Georgetown area include Low Country Expeditions (843-546-2107; www.lowcountryguides.com) and Captain Fred Rourk's Sweet Tea Charters (843-241-4767; www.sweetteacharters.com).

Kingfisher Guide Service (843-318-0474; www.gtownkingfisher.com), based in Georgetown, specializes in going after the big summer tarpon, which often weigh in at over 100 pounds.

For light tackle and fly fishing on the North Strand, contact Capt. Patrick Kelly aka Smiley (843-361-7445; www.captainsmileyfishingcharters.com), who also offers family crabbing trips and ecotours.

Kayak fishing is an increasingly popular activity in the area, perfect for sneaking up on big fish in shallow inlet waters. Black River Outdoors (843-546-4840; www.blackriveroutdoors.com) will provide all the equipment you need and guide you to the best fishing holes.

Fishing Piers

The Grand Strand is home to numerous fishing piers where you can catch your dinner or just watch this traditional beach activity. Our listing visits the piers north to south.

Cherry Grove Pier (843-249-1625; www.cherrygrovepier.com) is open 24 hours a day when the fish are biting, but closes down in December and January. The two-story observation deck offers a fine view, and a café on the pier serves casual meals.

Located inside the Apache Family Campground on Lake Arrowhead Drive, the ⚓ ⛾ Apache Pier (843-497-6486; www.apachefamilycampground.com) has a lot going on, especially in the summer when there's live entertainment and dancing on the pier. The Apache Family Fun Zone arcade, a full-service bait and tackle shop, and Croakers at the Pier (843-497-5331), serving breakfast, lunch, dinner, and cocktails, are onsite. There's a $2 parking fee, paid at the campground gate, then another $2 for those over 12 to stroll on this very long wooden pier. A snack bar on the pier serves beer, wine, hot dogs, and snacks.

Down in Myrtle Beach, the ⛾ (ᵖ) 14th Avenue Pier (843-448-6500; www.pier14.com), at the north end of the Myrtle Beach Boardwalk behind

The Second Avenue Pier sits in the heart of the Myrtle Beach action.

the Yachtsman Resort, has a restaurant with free WiFi and a casual deck menu, plus a gift shop selling beer, bait, and souvenirs. Rod rental packages are some of the least expensive on the Strand.

Second Avenue Pier (843-445-7437; www.secondavenuepier.com), a new hot spot near the south end of the boardwalk, boasts a popular restaurant and a second-story deck with a trendy open-air lounge. King mackerel fishing is not allowed.

Springmaid Pier (843-315-7100; www.springmaidbeach.com), centerpiece of the ❧ Springmaid Resort at the southern end of Myrtle Beach, was originally built as a recreational facility for textile workers in the Springmaid factories around the Carolinas. Today it's open to the public, one of the longest piers on the Strand. BARnacles Bar & Grille offers light meals, with cocktails served in the oceanfront bar.

Pier walking is free on the ✍ (ⁱ) Myrtle Beach State Park Pier (843-238-5325; www.myrtlebeachstatepark.net). You must pay for entering the park, and for fishing from the pier, but rates are low, with senior and kid specials. As a state facility, no alcohol is allowed, but you can get snacks and ice at the bait and tackle store at the pier.

The city-owned Surfside Pier (843-238-0121; www.surfsidepier.com) is open daily until midnight. The Pier Outfitters Tackle Shop rents rods and sells snacks and other supplies.

Locals vote the ✍ ♿ Ⓨ Garden City Pier (843-651-9700; www.pierat gardencity.com) the region's best fish-

Quick tip: Pets are not generally allowed on piers, due to the many hooks lying around that might injure paws.

Fast fact: Fishing pros say that fish are most active around the time of high tide and at sunrise and sunset.

Classical sculptures at Brookgreen are set in a natural paradise.

ing pier year after year, and for good reason. Open 24 hours a day during the high fishing season, and free to walk on, this landmark has two bars at either end of the pier, both with nightly live music during summer. The Cafe Deck Bar at the pier's entrance serves meals beginning with breakfast.

Garden City has a second public pier located on the mainland at the end of Pine Avenue. Stretching far out into the marsh, this little-known pier is a perfect place for crabbing, and it also has a playground and picnic area. A fishing license is required.

In Murrells Inlet, the free Veterans Pier (www.murrellsinletsc.com) next to the marsh walk is a good place to drop a line, but you'll need a South Carolina saltwater license. Crabbing is good at Morse Park Landing, just down Business 17.

Located off US 17 just before you reach Georgetown, the Winyah Bay Fishing and Observation Pier and the Hobcaw Point Observation and Fishing Pier (843-545-3275; www.georgetowncountysc.org) face each other across the Great Pee Dee River, just before it empties into Winyah Bay. These piers are the remnants of the old Ocean Highway bridge left in place for fishing, and are free to use, for fishing or for a stroll, but you'll need a South Carolina Freshwater Fishing License to cast a line. A gazebo on the pier on the northeast side of the river makes a scenic setting for picnics.

While you don't need a fishing license at commercial piers or on charter boats, you'll need one to fish, crab, or shrimp from the beach, banks, bridges, or free public piers. Contact the South Carolina Department of Natural Resources (1-866-714-3611; www.dnr.sc.gov) for current rules and rates and to buy licenses online.

Hiking

Brookgreen Gardens (843-235-6000; www.brookgreen.org) is a great place for a hike. The free "Walking Program" guide details several paths with mileage, from a Zoo Strut to a Beyond the Garden Wall walk. Or visit the Chartres-style Labyrinth for a contemplative stroll. All are free with garden admission, although you need to take a $3 shuttle to hike at Oaks Plantation. Tickets to Brookgreen are good for seven consecutive days, so you can come back as many times as you like.

*If you like this . . . the Sculptured Oak Nature Trail at **Myrtle Beach State Park** (843-238-5325; www.southcarolinaparks.com) passes through one of the last stands of maritime forest along the coast.*

The Cox Ferry Lake Recreation Area (843-527-8069; www.fws.gov/waccamaw), off SC 544 near its junction with US 501 in Conway, has nature trails and boardwalks providing excellent opportunities for birding and wildlife observation. This is the northernmost nesting area for swallow-tailed kites.

The Lewis Ocean Bay Heritage Preserve (843-546-3226; www.dnr.sc.gov), off International Road on the west side of the ICW, contains 23 Carolina bays, the largest number in the state, as well as bald eagles, red-cockaded woodpeckers, and South Carolina's largest population of black bears. Hiking, driving, and horse trails lead through this natural gem, just off US 501.

Horseback Riding

Inlet Point Plantation Stables (843-249-2989; www.inletpointplantation.com), in North Myrtle Beach, offers trail rides across a pecan grove to a private island where you can ride on the beach. Younger riders can enjoy a pony ride. You can also bring your own horse to ride here in the off-season. Stabling available.

If you like this . . . Horseback Riding of Myrtle Beach (843-294-1712; www .myrtlebeachhorserides.com) has daily rides: in the summer through a nature preserve and in the winter along the sand at Garden City, Litchfield, or Myrtle Beach.

You can help rescue horses in need by taking a trail ride at ♿ Tranquility Farm (843-246-4502; www.horsebackridingmyrtlebeach.com) in Conway. Rates are the most reasonable on the Strand.

Skate Parks & Disc Golf

Skate parks in the area include the free Matt Hughes Skateboard Park (843-918-1188; www.cityofmyrtlebeach.com), operated by the city of Myrtle Beach, next to Doug Shaw Stadium at 33rd Avenue North.

Horseback riding is permitted during the off season on some area beaches.

If you like this . . . Cornerstone Skate Park (843-280-5071; www.stability skateboard.com), next to the Stability Skate Shop and North Shore Surf Shop on US 17 in North Myrtle Beach, offers a variety of facilities for both transition and street skaters.

You can toss your discs for free at the waterfront disc golf course in East Bay Park (843-545-3275; www.georgetowncountysc.org) in downtown Georgetown. Another free public course can be found in the Loris Nature Park (943-915-5330; http://parksandrec.horrycounty.org), just off SC 9, on the north end of the Strand. Harbor View Golf Complex (843-249-9117; www.harbourviewgolf.com) in Little River and Tupelo Bay Golf Center (843-215-7888; www.tupelobay.com) in Garden City both have disc courses that are pay-to-play, but they're lighted for night action.

Scuba Diving

The ocean waters along the Strand harbor a wide variety of dive sites for all skill levels. Limestone ledges just offshore provide views of sea turtles, stingrays, and cobia. Man-made reefs, made of everything from decommissioned landing craft to NYC subway cars, attract numerous species of fish, including grouper, spadefish, snapper, queen angels, and barracuda. Plenty of natural wrecks lie on the ocean bottom as well, including tugboats, submarines, paddlewheelers, even an airplane. The *Sherman*, a blockade runner from the Civil War era, is a favorite destination for both new and experienced divers, thanks to the wide variety of artifacts found there.

Fast fact: Myrtle Beach State Park and Surfside Beach are popular spots for shore dives or snorkeling, with coral formations not far from the beach.

On the South Strand, 🐟 Scuba Express (843-357-3337; expresswatersports .com) offers equipment rentals, trips to many local wrecks, Discover Scuba sessions, and the Bubblemaker program, a snorkel and scuba activity for 8 to 12 year olds.

Surfing & Kiteboarding

The Grand Strand Chapter of the Surfrider Foundation (1-800-743-SURF; www .surfridergrandstrand.org) sponsors events for surfers year-round. Annual surfing events include the October Happy Hendriks Memorial Surf Off, sponsored by the Pawleys Island Surf Club (www.surf-the-earth.com), and the Guy Daniels Memorial Surfoff (www.surfoff.com) held every August.

At Island Inspired Surf Board Factory and Surf Shop (843-236-2841; www.islandinspired.com), you can watch board shaper Todd Sutz, who got his start on the North Shore of Oahu, at work on custom surf and paddleboards. The Island Inspired Surf Café and Surf Gallery (843-692-SURF; 5901 N. Kings Hwy, MB) offers coffee and healthy snacks, surf gear, and rental boards and bikes, as well as surf clinics and lessons.

If you like this . . . in Murrells Inlet, the funky Village Surf Shoppe (843-651-6396; www.villagesurf.com) on Atlantic Avenue, established in 1969 by and for hardcore surfers, makes and sells Perfection Surfboards, created by local legend Kelly Richards.

Carolina Wake Sports (843-855-0024; www.carolinawakesports.com) will take you waterskiing, wakeskating, wakesurfing, or tubing on the ICW from Osprey Marina (www.ospreymarina.net). Camps for ages 7–19, lessons in wakeboarding, slalom and barefoot skiing, and equipment sales and rentals are also available.

Contact Sail and Ski (843-626-7245; www.sailandskiconnection.com) to arrange lessons in kiteboarding, wakeboarding, Hobie sailing, and paddleboarding for children and adults.

Tennis

The Myrtle Beach Tennis Center (843-918-2440; www.cityofmyrtlebeach.com), next to Myrtle Beach High School on Grissom Parkway, is the area's largest public tennis facility, with ten courts, including eight with lights, and a pro shop. Court rental is $2 per person, per hour.

If you like this . . . additional lighted courts can be found at Midway Park at 19th Avenue South and US 17 in Myrtle Beach; at Central Park and McLean Park in NMB (843-280-5684; http://parks.nmb.us); and at Fuller Park (843-650-4131; www.surfsidebeach.org), at the corner of Surfside and Myrtle Drives, in Surfside Beach.

The Litchfield Racquet Club (843-237-3411; www.litchfieldbeach.com), at the Litchfield Beach & Golf Resort, was named among the top 50 tennis resorts in the United States by *Tennis* magazine.

SHOPPING

The Grand Strand is noted for its wide range of shopping options. Leading the way are huge mixed-use projects Broadway at the Beach (www.broadwayatthebeach .com), Barefoot Landing (www.bflanding.com), and the Market Common (www .marketcommonmb.com). Coastal Grand (843-839-9100; www.coastalgrand.com), located on US 17 Bypass near the airport, is one of the largest enclosed malls in the South.

Myrtle Beach Mall (www.shop myrtlebeachmall.com), and one of the area's Tanger Outlets (843-449-0491; www.tangeroutlet.com) can be found between NMB and MB where SC 22 meets US 17.

Tommy Bahama's in Market Common offers both indoor and outdoor seating.

Once Myrtle Beach's iconic shopping destination, the Waccamaw Pottery, on US 501 just before the ICW, has closed; but the second Tanger Outlet Center (843-236-5100; www .tangeroutlet.com) is still going strong just down the road, along with other shopping options such as Wild West (843-347-WEST; www.wildwestmyrtle beach.com), which stocks Western boots, clothing, and gifts.

B&B Antique Mall (843-361-0101; www.bbantique.com), on US 17 in NMB, has 50,000 square feet of everything under the sun, from life-size Elvis figures to Pecan Pie In-A-Jar.

If you like this . . . shoppers at Toby's World Gifts (843-249-2174; www .tobysworldgifts.com) in Little River enjoy tunes from a vintage player piano in an old-fashioned general store stocked with collectibles.

Nostalgia City and Museum (843-444-0058; www.nostalgiacityandmuseum .com), on South Kings Highway next to Whale's Nautical Gifts in Myrtle Beach, carries vintage and reproduction collectibles, including antique fire engines, signs, and toys. Second location in Surfside Beach (843-650-2432).

The Myrtle Beach Flea Market (843-477-1550; www.myrtlebeachfleamarket .net), occupying five buildings across US 17 from Myrtle Beach State Park, pro-vides great browsing for a wide variety of goods.

Tara Grinna Swimwear (843-365-2894; www.taragrinna-swimwear.com), on US 501 in Conway, was featured on the ABC News *Made in America* series.

Bookstores

Bookends (843-280-2444; www.bookendsonline.com), on Main Street in NMB, stocks 15,000 new and used books in every category, and accepts books in trade.

On the South Strand, the locally owned Litchfield Books (843-237-8138; www.litchfieldbooks.com), in Litchfield Landing, features regional authors and frequent book signings.

Moveable Feast Literary Luncheons (843-235-9600; www.classatpawleys.com), sponsored by Litchfield Books, include lunch with regional authors, followed by book signings.

Harborwalk Books (843-546-8212; www.harborwalkbooks.com), an independ-ent bookstore in Georgetown's historic district, sells new and used books specializ-ing in regional history, the Civil War, and local authors. The on-site Waterfront Gallery hangs local art.

SPECTATOR SPORTS

From April through September, baseball fans can watch the Myrtle Beach Pelicans (843-918-6000; www.myrtlebeachpelicans.com) take on their opponents in the Carolina League at BB&T Coastal Field next to Broadway at the Beach. The team, affectionately known as the Birds to its fans, hosts a full roster of special events, including Thirsty Thursdays, Weiner Wednesdays, and frequent fireworks shows and giveaways.

If you like this . . . visit the Ripken Experience (1-888-747-5361; www .ripkencamps.com), a state-of-the-art baseball training center where young athletes compete in tournaments February–November.

The Myrtle Beach Speedway (843-236-0500; www.myrtlebeachspeedway .com), a NASCAR-sanctioned short track located off US 501 just west of the ICW, hosts high-speed action, car shows, and swap meets, April– September. NASCAR stars of tomorrow race on Saturday nights, while drifting competitions with plenty of smoke take over the oval on Sundays.

For college action, the Coastal Carolina University Chanticleers (843-347-8499; www.goccusports.com) field teams in a number of sports and have won over 80 Big South Conference championships.

Golf

So many golf courses wind along the Strand that it's hard to know where to start. The area has close to 150 courses, including signature courses by all of golf's top designers, courses with venerable traditions, and brand new courses with all the latest bells and whistles. *Golf Digest* awarded 36 of them four-and-a-half stars—or more. Presented with an eye to interesting details, our listing covers some of the most popular spots with locals, divided by region.

One not to miss, whether you're a lover of golf or a lover of history, is &

Baseball is a popular sport on the Strand.

♂ Pine Lakes Country Club (843-315-7700; www.pinelakes.com), the first golf course on the Strand, and originally part of the Ocean Forest Resort, a Jazz Age showplace. The granddaddy of them all, Pine Lakes offers the same traditional Scottish golfing experience it did when it opened to the public in 1929, enhanced by a 2009 restoration and expansion. It's also the birthplace of *Sports Illustrated*, first envisioned by Time Inc. execs on a retreat at Pine Lakes in 1954.

During your visit to Pine Lakes, check out the Myrtle Beach Golf Hall of Fame (www.themyrtlebeachgolfhalloffame.com), honoring folks who have made a difference in the development of the game. Among them: Robert White, first president of the PGA and the original architect of Pine Lakes. Afterward, celebrate his achievement at the Pine Lakes Grill, host of a daily happy hour and open to the public.

North Strand

Barefoot Resort & Golf (843-390-3200 or 1-866-638-4818; www.barefootgolf .com), with four award-winning courses by golf's top designers—Greg Norman, Davis Love III, Tom Fazio, and Pete Dye—is on the west side of the ICW, across from Barefoot Landing. Locals consider the unique Love course, set amid replicas of antebellum plantation house ruins, one of the Strand's best.

The Glens Golf Group (1-888-999-9520; www.glensgolfgroup.com) includes one of the Strand's most talked about (and toughest) courses, Glen Dornoch, designed as a tribute to the great Donald Ross. Don't miss the view of the ICW from the patio at the course's pub. Across US 17, near the North Carolina border, its sister course, Heather Glen Golf Links, offers three Scottish-inspired nines.

Fast fact: The "I Played Possum" logo at Possum Trot, another Glens Golf Group course, makes its pro shop one of the Strand's favorite stops for a memento of a Myrtle Beach golf vacation.

Quick tip: See our chapter on the North Carolina coast for information on the top public courses in nearby Brunswick County, including the course on Bald Head Island, and the top-rated River's Edge along the Shallotte River. And don't miss a round at the **Farmstead Golf Links** (910-575-7999; www.farmsteadgolflinks.com), where the 18th hole, spanning the border between North and South Carolina, is the region's only par 6.

Accommodations are available in Village at the Glens.

The Long Bay Club (1-800-344-5590; www.longbaygolfclub.biz), located off SC 9 in Longs, South Carolina, is one of the few Jack Nicklaus Signature courses in the world that welcomes public play. Golfers consider it one of the toughest on the Strand, with bottomless bunkers and vast wastes.

River Hills Golf & Country Club (843-399-2100; www.riverhillsgolf.com), designed by Tom Jackson on rolling hills in Little River, was selected as one of *Golfweek's* top 50 in the Southeast.

Tidewater Golf Club & Plantation (843-913-2424; www.tidewatergolf.com), nicknamed the Pebble Beach of the Strand, overlooks the Atlantic Ocean, the ICW, and the Cherry Grove marsh. It's highly ranked in regional and national polls by *Golf Digest* and other golf publications.

Waterway Hills (1-866-442-8417; www.waterwayhills.biz), three nines designed by the famed Robert Trent Jones, in on the west side of the ICW. Access to this unique course is via gondola over the waterway.

Myrtle Beach

Arrowhead Country Club (843-236-3243; www.arrowheadcc.com), South Carolina's only Raymond Floyd signature course, takes a special interest in young golfers. Juniors 8–16 play free with an adult year-round at this daily fee course.

The Dunes Golf & Beach Club (843-449-5236; www.thedunesclub.net), designed by the legendary Robert Trent Jones in 1948, ranks among the top courses in the country and the best on the Strand. It's available for public play.

& Grande Dunes Resort Club (1-888-886-8877; www.grandedunesgolf.com) is the longest on the Strand, with huge greens, spectacular views along the ICW, and a GPS system to keep you on track.

Legends Golf & Resort (1-800-299-6187; www.legendsgolf.com), a stay-and-play resort, offers golf in a setting inspired by the Royal & Ancient Golf Club of St. Andrew's, with play on the Moorland, Heathland, and Parkland courses, and postround refreshments in a Scottish pub, Ailsa, selected

as a best 19th hole by *Golf Digest.* The Pete Dye–designed Moorland, with its Hell's Half Acre 16th hole, is rated among America's toughest.

Myrtle Beach National Golf Club (1-866-442-8417; www.mbn.com) features three courses designed by golf great Arnold Palmer, including King's North, ranked among the top 100 courses in the country by *Golf Digest* and home of the Gambler, one of the Strand's most famous holes.

 ♿ Myrtlewood Golf Club (843-913-4516; www.myrtlewoodgolf.com), a local favorite, includes two courses, PineHills, the area's only Arthur Hills design, and the venerable Palmetto course, providing top-class golf in a convenient central location.

Mystical Golf (843-282-2977; www.mysticalgolf.com) includes three courses located between MB and Conway. Course designer Dan Maples is at his most creative here: Man O' War is built in the middle of a lake, the Wizard creates a bit of mountain golf in the Lowcountry, and the Witch winds over a mile of wooden bridges and through an enchanted forest.

Many area golf resorts also offer accommodations.

World Tour Golf Links (843-236-2000; www.theworldtourgolf.com) re-creates 27 of the world's most famous golf holes, including St. Andrew's No. 18, complete with its ancient stone bridge; Augusta National's Amen corner; Doral's Blue Monster; and many more. Bronze plaques at the tee boxes give the background of each hole. Inside the clubhouse, visit the hall of fame, honoring top courses and holes around the world.

South Strand

Blackmoor Golf Club (1-866-952-5555; www.blackmoor.com), Grand Slam winner Gary Player's only course along the Grand Strand, occupies a former rice plantation complete with alligators and a pre–Civil War cemetery.

Did you know? Kids 16 and under play free with a paying adult at many area courses. Visit the website of **Myrtle Beach Golf** (www.myrtlebeachgolf.com) for a list of participating courses.

Quick tip: The website www.northmyrtlebeachgolf.com has profiles of the many golf architects who have designed courses on the Strand. **Myrtle Beach Golf Resorts** (www.myrtlebeachgolfresorts.com) provides links to many golf-friendly local establishments.

The Grand Strand's numerous courses make it a top year-round destination for golfers.

Caledonia Golf & Fish Club and its sister club, True Blue Golf Plantation (843-235-0900; www.fishclub.com), two courses designed by Mike Strantz, occupy stunning property on former rice and indigo plantations studded with ancient live oaks and tidal marshes. Both Pawleys Island courses are ranked among the top 25 in the South by *Golf Digest*.

The Heritage Club (843-237-3424; www.legendsgolf.com), part of the Legends Group, is a beautiful Dan Maples design set amid old magnolias, camellias, azaleas, and live oaks.

♂ Litchfield Beach & Golf Resort (843-237-3000; www.litchfieldbeach .com), selected as one of the world's 50 best golf resorts by *Condé Nast Traveler*, includes three signature courses: Willard Byrd's Litchfield Country Club, Tom Jackson's River Club, and Dan Maples's Willbrook Plantation, all rated four stars or more by *Golf Digest*.

♂ Pawleys Plantation Golf & Country Club (1-800-367-9959; www.pawleys plantation.com) boasts a recently renovated Jack Nicklaus signature course rated among America's best.

The Tournament Players Club of Myrtle Beach (843-357-3399; www.tpc myrtlebeach.com), designed by Tom Fazio, is the only course on the Strand to receive five stars from *Golf Digest*. Keep an eye out for wild turkeys roosting near the ninth tee, and rising PGA Tour star Dustin Johnson in the TPC clubhouse.

Wachesaw Plantation East (1-800-344-5590; www.wachesaweast.biz), a Scottish-inspired Clyde Johnston course in Murrells Inlet, hosts many LPGA events.

If you like this . . . the award-winning Waccamaw Golf Trail (1-888-293-7385; www.waccamawgolftrail.com) offers deals on a dozen South Strand courses, maximizing your time amid the ancient live oaks and marshlands of these former rice plantations.

Sidetrips

HISTORIC GEORGETOWN: HEART OF THE RICE EMPIRE

FOUNDED IN 1729, Georgetown is the third oldest town in South Carolina, a major port for the long-grain Carolina Gold rice grown on the plantations that thrived from Colonial days to the Civil War. By 1840 Georgetown County produced half the rice grown in America, and the port exported more rice than any other in the world.

Located where four major rivers—the Great Pee Dee, the Waccamaw, the Black, and the Sampit—combine to form Winyah Bay, the town grew in wealth and influence for two centuries before subsiding into a historic but quiet riverfront town. Today Georgetown is experiencing a renaissance fueled by tourism and its attractive, laid-back lifestyle.

Nowhere else can the history of antebellum rice culture be better experienced. A stroll through Georgetown's compact historic district, located south of US 17 between the Great Pee Dee and Sampit River bridges, leads past dozens of pre–Civil War mansions, townhouses, churches, and commercial buildings, many listed on the National Register of Historic Places (www.nationalregister.sc .gov). Blue markers provide information on historic structures.

Georgetown retains its antebellum charm thanks to the collapse of the rice economy after the Civil War. With no local economic boom like that seen in many parts of the South, Victorian architecture is rare.

> **Fast fact:** Named one of the top small towns in America, Georgetown is situated about halfway between Charleston and Myrtle Beach, making it the perfect day-trip destination. Contact the **Georgetown County Tourism Management Commission** (843-546-8436; www.hammockcoastsc .com) at 531 Front Street for more information.

LEFT: Just beyond the crowds, the Carolina Lowcountry reverts to rural charm.

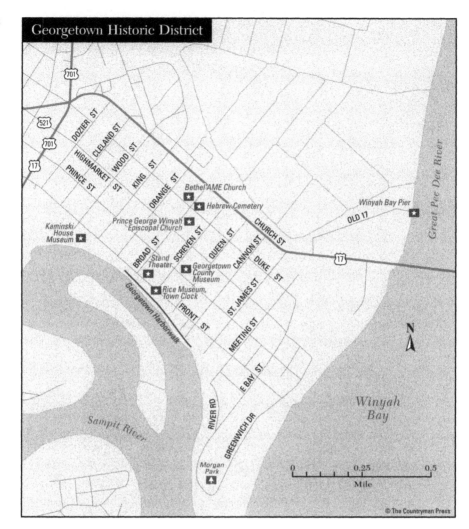

Georgetown Historic District

Front Street, lined with shops, restaurants, and museums, is the heart of the action, along with the parallel Harborwalk (www.theharborwalk .com), a 12-foot wide boardwalk running behind the shops along the waterfront between the Rice Museum (633 Front) and the Kaminski House Museum (1003 Front). Francis Marion Park, at the foot of Broad Street, is a good place to get your bearings. The new South Carolina Maritime Museum (843-545-0015; www.scmaritimecenter.org) is scheduled to open here in 2012. The visitor center, with parking, is at the foot of Queen, a few blocks east.

Housed in the former city market topped by the 1845 town clock, the

Quick tip: For up-to-date information on events, shopping, and dining in Georgetown, consult the websites of the Georgetown Business Association (www.seaportgeorge town.com) and the *Georgetown Times* (www.gtowntimes.com).

Sweetgrass baskets, developed for winnowing rice, are a major product of the Gullah culture.

A Gullah bottle tree, believed to ward off evil spirits

☗ Rice Museum (843-546-7423; www.ricemuseum.org) explores the culture created by rice from both the planters' perspective and that of the enslaved peoples who made that culture possible. Visits include a guided tour of the 1842 buildings, a video on rice production and history, a gallery hanging local art, and exhibits featuring Miss Ruby Forsythe, an early African American educator on Pawleys Island, and other prominent people descended from the enslaved community. Closed Sunday.

Lafayette Park, surrounding the Rice Museum, provides an oasis of beauty with flower beds tended by the local garden clubs. A walkway lined with fragrant herbs leads to the Harborwalk. Stroll along the boardwalk, passing the back entries of Front Street shops and restaurants, many with charming patios inviting you to stop for refreshment.

Several restaurants along the Harborwalk provide dining options with a view. The River Room (843-527-4110; www.riverroomgeorgetown.com), at Front and Broad, is the most revered, serving famous shrimp and grits, McClellanville lump crabcakes, and bread pudding with bourbon sauce, at lunch and dinner for the past three decades. Closed Sundays.

A more casual choice, and a must for breakfast or lunch, is the nearby Thomas Café (843-546-7776; www.thomascafe.net), founded in 1929 in a 100-year-old building at 703 Front. Now chef-owned and operated, the café's cuisine runs to country classics perfectly prepared, including a breakfast shrimp and grits with red-eye gravy, local specialty chicken pilau, and meat-and-two lunch plates, all at prices that won't break the budget. Closed Sundays.

Most Georgetown menus feature the Lowcountry classic: shrimp and grits.

If you like this . . . Aunny's (843-461-4750; www.aunnys.com) at 926 Front plates up authentic soul food specialties for lunch daily. Closed Mondays.

At Ⓨ Buzz's Roost Rooftop Restaurant and Bar (843-545-1595; www.buzzs roost.net), you can dine indoors or on the second-floor deck overlooking the Harborwalk. Other eateries with waterfront views include Portofino's on the Wharf (843-485-4210; www.portofinosonthewharf.com), serving Northern Italian cuisine; the Old Fish House Restaurant (843-546-1045), known to locals as the Big Tuna; and Limpin' Jane's Old South Eatery and Taproom (843-485-4953; www.limpin janes.com).

Several shops along the Harborwalk are worth a look, including Harborwalk Books (843-546-8212; www.harborwalkbooks.com), an independent bookstore specializing in local history and authors. The Georgetown Art Gallery (843-527-7711), at 705 Front, displays works by 20 local artists, each giving a unique interpretation of the Lowcountry. At Sweeties Pralines & Chocolates (843-545-5400; www.sweetiessweets.com), stock up on authentic Southern confections made in-house, or cool off with some homemade pecan praline ice cream.

Along Front Street you'll find a variety of bakeries, cafés, art galleries, and antique shops, including Augustus & Carolina Interiors (843-545-9000; www .augustusandcarolina.com), an antique store displaying a dazzling selection of high-end furniture and chandeliers. Outlaw's Originals (843-520-4462; www.outlawsart .com) displays the wood carvings and paintings of black folk artist Alvin Outlaw.

Throughout the historic district you'll enjoy sidewalks shaded by live oaks. The Champion Oak, estimated to be over 500 years old and recognized by the American Forestry Associates as one of the state's oldest, can be found between 513 and 515 Prince Street. A block away, the Georgetown County Museum (843-545-

7020; www.georgetowncountymuseum.com), at 632 Prince, explores more than 300 years of local history.

On a bluff overlooking the Sampit River, the ⛴ ♂ Kaminski House Museum (843-546-7706; www.cogsc.com) offers tours of two historic houses, the antique-filled 1769 Kaminski house and the 1740 Parker House, both overlooking the scenic harbor. Don't miss the gift shop here, where traditional local crafts such as sweet grass baskets and China berry jewelry, plus a wealth of books on local history, are available to take home.

Quick tip: Like many riverfront towns, Georgetown's layout follows a simple pattern: Front Street runs closest to the water; the parallel Prince Street contains many public buildings. The historic district is eight blocks long and five blocks deep, bordered by Meeting Street, Church Street/US 17, Wood Street, and the Sampit River. Street parking can fill up during busy times; additional large public lots can be found in East Bay Park, at the east end of Front Street.

If you like this . . . journey a few miles south to the town of Andrews on the Black River, where the Old Town Hall Museum (843-264-3715; www .townofandrews.org) re-creates a Victorian mansion of 1909. Free.

Other landmarks in Georgetown's historic district include the Prince George Winyah Episcopal Church (843-546-4358; www.pgwinyah.org), built about 1750 with brick from the ballasts of ships; the 1882 Bethel African Methodist Episcopal Church (843-546-4898); and the circa 1772 Hebrew Cemetery. A guided introduction aboard the tram operated by Swamp Fox Tours (843-527-1112; www.swampfoxtours.com) is highly recommended. Tours begin at Bienvenue Home Accents, in a historic house at 624 Front Street.

Other tours explore Georgetown by horse-drawn carriage, by foot, and by boat. The costumed guides at Ghosts of Georgetown (843-543-5777; www.ghosts ofgeorgetown.com) lead lantern tours of the historic district on Friday evenings. Miss Nell (843-446-4777; www.missnellstours.com), a former director of the county museum, leads daytime tours from Harborwalk Books. Or catch a ride with Low Country Carriage (843-567-7167; www.lowcountrycarriage.com) at the corner of Front and Cannon Streets.

Popular excursions from the Harborwalk docks take visitors out to the 1811 Georgetown Lighthouse (www.lighthousefriends.com), located on an island at the entrance to Winyah Bay and accessible only by boat. The beach here provides excellent shelling. Stroll the Harborwalk to select your vessel or contact Rover Boat Tours (843-546-8822; www.roverboattours.com) or Cap'n Rod's Lowcountry Plantation Tours (843-477-0287; www.lowcountrytours.com) for schedules and fees.

If you like this . . . follow the riverfront to the southern end of Bay Street and take the boardwalk across the marsh to discover a secluded beach and picnic area at the junction of the Sampit River and Winyah Bay.

The Sampit riverfront in downtown is lined with public docks, if you're arriving by boat. For a longer stay, rent a slip at the full service 🐾 (📶) Harborwalk Marina (843-546-4250; www.harborwalkmarina.com).

For a fun evening in Georgetown, begin with cocktails in the lounge at the Rice Paddy Restaurant (843-546-2021; www.ricepaddyrestaurant.com), housed in a historic bank on Front Street, then stroll down the street to the art deco Strand Theatre for the screening of an independent film or a performance by the Swamp Fox Players (843-527-2924; www.swamp foxplayers.com). The ♉ Backstage Cafe (843-546-4900) at 816 Front hosts live music several nights a week.

Did you know? At one time, seven different movie palaces lined Georgetown's Front Street.

Quick tip: Score some shrimp right off the boat at **Independent Seafood** (843-546-6642), located at the foot of Cannon Street, just past the Harbor House.

If you like this . . . plan a trip to a Wednesday night Barn Jam at Awendaw Green (843-452-1642; www.awendawgreen.com), one of the area's most enjoyable music venues, located next to the Seewee Outpost in Awendaw, on US 17 about 30 miles south of Georgetown.

Another great place to party is the ⚓ ♉ Land's End Restaurant (843-527-1376; www.landsendrestaurant.com), located off US 17 just west of the Pee Dee River bridge in Georgetown Landing Marina (843-546-1776; www.georgetown landingmarina.com). Fabulous water views here are complemented by shag dancing on Thursday nights and jazz on the weekends.

If you'd like to extend your stay, the 1765 (ψ) Harbor House Bed & Breakfast (843-546-6532; www.harborhousebb.com) offers a wide veranda overlooking the water, where you'll enjoy a complimentary "afternoon delight" of Southern hors d'oeuvres and hospitality.

Georgetown hosts a number of popular festivals every year, including the Winyah Bay Heritage Festival (843-833-9919; www.winyahbayfestival.org) in March, with duck calling, net casting, and dog dock diving competitions; the Harborwalk Festival (843-546-1511) in May; the Wooden Boat Show (843-545-0015; www.woodenboatshow.com) in October; and Taste of Georgetown (www.tasteof georgetownsc.com), a restaurant crawl along historic Front Street, in November.

EXPLORING RICE COUNTRY

The golden rice exported from Georgetown's harbor was grown at plantations that lined the rivers converging in Winyah Bay. To grow the rice, plantation owners imported Africans who were accomplished in rice cultivation from Sierra Leone and other Windward Coast countries. These enslaved people cleared the huge cypress trees that grew in the tidal swamps, then constructed dams, dikes, floodgates, and canals that allowed the fields to be

A nearly intact slave village can be seen at the Howcaw Barony, just north of Georgetown.

Did you know? The rice grown on the plantations around Georgetown was the famed Carolina Gold (www.carolina goldricefoundation.org), a long-grain variety revered for its unique ability to produce fluffy individual grains, sticky Asian-style rice, or creamy risotto, depending on how it's cooked. Nearly lost after the Civil War and a series of devastating hurricanes in the 1890s, the Carolina Gold cultivar has been res- cued and is once again produced com- mercially in South Carolina.

flooded periodically to irrigate the young plants and kill insects. Later they planted, hoed, and harvested the rice by hand, then milled it in wooden mortars and winnowed it with sweetgrass baskets—a highly labor-intensive process.

Today, heirloom Carolina Gold rice is available by mail order from ✧ Anson Mills (803-467-4122; www.ansonmills.com) and Carolina Plantation Rice (877-742-3496; www.carolinaplantationrice.com), or at Lowcountry groceries and gift shops.

Meanwhile the plantation owners lived high on the profits brought by rice, building lavish homes along the banks of blackwater rivers. Guests arrived from around the world to admire the long alleys of live oaks that led up to the mansions, the elegant camellia gardens, and the groaning boards of Lowcountry dishes featuring fresh seafood, wild game, and, of course, rice.

This world disappeared with the Civil War, as owners couldn't afford the labor to grow rice or repair irrigation systems destroyed by storms. Many sold their plantations to rich industrialists from the Northern states, who found the old rice fields to be the perfect habitat to attract wild waterfowl and came south every winter to hunt.

A number of the plantation houses that once flourished along these rivers have survived into the 21st century— mostly seasonal residences, now as then, of the wealthy. Several tour companies offer river trips past these relics of the antebellum age, dreaming

Free-standing chimneys once attached to rice factories dot the shores of the Wacca- maw River.

Alleys of oaks are all that remain of most rice plantations.

beneath moss-draped oaks of a vanished time. Other plantations have disappeared into the swamps, marked only by a lonely rice mill chimney or derelict rice fields, now home to alligators, wild geese, and ospreys.

The *Waccamaw Lady*, a pontoon boat operated Plantation River Tours (843-651-2994; plantationrivertours.com), departs from the Wacca Wache Marina on the Waccamaw River in Murrells Inlet before heading south through Brookgreen Gardens and traveling up the Great Pee Dee to see Arundel and other plantations there. Cap'n Rod's Lowcountry Tours (843-477-0287; www.lowcountrytours.com) follow a similar route after departing from the Georgetown Harborwalk.

*If you like this . . . explore the remains of former plantations at **Brookgreen Gardens** (843-235-6000; www.brookgreen.org) and the **Hobcaw Barony** (843-546-4623; www.hobcawbarony.org). Between them, they preserve more than a dozen old plantation sites on the Waccamaw Neck. Brookgreen has a restored rice field and an audio trail examining rice cultivation. Tours of Hobcaw feature the 1930 mansion built as a winter retreat by Wall Street financier Bernard Barush and a slave village dating to the 1800s.*

Get a more ecofriendly look at the plantations by paddling a kayak along these quiet rivers. Black River Outdoors (843-546 4840; www.blackriveroutdoors.com) conducts guided ecotours or will rent you a kayak or canoe and deliver it for free so you can explore on your own. You can also rent a kayak or party barge at Wacca Wache Marina (843-651-7171; www.waccawachemarina.com) on the Waccamaw River in Murrells Inlet.

Getting inside of one of the old plantation houses is another matter; most are privately owned and don't welcome tourists. However, once a year, usually in

Restored rice field along the Waccamaw

March, the women's organization of Prince George Winyah Episcopal Church (843-546-4358; www.pgwinyah.org) sponsors an annual plantation tour when more than a dozen homes, many on the National Register of Historic Places, open their doors to guests.

If you like this . . . one of the plantations on the tour is open to the public year-round. ♂ Hopsewee Plantation (843-546-7891; www.hopsewee.com), 12 miles south of Georgetown off US 17, was the birthplace of Thomas Lynch Jr., a signer of the Declaration of Independence. After your tour of the home, enjoy a Southern tea or Lowcountry lunch at the River Oak Cottage Tearoom on the Hopsewee grounds.

To experience a taste of what life was like on the old plantations, book a stay at ♂ (👁) Mansfield Plantation (1-866-717-1776; www.mansfieldplantation.com), ranked by many as one of the top bed & breakfast inns in the country. Used as a film location in *The Patriot,* Mansfield sits on 1,000 acres and retains many early features, including a magnificent alley of live oaks leading to the 1768 manor house, a slave village and chapel, and the only winnowing barn remaining in Georgetown County. Guests set their own pace here, exploring miles of nature trails by foot or bike, bird watching in the old rice fields, kayaking on the Black River, or just relaxing in a riverside hammock.

But the white-pillared plantation houses tell just one side of the story. The descendants of the enslaved peoples that worked the fields continue to inhabit the region and have developed the unique Gullah/Geechee culture, preserving elements of their inherited African crafts, cuisine, and customs, and speaking their own Creole language.

One of the remaining Gullah communities in Georgetown County lives on Sandy Island, accessible only by boat. While visitors are welcome to

The Carolina Lowcountry is at its most lovely along the lower Waccamaw.

Fast fact: **The Gullah/Geechee Cultural Heritage Corridor** (843-881-5516; www.nps.gov/guge), under development by the National Park Service, will stretch from Jacksonville, Florida, to Wilmington, North Carolina.

walk the nature trails in the Sandy Island Nature Preserve (843-937-8807; www.nature.org) on the north end of the island, uninvited guests are not encouraged in the Gullah village at the south end. To visit with the residents and get a taste of their culture, arrange a tour with local Rommy Pyatt, operator of Tours de Sandy Island (843-408-7187; www.toursdesandy island.com).

If you like this . . . the Gullah O'oman Museum and Shop (843-235-0747; 421 Petigru Drive) in Pawleys Island exhibits sweetgrass baskets, dolls, wood carvings, and other traditional Gullah crafts, including a "story quilt" that depicts First Lady Michelle Obama's Gullah roots.

An audio trail explains rice cultivation at Brookgreen Gardens.

CONWAY: HISTORY ALONG THE WACCAMAW

Just 15 miles west of downtown Myrtle Beach, the historic city of Conway is far older than its younger neighbor. Founded in 1732, this river port is Horry's county seat, occupying a prime spot on the Waccamaw River. Legend has it that the streets were laid out around the huge oaks, some 400 years old, that grow along the banks.

The river and the oaks remain two of the best reasons for a day trip to Conway. The Conway River Walk, a complex of sidewalks and boardwalks, makes for a pleasant stroll along the riverfront. Get a closer look at the ecology and history of this blackwater river and the surrounding swamps on a guided tour with Conway Kayak (843-488-0999; www.conway kayak.com), offered year-round. Or you can rent a kayak and explore on your own. Signs along the river identify historic spots; download a paddle trail map from Conway Parks and Recreation (www.conwayparksandrecreation .com).

A trip into the depths of the swamp with Conway Kayak introduces local flora and fauna. Karen Wright

If you like this . . . Conway native Jim Holbert conducts historical cruises on the river aboard the River Memories (843-246-1495; www.river memories.org), a boat with a quiet electric motor that doesn't disturb the majesty of the swamp—or pollute its fragile black waters.

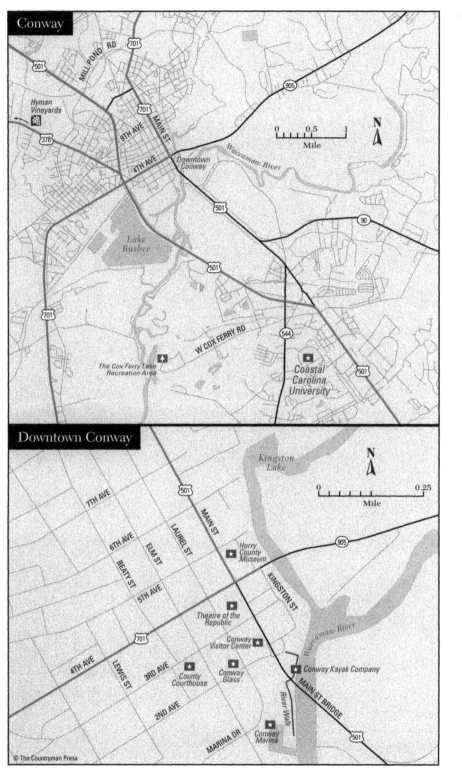

Conway

Hyman Vineyards

MILLPOND RD

501

701

378

9TH AVE

MAIN ST

4TH AVE

701

Downtown Conway

Waccamaw River

905

0   0.5   1
          Mile

N

90

Lake Busbee

501

501

701

W COX FERRY RD

544

501

The Cox Ferry Lake Recreation Area

Coastal Carolina University

Downtown Conway

Kingston Lake

N

0   0.25
          Mile

7TH AVE

501

6TH AVE

LAUREL ST

MAIN ST

ELM ST

BEATY ST

5TH AVE

Horry County Museum

905

KINGSTON ST

Theatre of the Republic

Conway Visitor Center

Waccamaw River

4TH AVE

LEWIS ST

3RD AVE

County Courthouse

Conway Glass

Conway Kayak Company

MAIN ST BRIDGE

2ND AVE

River Walk

501

MARINA DR

Conway Marina

© The Countryman Press

Several of the ancient live oaks that line Conway's streets are named. Get a self-guided walking tour map of the legacy oaks or local historic properties at the Conway Visitor Center (843-248-1700; www.visitconwaySC.com) at 903 Third Avenue or in the visitor's lobby at the Conway Area Chamber of Commerce (843-248-2273; www.conwayscchamber.com) at 203 Main Street.

Quick tip: Plan your visit to Conway for the first Thursday of the month when the **Conway Crawl** fills downtown with live music, open houses, and other special events from 7:30 to 9 PM. The **Conway Farmers Market** (843-365-6715; www.waccamaw markets.org) takes place Saturday mornings at 217 Laurel Street in the historic downtown district.

History buffs find plenty to keep them busy in Conway's Historic Downtown (www.nationalregister.sc .gov), where 33 buildings are listed on the National Register of Historic Places. Notable among them: the 1824 city hall, formerly the county courthouse, at Main and Third, designed by Robert Mills, who is best known for designing the Washington Monument. Also on Main Street, the ♂ ☂ Horry County Museum (843-915-5320; www.horrycountymuseum.org) and the 1912 Historic Bryan House (843-488-1966; www.hchsonline.org), headquarters of the Horry County Historical Society, provide insight into the history of the area.

Numerous shops and restaurants line the streets of the historic district. Conway Glass (843-248-3558; www.conwayglass.com) at 209 Laurel Street is one of the most interesting, with a gallery of handblown and stained glass, plus glass-blowing demonstrations and classes. At Bodega (843-248-9271; www.shop bodega.com), located at 301 Main Street, shoppers enjoy gourmet food and wine tastings while they browse the largest family-owned kitchen and tablescape store in the state.

Rivertown Bistro (843-248-3733; www.rivertownbistro.com), at 1111 Third Avenue, is the don't-miss dining experience in downtown Conway. Innovative cuisine ranging from sushi rolls to Southern classics is matched by a contemporary decor that includes an upstairs deck overlooking downtown and a cozy lounge with daily happy hour. Closed Sunday and Monday.

For a casual, but very historic lunch, travel down Third Avenue to the river where the Ocean Fish Market (843-248-4334; 302 Kingston Street) has been selling seafood and shucking oysters since 1940. The spot sandwich is the house specialty.

The best Sunday brunch in Conway is served at Crady's Restaurant and Bar (843-248-3321; www.cradys .com), located at 332 Main Street, directly across from the Theatre of the

The Ocean Fish Market has been shucking oysters since 1940.

Conway's Main Street Theatre hosts plays by the Theatre of the Republic and classic movies.

Republic (843-488-0821; www.theatreoftherepublic.com). Famous for the fine baked goods produced by Barbara Whitley, matriarch of the clan that owns and operates Crady's, the eatery also serves lunch daily. Dinner and a late-night menu are available only on nights of theater performances. Reservations are highly recommended.

For a fun evening, join the alumni and students of Coastal Carolina University at their favorite hangout, the ♂ ♉ Crafty Rooster Bar & Grill (843-438-8330; www.craftyrooster.com), just a few doors down from the Rivertown Bistro on Third Avenue. Chanticleer team spirit joins an interesting list of beers on draft, a bar menu featuring chicken bog, and frequent live music and open mike nights to give guests something to crow about.

If you'd like to extend your visit to Conway with an overnight stay, the ♂ (ဇ) Cypress Inn (843-248-8199; www.acypressinn.com) on the banks of the Waccamaw River at the end of Elm Street makes an excellent and convenient choice.

Several fun family festivals take place annually in downtown Conway, including the Rivertown Music and Arts Festival on the first Saturday in May; Bluegrass on the Waccamaw (843-455-6161; www.rivertownbluegrasssociety.com), a free music festival on the second Saturday in May; Riverfest in late June; the Conway Fall Festival on the first Saturday of October; and Rivertown Christmas on the first three Thursdays in December. Visit the websites of Conway Downtown Alive (843-248-6260; www.conwayalive.com) and the Conway Area Chamber of Commerce (843-248-2273; www.conwayscchamber.com) for details.

Index